The Family Silver

SUSAN KRIEGER

The Family Silver

Essays on Relationships
among Women

UNIVERSITY OF CALIFORNIA PRESS
BERKELEY   LOS ANGELES   LONDON

University of California Press
Berkeley and Los Angeles, California

University of California Press, Ltd.
London, England

Library of Congress Cataloging-in-Publication Data

Krieger, Susan.
    The family silver : essays on relationships among women / Susan
Krieger.
      p.   cm.
    Includes bibliographical references.
    ISBN 0-520-20310-0 (hardcover : alk. paper).—ISBN 0-520-20311-9
(pbk. : alk. paper)
    1. Krieger, Susan. 2. Women—United States. 3. Lesbians—United
States. 4. Women college teachers—United States. 5. Gender
identity—United States. 6. Interpersonal relations—United States.
7. Feminist theory—United States.   I. Title.
HQ1421.k75 1996   96–788
305.3—dc20

Printed in the United States of America
9 8 7 6 5 4 3 2 1

For Estelle

CONTENTS

PREFACE

I HAD NOT INITIALLY planned to write a book called *The Family Silver,* nor expected, at the start, to be discussing my life in such an intimate way. I had thought that I would be writing about women and organizations, and that I would present insights about female gender that I had learned from teaching feminist classes. The rest evolved gradually. I often felt I was writing what I could not avoid writing, or simply what I was able to do at the time. There were welcome surprises. For instance, my interest in female gender soon led to chapters about my women relatives and my first lesbian love. It led to a sense that my struggles in academia had to do with my being a woman, and with my having roots in a private female world that is all too often forgotten when one enters the male world of a university. In a previous work, *Social Science and the Self,* I spoke of my father and of men who had influenced me. I am now glad to speak of my mother and of intimacies with women, no matter how complex and difficult our relationships have been at times.

In writing these essays, I sought to come to terms with my own feelings on sensitive issues of gender, status, family, lesbianism, and my place in the academic world. I worked a great deal on the wording of each essay and I worried a great deal about how they would feel to others. Fortunately, as I wrote, I had friends who were willing to reassure me that my work was worthwhile. For their good humor and encouragement in reading drafts of each essay as soon as each was written, I want to thank Laura Carstensen, Estelle Freedman, Paola Gianturco, Carolyn Hallowell, and Martin Krieger.

Other readers, also friends, provided encouragement and helpful responses to selected essays and to the work as a whole. I want to thank Kenneth Arnold, Susan Christopher, Jane Collier, Norman Denzin, Marjorie DeVault, Julie Duff, Ilene Levitt, Linda Long, Sue Lynn, James G. March, Laurel Richardson, Judith Stacey, Nancy Stoller, and John Van Maanen. For insightful comments on the collection at a critical final preparation stage, I am indebted to Sorca O'Connor and Verta Taylor. I thank Peggy Pascoe for her exceptionally valuable suggestions for revisions. I am grateful to Naomi Schneider for her bravery in taking the book for the University of California Press.

Students in my classes on feminist research and on women and organizations have provided encouragement for this work and have generously shared their experiences with me. Their voices and concerns appear in many of the essays. I deeply thank these students for giving so much to me and for teaching me.

For sharing important experiences that appear in these essays, I am grateful to Nancy Martin, Nicole Raeburn, and Sylvia Yanagisako; to my friends, both from the past and in the present; and to Barrie Thorne, Barbara Laslett, and the group of feminist sociologists who met together one long winter's weekend providing an occasion that encouraged two of these essays, "Hurts of the System" and "Lesbian in Academe," which were hard to write because of their subject matter.

For family experiences, I am grateful to my mother, Rhoda Cahn; my sister, Kathe Cahn Morse, and her family; and to my aunt Minnie Wasserman, who died too soon, at age eighty-five, and before ever reading the essays in which she appears. I am indebted to another aunt, Estelle Freedman's aunt Ann Braker, whom I met when I sorted through her clothes after her death, and to Martha Freedman, Estelle's mother, who gave me my title quite by accident. My mother, of course, told me how to take care of family silver and what it meant sentimentally in terms of relationships with female relatives. "You'll remember me every time you clean these," her mother told her upon handing down a set of ornate silver candlesticks with a bold floral pattern. Those candlesticks, which tarnish easily, now sit on my kitchen table and I think of both my mother and her mother when I see them.

My female relatives and others who appear in these essays appear with pseudonyms or anonymously, as if I could thus protect them from any hurt that might result from my very purposeful stories. My use of others in the service of my feminist sociology, or of my own self-expression, is, I hope, forgivable by those close to me, who may not be comfortable with parts of what I have written.

I want to thank Carolyn Hallowell for her abiding commitment to me. Finally, I want to thank Estelle Freedman, who understood the importance of seeing gender long before I did, and whose commitment to feminist teaching and scholarship, and to the softer side of our joint life, means so much to me. I always knew this book would be for Estelle.

INTRODUCTION

THE FAMILY SILVER IS an unusual collection of essays. It is at once an intensely individual and emotional set of reflections and a more general sociological study. These essays were written as a collection and are intended as a contribution to feminist scholarship and feminist teaching, to the ethnographic tradition in sociology, and to emerging scholarship in lesbian and gay studies. I also intend them to be emotionally moving personal reading. *The Family Silver* draws on my particular life experiences—as a woman, a lesbian, a teacher—in order to contribute to our understanding of female gender. In previous work, I have studied others, and it seems to me that it is far easier to look at others and think one sees what is occurring than to look at oneself and try to see themes, explanations, interpretations, to offer stories that are both true and acceptable. When one looks at oneself, the picture becomes more complex, more intimate. The easy answers disappear.

In *The Family Silver,* I start by describing my specific experiences and then develop insights about gender from a careful consideration of them. I build my interpretations from the ground up, very much in the tradition of an ethnographer (rather than by beginning with more general ideas and then applying them). The book thus has an emergent, discovery-like character. It moves back and forth between events and insight, between emotion and thought. My experiences are never uninterpreted, and I often interpret them closely. Because these essays draw on my internal emotional life and deal with issues of sexual preference, they result in a study that is intimate far beyond my prior works, and beyond what is usually found in the social sciences and considered acceptable in academic discourse. The intimacy of the essays is their central challenge.

It is not, however, their only challenge. *The Family Silver* focuses on female gender, on how women organize social life, and on how lesbianism encourages us to value the female in ourselves. My quest for understanding is shared with other feminist scholars. Over the past few decades, feminists have sought to increase our substantive understanding of women and to experiment with how we go about producing our knowledge, seeking to free it from male definition. A desire to create our own unique forms of expression—to describe women's experiences in ways that reflect women's voices and visions, and that faithfully depict particular social realities—has become important not only among feminists, but also in branches of the traditional disciplines, in new fields such as lesbian and gay studies, and in African American and other specialized group studies. In all these areas, one assumption is that a field of knowledge that looks at previously forbidden choices, ways of being, or overlooked aspects of experience, that seeks to revolutionize our knowledge in some way, had best attend to the forms it uses in doing so, so that it does not simply reproduce an old hierarchy.[1]

Structured in a way that contributes its own form of expression, *The Family Silver* is organized in three parts. The first section contains a set of highly personal essays that draw the reader into my relationships with friends, lovers, and family. The second part moves to institutional settings, where I try to understand how my gender has affected me as a teacher in universities and in an academic career. In the third section, I describe a course I taught on women and organizations, and I take the reader along in the learning process. Here the ideas that organize the entire volume are spoken of in general terms, providing a kind of summary, or a way to reflect back on the earlier sections of the book. One could read this book back end first, but my approach is to speak more personally at the start.

In following my stories, the reader will be in a position of puzzling through situations, much as I was as I wrote each essay. At times, the reader may take a different route than I do, and may think of her own experiences and make up her own interpretations concerning gender. She may come to different conclusions, be surprised by the twists and turns of my inner thinking, be discomforted by what are for me familiar facts of my intimate life, or be overwhelmed by my attention to pain and vulnerability. But the point is to follow along, to use these essays to help see how gender operates in one's own life. None of us can speak for all women, but we can certainly share our different kinds of insights and borrow understandings from one another where that seems helpful.

I do make generalizations about the situation of women in these essays, but never lightly. I do this because it helps me interpret my own life experiences and because—although I claim no universality—I think similarities exist among different women's experiences, despite crucial differences of race, class, culture, and more. I think similarities appear because women occupy subordinate statuses in our various contexts, and because we have had certain types of functions through history, some associated with reproduction and physical attributes, and others not. I think that lesbianism, too, is both a similarity and a difference. It reflects a desire that many women have, but that only some of us commit our lives to; and among lesbians, each of us interprets herself in a distinct way. A similarity/difference dilemma runs through all my stories. At one moment, the reader may feel a difference among women, or between her life and mine; at another time, a similarity may seem more prominent. Both are useful to consider.

In these essays, I speak emotionally and as plainly as I can. Usually, academics speak in a more abstract or explicitly theoretical language, use a technical vocabulary, and refer often to work by other scholars. The academic style is designed to produce distance and to exclude emotion—to speak from above and outside an experience, rather than from within it. Although feminist writers often desire to be intimate and to celebrate women's subjectivities, in recent years, feminist work has tended to merge back into the academic mainstream and to use theoretically distancing and abstract, or obscuring, language. Lesbian and gay studies, especially the literature of queer theory, has tended, also, to use complex and distancing language in an effort to become legitimate, in part to compensate for a subject matter that is hardly considered so. *The Family Silver* is more direct than much current work in these fields. Because it lacks camouflage, it may seem vulnerable. I hope it will be received protectively. I offer it as a reminder of our need for authenticity, or for speaking candidly about our experiences despite the risks involved.

Although I avoid academic jargon—whether a language of deconstruction or of structural functionalism—I am well aware that I am taking my place among other scholars.[2] In the academic context, there has been much recent debate over how we should talk about women, gender, and same-gender sexual relationships.[3] To simplify somewhat, two basic camps dominate these debates. One consists of those who see gender in largely binary terms—whether as a social structural fact, or as a biological given—who see a world of women and men, of unequal opportunity and unequal people. This group includes many feminist social scientists, who view their task as describing and explaining the social reality of gender. The second group consists of those who argue that gender fluidity and ambivalence are the more underlying facts, that a binary view oversimplifies unstable and overlapping categories, and that cultural possibilities count more than social structure. Often, those in the second camp are from literary or humanistic disciplines and view the world as made up of texts, discourses, or systems of ideas.

Like those in the second camp—deconstructionists, postmodernists, queer theorists, and many feminists—I see much fluidity and complexity in the way that gender is enacted and defined. Definitions of gender vary across individuals, subgroups, cultures, and times. I see gender as socially constructed, something we create. However, I also have a profoundly sociological view of gender, which is to say, on the one hand, that I am not a biological determinist, and on the other, that I am not an absolute relativist. I view gender as a hierarchical form of social organization, a system in which superiority has traditionally been assigned to men and male ways, and inferiority to women and female ways. I think gender systems have a structural existence quite apart from our ideas about them. We cannot change these systems merely by thinking them away. While each of us has a choice with regard to how we define our gender, the range of discretion available to us seems to me not very wide. I think that if we wish to change our gendered experiences and the structures that support them—so that women are less disadvantaged, and so that the principles that rule the world are less strictly male—we must first recognize the powerful hold gender has on us.

This book is very much about the hold of gender in an individual life. In it, I argue for acknowledging gender rather than denying it, and for valuing, rather than devaluing, both the inner realities of women and the outer ways that women do things. The book's title, *The Family Silver,* refers to women's ways, to the wealth women have and pass on to one another and try to keep from being stolen or melted down by men. There are many forms of women's wealth; family silver is one suggested by my own familial experiences and used here as a metaphor. I think women's wealth is like women, considered second best and "not as good as gold" in a world that values gold more highly, but it is our wealth and we have to learn to cherish and use it. My effort throughout this book is to cherish women's ways, to make them more visible in order better to value them.

In each of the essays, I speak personally, offering imagery from my own life. I refer to literature by others only in the endnotes and in the teaching chapters. My purpose in doing so is to demonstrate a process of developing insights from a consideration of one's own experience. The usual academic style is to take someone else's ideas and apply them to a situation one is studying, and to view an individual reality as not worthy enough to stand alone. Women's realities, especially, have been seen as unworthy. I wish to challenge that view. Women often struggle to give the inner emotional life external form, to put the unspeakable into words. I wish to contribute to that process and to encourage others to do so as well. My method is to speak about a level of experience just beneath the surface of what is usually seen, a level where feelings are highly important and where emotional evidence prompts complex interpretation.

Each of the essays in *The Family Silver* was written to stand as a complete statement. Because each reflects the events it describes, none of the essays looks exactly like the others, and the whole has a very original shape. In each essay, I discuss events in depth; in some cases, I tell a step-by-step story. Such attention to detail seems to me especially important when discussing women's submerged experiences. Each essay merges personal and academic approaches and speaks of both public and private aspects of my life. Many of the stories that I tell are not the usual success story, and that may affect the reader's responses. It would be easier if I had written about triumphing over adversity, or about transcending the problems of my gender. But I have chosen to write about topics that are more difficult. Thus, I say things that are harder to hear.

Although the reader will find her own way through the volume and identify themes that seem meaningful to her, I want to comment briefly on each of the essays and some of their themes. "Gender Roles among Women" opens the collection and introduces the approach. My first attempt to examine gender in my own daily life, it reflects on a series of events that confused me about gender—experiences in which men acted like women, and women acted like men, and in which others mistook me for a man. I wanted to clarify my discomfort by asking, What is going on beneath the surface in terms of gender roles? "Becoming a Lesbian," the second essay, discusses a process of individual growth through intimacy with another woman. It suggests that lesbian relationships allow women to shed their male-defined skins and to develop their own ways of being women.

"The Family Silver" views gender in the context of my familial relationships. It tells a story of a time when my lover's aunt died suddenly and we went to Florida to clear out her apartment and settle her affairs. I soon found myself writing about that trip, and about my own female relatives and relationships among us, and things passed down across female generations—like silverware and a sense of responsibility and of female hardship, and a sense that women will improvise and triumph and find ways to do almost anything, a sense that we are, in fact, the invisible wealth we seek. The metaphor of the "family silver" soon seemed to unify this collection for me. Although all women do not have actual family silver, it is the idea behind this metaphor that seems important to me. Other objects, possessions, or qualities that are like family silver are suggested in the book. In "The Passing Down of Sorrow," I discuss my relationship with my mother and how one very important thing she passed on to me was inner sorrow. I think that daughters often inherit sorrow, as well as strength, from their mothers as part of their femaleness.

In "Hurts of the System," which opens the section on academia, I discuss the fact that, for twenty years, I have done academic work, but I have never been awarded a regular academic job. Why, I ask, and why is the hurt I feel so deep? What does this lack of institutional support have to do with my being a woman, and with the female, and unconventional, nature of my work? "Saying No to a Man," the next essay, describes a situation in which I denied permission to a hostile male graduate student to take one of my classes. That action caused controversy among students and feminist faculty, and, in this essay, I try to understand what happened. Why was I so vulnerable, both to inner feelings of pain and failure, and to external attack? The consequences of saying no to men are discussed further in "Lesbian in Academe," an essay about how my being a lesbian has influenced my academic career over time. I wrote this essay to consider the possibility that who I had, and had not, slept with had had more effect on my professional life than I wished to know.

The book concludes with a series of essays on classroom teaching that traces interpersonal dynamics, changes in student views, and the central ideas of a course called Women and Organizations. I encourage the reader to take the course vicariously as she reads this series. The first essay, "A Feminist Class," presents the fundamentals, focusing on my attempts to overcome the students' initial resistances to seeing gender. "Separatism" discusses my struggle to get the students to see the need for separate women's organizations. "Desires for an Ideal Community of Women" suggests the deep wishes, on the parts of both the students and myself, that a feminist course be an ideal world and that we create, in all our female relationships, a more perfect and nourishing community. Themes of lesbianism recur through this entire series. How does my being a lesbian teacher increase my own fear? I ask. How does it affect what the students think of me?

Themes of feminist teaching and of women teaching women weave through all the essays, whether the teaching occurs in a classroom, a family, or an intimate love relationship. I think that the effort of feminist teaching that many women are now engaged in is a way that women learn from each other to value female realities. Especially when it occurs within the male preserves of higher education, this teaching is often a difficult and vulnerable activity, yet I think it is extremely important. Like talks between mothers and daughters about what to make for dinner, or what to do when the relatives come to visit, it is one way that we pass down women's culture to one another across the generations, which returns me to this book's title—about the wealth of women, and women's work, and the ways we seek to be generous with our lives.

Here then is *The Family Silver*, a collection of lesbian-feminist personal essays written from 1991 through 1994. These essays were responses to circumstance, and they reflect very much the times in which they were written. Perhaps one day lesbians will no longer lose their jobs, and women students will not need to be taught to value themselves, and I will be more accepting of my choices. But for now, I think it is important to describe things as they are. At least, that is what I know how to do. I hope that the reader will be able to identify with some of my experiences. We each have our own pain, our own mothers, our own ways of finding comfort, our own struggles to be women in worlds of men and in our more intimate communities of women. We each have our own unique feelings about being women. Yet I hope there may still be identification across the differences, and that my stories may lead other women to tell theirs.

The Family Silver

PART ONE

Personal Settings

One

GENDER ROLES AMONG WOMEN

I AM INTERESTED IN HOW ideas about gender organize identity and social relationships among women. Perhaps because I am a lesbian and have noticed how women who are lesbian adopt one gender role or the other (female or male), then discard it, combine roles, and act in ways that confuse me, I feel a need to come to better terms with the use of gender roles by women. Why am I fascinated, confused, repulsed, and drawn in when a woman acts like a stereotypical man, or like a stereotypical woman, for instance? Why do I hate, at one moment, to see stereotypical gender roles among women, and then take satisfaction from seeing these same roles the next?

Do I want to be a woman or a man? To be seen as a woman or a man? Do I have to be seen as one or the other? Do I have to choose; do I have a choice? Do people like me because I am a woman, or because I am a woman who is also like a man? Do I really know which gender I am? Why do I perpetuate a rigid gender system despite my wishes to the contrary, saying, with my choice of women, that gender really does define people? If gender did not matter, I might as well choose a man. I might as well be a man. Yet gender matters more than it might seem.

Even attempts to make one's gender ambiguous or to push away conventional gender roles suggest the formative nature of those roles.

By gender roles, I mean ways of defining oneself that are congruent with common ideas about how a person of one's perceived sex type behaves and feels—so that the outside world sees a woman, for instance, and so that the inner sense of self is that of a woman. Ideas about how to be of one's gender vary with time and culture. In this essay, I wish to identify neither universals nor variations, but rather to discuss what an individual does to come to terms with the fact of her gender, however that is defined. I focus on particular social settings with which I am personally familiar.

I think that coming to terms with gender is a process never settled once and for all but one that is ongoing—a series of repetitive motions much like "coming out of the closet" (it is never enough to announce only once that one is a lesbian). Repeated attempts at defining oneself by one's gender are integral to defining oneself as a person, in my view, although gender is often talked about as if it were secondary to a nongendered status—that of being a gender-neutral "person," for instance—and as if one's gender were a relatively trivial aspect of oneself, something one could easily be without. The importance of gender, in other words, is frequently denied.

When I teach about gender socialization among women, or think about it in my own life, the denial of gender—that it makes no difference, is not important, or not as important as something else—is the biggest fact I have to confront and the most persistent. Students in my classes on women become disturbed when required to see gender everywhere, particularly female gender, because doing so reveals a world not congruent with ideals of equality. When looking at gender in my own life, I feel a similar discomfort. I want to believe I can be separate from my gender and that I am not a victim of it. I do not want to be reminded of my female subordination or of the gender role-playing in my life— the ways I try to be like a woman, or like a man, and the uncomfortable responses I often feel upon seeing others who act as I do, or who act in ways that are more extreme or deviant. These include both those who play the femme or the butch more strictly and those who say they follow no gender roles at all. My discomforts with gender-related behaviors are key to the comforts of gender. They suggest reasons for the enormous hold of it in my life.

DISCOMFORTS WITH GENDER AMBIGUITY

Each year, I attend the annual lesbian and gay parade in San Francisco, where I see gay men in drag pretending to be women. I become uncomfortable when I see them because I want them to be one gender or the other, male or female, not the two mixed up. If they are to be women, I want them to be real women, authentic and appealing, rather than caricatures of certain aspects of female styles that I usually stay far away from—high heels, stockings, made-up faces, and ways of saying "dahling" and gesturing broadly to crowds. The superficiality of these men playing women scares me, much as it probably comforts others who like it precisely because it is superficial.

Over time, I have become more used to men in drag, but I still feel hurt and left out by them. The women these men like, those who seem to matter to them, are glamour queens, not me. Having grown up wanting boys and, later, men to like me, and having felt that the right ones—the popular and handsome ones—never did, I have always felt awkward as a woman around men. It was with relief that I turned from the heterosexual world to a lesbian one where I could forget men and seek only the affections of women. However, even among lesbians and gay men, occasionally at a party, or a political gathering, I would find myself with men and feel uncomfortable again: Why should gay men like me? I would feel. They have no use for me, they only like men. When they like women, they like the desperately outgoing types—the kind of woman I could not be when I was straight and cannot be now. They like the trappings of being a woman—the effusive, stylized parts—because that is all most of them can grasp. When they imitate women, I feel it is a way of putting on a show, or externalizing. It does not present a fundamental challenge to being a man. It is more like putting on a new pair of clothes, a new act, annexing a new country. Yet, however crude the caricature, a man putting on a female act may feel a greater sense of freedom. He may feel more himself.

The year before last, my favorite part of the gay parade was a marionette of a man in a purple sequinned dress riding a unicycle. He had long teased-out blond hair swept back, wore makeup, very high heels, and stockings, and he gestured to the crowd occasionally, throwing kisses and showing off his legs. High above him, a man on stilts worked him with strings, walking the entire length of the parade near the edge of the street, his attention riveted to the ground far below him where the little lady on the unicycle had to be kept upright and in constant motion.

To me, this marionette of the woman in the purple dress was wonderful. I liked it because the woman on the unicycle was not real. She was not even supposed to be real (in the sense of being a flesh-and-blood person), and so did not confuse me about reality—about whether she was a woman or a man. She was clearly a doll who looked like a woman but who was actually a gay man in drag. Because she was not a caricature of a woman so much as she was a caricature of a gay man dressed in women's clothes and makeup to be in the parade, the doll did not make me question whether she was fully enough a woman, or the right kind of woman—someone I could be. The questions she raised were, instead, about men. When I saw this little woman in her purple dress riding her unicycle down the street, I saw her as a comment on gay men parodying women. "You might as well be a doll" was one possible message to them. Although she was a doll, the marionette was lifelike to me. I liked her because she let me see, without confusion, something that really existed—a man dressed in drag as a flamboyant type of woman who, nonetheless, was still a man.

Before I ever saw a gay parade, I saw a movie called *Tricia's Wedding,* featuring a song and dance group called the Cockettes—men who played women's parts and dressed in women's clothes and hats and generally went wild. The movie was a takeoff on a wedding party for Tricia Nixon. What most bothered me as I watched it was that although the men in the movie impersonated women, imitating female mannerisms and styles, they did not change their voices (they still used deep men's voices), and they did not put makeup over their beards or appear to have shaved closely. The hair of a woman and a woman's hat and dress would be seen from behind, then the face would turn around and it would be an unshaven man's face. I thought, at the time, this must indicate a cheaply made movie, or that the men in the movie were simply slobs and had not finished applying their makeup.

Now I think there were probably other reasons, having to do with maintaining male gender visibility, rather than completing the act of appearing to be a woman. Different would be the case of a male-to-female transsexual who tries hard to complete the act of passing as a woman, or the case of any everyday woman whose behaviors are aimed at constructing a convincing appearance of being a woman because her life—and getting proper treatment and not ridicule—depends on it. Watching the Cockettes, I felt these men were not taking the pains they should have with the female gender, or that I, or most socially-constructed women, would have taken, and are required to take, and that seem necessary for our safety. When I stepped outside the theater after seeing the movie, I was shaken. The images of women the Cockettes had presented scared me and made me angry. They certainly looked ugly under their hats.

About the time I saw the Cockettes, I saw the Andy Warhol movie star Holly Woodlawn in a monologue-type movie, *Trash*. Holly Woodlawn was a man who played a woman so well that in watching her, I did not feel distress. Her gender moved into the background, and her qualities as a person—down to earth, honest, interesting—were most important. Woodlawn enacted a woman in such an understated way that hers seemed not an impersonation but a way of being. I felt comfortable with her and accepted her gender switch, suspending my anxieties about whether, indeed, she was truly, and once and for all, a woman or a man. The difference, I think, between my responses of uneasiness to men who pretend incongruously to be women, and my more accepting responses to others, like male-to-female transsexuals, everyday women, or Holly Woodlawn, is a difference tied to my experience of my own gender.[1]

Because I have been socialized intimately as a woman—taught that what is female is me, and that what is male ought not to be me—I identify much that is male as foreign and artificial, and much that is female as natural and good. I tend to understand women better than I do men, and to value women more. I seek my protection with women, I want men to be women, I do not want women to be men. My gender thus splits the world in two—providing a line I feel I should not cross, or that I cannot cross, and that I feel others should not cross either, unless they are very convincing about it. Most fundamentally, I think, I do not want the boundaries between the two genders to be confused because my sense of gender is closely tied to my sense of social order and personal safety. If the genders get confused, I get confused about who I am and I cease to know how to be safe: for if I am not a woman and cannot do things women do to protect myself, what can I do? I fear I will be left wide open, that I will easily become the victim of abuse. To be left genderless is to be left defenseless, or it feels that way to me, perhaps because the basic defenses I have learned are gender-linked. These defenses hinge on my ability to feel and act like a woman—to speak quietly, appear innocuous, or defer to others, for instance, and to feel "not myself" when I behave differently.

I think it is worth keeping in mind that while felt in such ways very personally, and as integral to the self, gender is more than personal. Because it is essentially about dominance and subservience, visibility and secrets, gender is political. To be male is to be powerful, to be a woman is to be weak. Given such a context, it is useful, if not necessary, especially if one is a member of the subordinate group—which is kept subordinate, in good part, through camouflage, through confusion of the difference that gender makes—to clarify relationships and not to forget who is who. A man appearing to be a woman may still be a dominant and dominating man; a woman appearing to be a man may be simply ignoring the chains that bind her, or ignoring what is noxious about perpetuating a style of dominance. In a system where women are neither equal nor safe, and where a great deal of one's safety depends on knowing the right ways to behave—how to dress, how to speak—it is good to see clearly the gendered structure of one's relationships. At the same time, such a vision is difficult, for gender distinctions are often hidden. Their significance is understated because these distinctions are thought of as trivial and because they are embedded in personal identity and in much that is taken for granted about daily life. The embeddedness of gender in daily life can be seen in instances of mistaken gender identity. These disturbances in the surface of gender expectations raise questions about the relationship between gender appearance and inner gender identity.

ON BEING MISTAKEN FOR A MAN

I used to like to be mistaken for a man. I do not anymore. In the past month, I have been mistaken for a man, in person, at least three times. The first was in a hospital waiting room where, when I emerged from using a women's bathroom, a small boy asked me, "What'cha doing using the women's? Why didn't you use the men's?" His comment made little sense to me when I heard it. I thought he was talking to someone else. However, there was no one else behind me and he was standing in front of me, looking straight at me. I felt uncomfortable, and ridiculed. I did not wish to be seen as a man. There might be grounds for it in my style of dress, but would a man wear two gold earrings and have a face like mine? Curiously, on each of these recent occasions when I have been mistaken for a man, it is my earrings I have focused on. I think my earrings surely show I am a woman. A man would wear one earring or a mismatched pair. I forget that the two gold hoops I wear are relatively small and perhaps not what the person facing me sees. Instead, that person sees an image suggested by short hair, jeans, a sweater or jacket, oxford shoes, a physical stance. Yet so much do I feel not a man that when mistaken for one, I doubt I have heard correctly the person speaking to me. I become confused and wonder what I have done wrong. I become, in other words, unclear about whether the mistake in identifying me is someone else's or mine. I usually do not question or correct the person who has called me a man, for I do not want to call attention to myself at that moment.

In my second recent experience of mistaken gender identity, I was buying bread in a bakery. A woman behind the counter addressed me as "sir." I mentioned this to a friend who was with me. "That can't be," she said. I thought of my earrings and thought I might be mistaken. I must have heard wrong. Still, I had felt some pride in being seen as a man, as if that made me more desirable than being seen as a woman, and I did not want my friend's disbelief to take that away from me.

When the woman behind the counter addressed me as "sir" a second time, I felt vindicated. I had heard correctly after all. Nonetheless, I still felt doubt: Was it really "sir" the woman had said? What about my earrings? What about my face? Why do people do this? Do they call me "sir" because when in doubt, it is better to assume maleness, better to call a woman a man than to insult a man by calling him a woman?

The third instance of this sort occurred one afternoon when I was walking down a street in the city. A man called after me from behind, asking what the date was. I was in an area where it is sometimes unsafe, and I did not want to turn around and find a strange man making faces at me, or making an obscene gesture referring to sexual parts, or a sexual act, simply because I was a woman. Why else, I thought, would this man be calling after me except to taunt me? It was late on a Saturday afternoon and I did not think he really needed to know the date from me. He could walk into any nearby store and find out. I kept walking. The man kept calling after me. I walked faster. He called out, "Sir, what's the date?" I thought his calling me "sir" was a ploy to get me to turn around so then he could make fun of me for being a woman. I kept walking. He kept calling after me. Now he was calling me, "Hey, sir, you with the gloves." I was wearing gloves because it was cold, but most people that day were not wearing gloves. By this time, I thought the man behind me probably did think I was a man. What kind of man, though, from the rear?

I thought maybe he saw me as a gay man, this being San Francisco, and that he was going to taunt me for that. Gay bashing came immediately to my mind and I was frightened. I had never been mistaken for a gay man and picked on for it. I felt I would rather be obscenely gestured at for being a woman. I was familiar with that. The man kept calling after me and I kept on walking, quickly and determinedly. He finally simply howled at me with no particular words. I felt he was frustrated that I would not obey him by turning around and answering him.

Afterward, I thought this man must have been troubled, that he wanted to be responded to, and that he was not a person who was planning to harass me for being a woman or a gay man. At the time, however, I did not want to take the chance of turning around and finding out. What stays with me from that episode in terms of gender, aside from my fundamental, and probably female, fear on the street, is my feeling that it was more frightening for me to be mistaken for a gay man than to be treated as a woman, and my more basic feeling that I did not want to be mistaken for a man at all. This mistake must have been made, I told myself, because of the jacket and pants I was wearing. These were men's clothes, chosen for a reason. Men's clothes are more durable than women's and I feel more physically protected in them. I also think these clothes make me look more like a man than a typical lightweight woman, and that people will treat me better as a result. However, although my clothes were men's, that did not mean I wanted to be seen as a man, a distinction that is sometimes difficult to grasp and that may seem to be asking for too much gender discernment. It is also a distinction that raises the question of what it means to want to look like and be treated as a lesbian. This question is related to the broader issue of lesbian invisibility. People are so used to seeing heterosexual women that a lesbian who looks different, who is, perhaps, more male in style, may pass unnoticed as a woman. People see the man in the image rather than the woman behind it. They say "sir" rather than something else they are perhaps afraid of.

THE CLOTHES OF MY GENDER

Both the pants and the jacket I wore on that day the man called after me on the street were purchased in men's sections of a department store, where, too, the issue of gender appropriateness arises for me. When I shop there, I always feel awkward: Will someone kick me out, look at me funny, think I am shopping for someone else—a man? Will they wonder what I, a woman, am doing here, think it strange? Have they seen other women do this? Didn't women used to shop in men's departments? Where are they now? I see women elsewhere wearing men's clothes. Is it not normal then? Is it not okay for me?

Clearly, the question of what is suited to my gender concerns me not only when I look at others (men in drag, for instance), but when I look at myself. A worry about gender appropriateness seems like something I have had all my life. I constantly think about whether I am acting enough like a woman, or in ways considered, by others and myself, as fitting to a woman, or as felt to be revealing of a woman. Am I dressing, speaking, feeling, moving, taking out the garbage like a woman? I wonder. Should a woman even be taking out the garbage? Am I assuming too many attributes of the other gender and, mistakenly, expecting good treatment for it? If I become too much like a man, what will happen to me? Will I be looked on as a freak, a bad person, a bad woman? Will I no longer qualify as a woman? One problem I have with thinking about these questions is that I easily become confused. There are so many injunctions—statements deeply learned about how I ought to be—and, at the same time, many factors interplay. It is hard to tell what is gender and what is not.

It is also hard for me not to see myself as a man when others see me that way. This is complicated because my own aims have often been to be a man. I think I have tried, since young, to be like men and boys, and not to be like women. My efforts have sources in my family. My mother, for instance, did not like frilly dresses and taught me not to like them and what they implied. She preferred a tailored look. She wanted to be taken seriously and not to be seen as a frivolous woman. I associate my mother's choice of clothing style with her wearing a light blue shirt-waist dress and silver jewelry. The shirtwaist style, a dress made like a man's shirt, was clearly not a ruffles and bows style; it commanded more respect. The silver jewelry, to my mind, meant my mother was a socialist.

I do not wear shirtwaist dresses and my mother has, for a long time, I think, found my style of dress inexplicable. "Why not wear brighter colors?" is the way she speaks of this. She does not say, "Why not wear more ladylike clothes?" The message I hear is the same, however: Why not wear something more complimentary—more expressive of you, more fitting to your gender? When visiting my mother, I try to please her with the colors of my shirts. I give up on my pants, my shoes, and my posture. Perhaps not surprisingly, I feel awkward when my mother looks at me, as if I am failing to be a woman and, for no apparent reason, masquerading in the clothes of the other gender. I feel that I am denying myself, that I am terribly uptight (which I am, since I am with my mother), and that I am denying others—my mother, most certainly— pleasure in me.

My relationships with the world at large are like those I have with my mother. Not that these relationships are the same, but there is a similar sense of failing to live up to what is expected of a woman, joined with a sense of being an imposter as a man. One solution to this sense of dual failure might be to change my clothing style, another to relax about it. However, I am not good at relaxing and I find that my costume cannot be switched easily, nor can the more fundamental imperatives that cause me to want protections associated with maleness. I am not trying to argue here that my basic nature is male, or even that part of it is, and that therefore a male costume is fitting to me; that I only feel such a costume false, or not truly mine, because others think so. Rather, I wish to speak of the hurt of being seen as a man, or as a woman trying to mime a man. Such hurt seems to me central to my experience of female gender.

THE HURT OF BEING CALLED A MAN

When on various occasions, I have been accused of being butch, a male-identified woman, a man, like a man, or, as once happened, a bulldyke, I have shuddered, feeling, "Of course I must be as they say" and, at the same time, feeling wronged and hurt. So central to me have been my efforts to be like a man, and not like a stereotypical woman, that I think I have succeeded. Thus the "Of course." In addition, so fundamental have been my identifications with important men in my life (my father, men in movies, boys when growing up) and not with the seemingly less adventuresome, more confused, less self-satisfied women (my mother, women in movies, women relatives) that I am surprised to find I am still a woman, that my attempts to outstep my gender have not worked. Often I know this only when called a man, or when ridiculed for being a mannish woman, for it is then I feel the hurt of having been over-looked as a woman for so long, the hurt of "you are not seeing me."

It was only a few years ago that a student in one of my classes told me that another student, a man, had called me a bulldyke outside of class. That was the first time I had heard that term applied to me. I felt I did not fit the image. In my mind, I pictured some other woman who was bigger and squarer than me, wore a leather jacket, rode a motorcycle, and slicked back her hair, and who did not make my little concessions to femininity—the earrings again, a woman's watch. Maybe that woman made her concessions, too, but, at the moment, I was mostly aware of mine, and of the degree to which the term "bulldyke" unnerved me. It made me anxious, as if it were indeed true of me, and uncertain about what kind of monster the student had seen.

At first, I thought it was the hate in the word that was so unsettling. The male student who said it was a ROTC officer, and he had not, I was sure, used the term bulldyke with pride, or with affection for me. There was fear in the word, I assumed, his of me, and I did not like to be feared. More importantly, however, although it took me longer to see it, I think the term shook me up because this fellow was calling me a man. In calling me "bulldyke," he was transforming me into a grotesque male thug, a person ostensibly a woman, but whose principal features were male— being brutish, for instance. There was something intrinsically horrifying to me about both the ridicule of my gender and the denial of me that were involved in the male bulldyke image. I was not well enough defended against the accusation of being such a mannish grotesque to disbelieve it entirely, however, or to keep it at a real distance from me.

Only when I spoke with a friend who was also a lesbian, and who, too, had experience being called a bulldyke, did I begin to see what bothered me. She said the term upset her because it made her feel she was being called a man and being told that she should not be like a man. My friend clearly looked like a woman to me, even in black leather with inch-length hair. Thinking of her, I was able to see myself also as a woman, rather than as the caricature in the bulldyke image. I was able to see that I could reject being called a man.

Nonetheless, after the name-calling incident, when walking the stairs and hallways of the building where I taught, I was more than usually self-conscious. What did people see when they looked at me? I wondered. Did they see a big, tough woman and hate her? Did they see a woman trying to be like a man? Did I look very odd? There was nothing much I could do about my discomfort except to try not to care. The discomfort was not really new to me, for it was about gender appropriateness and my own acceptability, about whether I could be a woman when seen as a man, and, most basically, about whether I had a right to be seen at all. In one sense, the story had a good ending. By the semester's end, the student who had called me a bulldyke came around to liking and trying to understand gay people, finding fault with his previous prejudices. He told me about this after the last two class sessions, pleased with himself for how he had changed. His ability to alter his prejudices seemed less unexpected to me, however, than my own response to a single word he had used. I would not have thought that being called "bulldyke" would have fazed me.

Another experience when being called a man hurt me occurred with a woman, a close friend whom I loved. In part because she was a woman and, in part, because of the context, I was hurt more deeply and for longer than when the male student called me a bulldyke. Why, I still wonder, did she do that? Why hurt me that way? Was I that bad? She was a straight woman. I was a lesbian. We had a minor sexual involvement. "It was like being with a man," she said. I heard, "It was not supposed to be that way with a woman. You were not supposed to be that way." I imagined I must have been barbaric, brutal, unfeeling, insensitive, like a living-room rapist. I felt terrible, as if part of me (the female part) was cut off by her comment. She had seen only my self-protective (male) shell. I felt there was more to me, but she no longer wanted my advances.

This straight woman did not want me to touch her, to be near her, to take her any further than a subdued sense of sexual arousal that she could experience by herself. During our sexual encounter, I had wanted her to respond to me so I could know that I mattered to her, that she was willing to be with me. She did not want to respond, to be a lesbian, to feel it was worth it. She wanted to lie on a couch, or a bed, and go into a trance, I felt, to be near oblivion, and then have a transcendent experience. I failed to provide that experience. I was a man for her. Are not lesbians really men? Are not butch lesbians, especially, stand-ins for men, to some women? Such questions keep haunting me.

At the time, and for some time after, I felt my friend's reaction to me implied that I had tried to make her feel more than she wanted to, and in doing so, that I had forced myself on her. Thus I had been like a man in a most offensive way. However, she did not give me a chance to be different; I also did not take the chance. I did not show my friend openly how I felt, but, instead, I wanted her to show her feelings to me.

I wanted her to be the yielding, revealing, expressive woman, while I was the one who shows little, who covers how she feels and tries to urge feeling in another. Only much later did I think, Why did I not see her in the man's role? Why am I so quick to put myself in that role? My friend was the one who lay there unwilling to feel, who would not respond. She felt hard and unyielding to me. I did not, therefore, say to her, "You felt like a man to me." Was that because she wore stockings and I wore pants? Because she lay beneath me and looked up? Am I fooled by such appearances? Do I see them and act like a man just so I can play the gender role I think will provide greater protection for me? Did I act like a man? Did acting like one make me one? Why does the hurt of being called a man run so deep for me?

That episode of my being seen as a man in an intimate encounter appears to me, eleven years later, in such highly gendered terms. The other woman seems the woman, I the man. I clearly associate maleness with self-protection and femaleness with a lack of it. When a man accuses me of being a bulldyke, or looks at me and sees a man, it hurts me far less than when a woman does so. A woman, I assume, knows me better. I take seriously what she says. I find it hard to rid myself of feeling I am the person another woman sees.

Much of my feeling that I am a man thus hinges on how I think I look to others. I feel often that my gender lies in my appearance. I also think such a feeling is deceptive. What is true of gender is not that it is primarily a matter of appearance, but that it is so important as to need to be signaled constantly by appearance. It is constantly necessary to tell who is female and male, to announce one's gender and be confirmed for it, for it is not only the outer but the inner world that asks, Which gendered terms describe me? How? Do these terms fit me well at all?

RESPONSES TO FEMME AND BUTCH STYLES IN WOMEN

I usually think it is other women, and not me, who adopt gendered roles, that these roles—femme and butch—do not describe me. I am clear that I would not call myself a femme. That style is, for me, too associated with what women traditionally stand for. However, I am less certain about the term "butch." I feel uncomfortable applying that term to myself and I am suspicious of my discomfort, as if it means I am trying to avoid who I am. I think I want to deny I am butch because of the male implications of the term, and because the goal people speak of always seems to be androgyny, a mix of gendered elements in which no one role is dominant. I also wish to deny I am butch because I have learned that a woman should not ape a man, because I think being butch is not true of me underneath, and because of how I often respond to other women I see as butch.

When I see a woman in a butch role, I recoil. I do not want to be near her. I see no point. What would I gain? I feel I am in search of a womanly woman. I do not fathom very well that the style might not be the person, that the whole might be more complex. I see male clothing, physical mannerisms, or style of speech, and I think, "This is a man," just as others may do when they look at me. Sometimes, I try to undress a butch woman in my mind. I think that if I can see a female body beneath this woman's clothes, I will feel differently toward her. If I can see breasts and a woman's rounded shape, I will feel this is someone soft and caring, capable of saying the gentle things I need to hear, which I often cannot say to myself because my mother did not say them. If I see a woman's body, I will be able to imagine myself curled up between this woman's breasts, my head nestled in them, myself as a child held and protected. I will know then that this is a woman. Of course, that is stereotypical thinking of an unreal sort. All women do not have breasts, all breasts are not nurturant, all mothers are not good, all mothers are not women. Yet I persist in looking for the most clichéd of female appearances.

When I see a woman wearing a dress, for instance, or with breasts whose shapes are visible through a shirt, a woman with a way of looking at, and speaking to, me that suggests she will be caring toward me, when I see long hair and a full-bodied figure, when I see the most standard displays of female style, I think, "Here is someone who will be kind to me. Here is a woman." I want to go to her, to be held, to go to bed with her. In that closeness, I think I will feel what I need. I fall for a symbol and move immediately to intimacy, and both the fall and the move can be disastrous for me.

One reason I think I look for femme-style women is that I do not feel

I myself am a woman. I have breasts, but they are not breasts. They belong to someone else. They are bumps, they are too small. My shape is not the shape of a woman. It is a man's shape, but it is not a man's shape. I have kindness in me, but it is not the kindness of a woman. Rather, it is my father's kindness. When people receive from me, they receive from him. What I offer is what a man offers. Usually, I think I am a young man, offering adventure and gentleness and a need for nurturance that some women will respond to. The sources that make me feel I am a man thus include my desire to be a man. This is so strong in me, in good part, because I have seen it is men who receive the affections of women. It is men in the movies whom women hold, men whom women are most caring toward. My mother slept with my father. My younger brother aroused much affection in people, and I always wanted to be him, to be male.

Heterosexuality has profound effects. It is more than an observation about who mates with whom. It is a theory about incompleteness and completion, about the desirability of women valuing men over women, and about the need for maintaining distinctions between the genders. I think it is a bad theory, but I am not immune to it, to the gender idealizations that come with it, and to the way it shapes the imagination.

LESBIAN IN A HETEROSEXUAL WORLD

Several years ago, for the first time, my lover, whom I will call Judith, and I spent a night in a country inn. We stayed in a room upstairs with a down comforter on the bed, wine and mints on the dresser, and antique dolls in the bookshelves. Nearby was a common room with a woodburning stove, and across the hall a bathroom with copies of magazines neatly set out. I was not accustomed to the deliberateness of the setting, but the least familiar part of the experience was the group breakfast in the morning. In the kitchen downstairs, around a big circular table sat all the people who had stayed at the inn the night before—ten people, five couples, including Judith and myself. The four other couples were heterosexual. One of the men was a coroner, another designed downtown department store windows. Over breakfast, while the innkeepers served us, the heterosexual couples discussed other inns they had stayed at, antique furniture they had bought at auctions, and large round globes that were the trend in department store windows that season. Judith and I felt out of place and very aware of the heterosexuality of the company.

Later that day as we drove away from the inn on our way to the ocean, I imagined a changed scene. No longer was the social climate of the inn heterosexual couples speaking of consumerism. Instead, the guests were lesbian couples and the inn was a setting for a mystery. My mystery began with a woman in dark clothes lurking in the doorway to a barn in a field behind the inn. But it was the nature of the couples whose paths might cross out by the barn that most fascinated me. In my mind, I saw one couple clearly. They were inside the inn talking in the common room by the woodburning stove—a small, dark-haired, butch-style woman and a larger, more outgoing, femme-style woman. I had little sense of the plot that would unfold. My focus was on the mystery of the attraction between these two women and, potentially, between these two and others staying at the inn.

What did the open-mannered, femme woman in the couple see in the smaller, dark-haired woman? I wondered. What did the quieter, dark-haired woman have to offer? What comfort did she find in the larger, more sociable woman? What was on the surface in each of them? What was underneath? Who gave what? Who needed what? What about the femme-butch aspect of their relationship? How important was it? What did it mean? Was the butch really the femme underneath, and the femme the butch, if one looked closely? Why would anyone value the butch woman when the femme, it seemed to me, had so much more to offer? Clearly, these questions were from my own life, but that was not the point for me at the time. The point was that I could not escape structuring my imagination in terms of gender roles—those female and male styles, highly variable and essentially heterosexual, here adopted by women.

Although I never was able to write a mystery plot set in the inn, the image of the lesbian couple by the stove stayed with me for a long time. It was a way that I reminded myself of a puzzle that bothered me. All of us, I think, have situations, or puzzles, in our minds in which the gendered behaviors we see are unsettling for us and not yet figured out. My mystery of the inn was a story of my own importing gender roles from one context, the inn (a heterosexual world), to another, a world of women, and then attempting to determine the meaning of these roles in the women's world. To what extent did female and male gender roles become different when adopted by women or, more accurately, when adapted by them, than when adapted by men, and different still when adapted by lesbians? To what extent did women adapting gendered roles perpetuate a system of male dominance and female subordinance in which women appear less substantial than men, and men are more important and more safe? Was a straight femme woman the same as a lesbian femme? Or was a lesbian different because she was more false in that role—less subordinate to men, although subordinate, perhaps, to women who acted like men? These distinctions seem important to me because women who act like men are not men, and because lesbians are again different, and the differences of women, and of lesbians, often are not seen. At the same time, what is seen—a surface gender style—is often not well understood, either in terms of what it means to an individual, or in terms of a deeper structure of gender.

In recent years, I have heard it said that gender roles are declining in significance both among lesbians and among heterosexuals. The gender differences these roles reflect are said to be increasingly superficial, rather than basic, reflecting people's attempts to hold on to old symbols of identity, even as these symbols lose social import. The two genders are said to be becoming more equal; women and men are becoming more the same. Gender role-playing among lesbians is often seen as something done years ago, in prior generations, when there was less of a feminist critique against reproducing heterosexuality. In prior years, the roles were supposedly taken more seriously: butch lesbians dressed in clear male ways, acted differently than femmes, chose femmes for lovers; and when they lived together, the two often divided labor according to traditional heterosexual marriage roles. Members of a more contemporary lesbian couple will usually not divide in such a strict manner, and there is a new "playing with gender" attitude. Yet it seems to me that gender roles persist and re-arise in many ways that are beyond our control and consciousness, some of them subtle, others blatant. The roles appear among working-class lesbians who take traditional gender roles seriously, as does the surrounding class culture; among younger lesbians who play at the roles, keeping, or feeling they keep, a more stylized distance from them (lipstick lesbians in the femme revival, for instance). The roles appear among women who wish to transcend gender roles in themselves and others, yet who see the roles everywhere, like myself; among career lesbians in male-style female clothes who must make great efforts to prove they are still women; among queer women and transgenderists, who often deal with gender by treating it as malleable, and by switching back and forth between female and male styles, as if they seek to do away with gender by mixing it up.[2]

My point is not how sharp the roles are, or how unchangeable, or how much the same from place to place, but the needs they speak to. More than announcing who is female or male, they represent a preoccupation with gender, a need to define oneself in gendered terms that is no less real for being unacknowledged, and that in women is often understated, or engaged in so quietly it seems to be natural. People who know me, for instance, think I look like myself, and that I am a woman. My clothes seem fitting to me. They are not aware of how much I feel, and fear, I am a man. When younger and wanting so much to be a man—in order to be free of being a woman, or like my mother, and in order simply to be free—I used to take greater pride in being mistaken for a man than I do now, and to feel less discomforted when called one. Maybe I got so accustomed to the pants and freedom that being called a man did not seem so much of a compliment anymore. I felt better when seen as a woman. But maybe the reason has more to do with a change in what the genders came to stand for in my particular world. At some point, the meanings switched, and good became female, and freedom became female, and so did I.

CONCLUSIONS

This is not a completed story but, rather, a suggestive one, providing a few illustrations to indicate the presence of inner conflicts in a female gender role. Although I have emphasized male elements in my gender style, my central concern is with my appropriateness as a woman—with whether I qualify, and what I must do, to be seen as female. My efforts to be a woman are harder to talk about than my efforts to be a man. They are more embarrassing, and less self-conscious, and they may be viewed as unnecessary—I cannot help but be a woman. However, I cannot remember a time when I could take that status for granted, nor when being seen as female was unrelated to feeling I was female. I know I gain a sense of protection when adapting elements of a male style— men's clothing, for instance. However, I feel touched most deeply when seen as a woman, as if being female is the most and least visible thing about me, and the most important thing.

I rely on women for both intimate and more formal relationships be- cause of qualities the gendered role of women provides for me. Among women, I find some who are, in style, like men, and others who are more like traditional women. I, myself, am often unsure of how to be. I feel that my gestures are either female or male, that a nongendered choice is not one I can make. At the same time, I often think that my actions are an individual matter and not gendered. Yet when I look closely, it seems to me that my needs for protection, the sense of vulnerability these needs are tied to, my compliance with a system that says I am unimpor- tant, my fear on the streets, my wanting to look tough like a man in my clothes, my seeking out femme-style women for comfort, my undress- ing butch women to find a similar comfort, my hurt on being called a man—all these are very much related to my being female. They are bound up with what I have learned is my gender, much as I wish they were simply signs of myself.

Clearly, I import heterosexual habits and perceptions into my female world. I would like to do differently. I would like to stop trying to be like a man, stop seeing femme and butch styles among women, stop thinking these matter. Yet I cannot easily do so, as if part of my self-pro- tection lies in not overlooking the signs—woman, boy, girl, man. These identifications emerge from a context in which women do not count for much, and in which the basic gender categories remain strict assign- ments for most people most of the time, even when gender roles other than one's own are tried on and partially adopted, blurring lines be- tween the genders. Gender categories are so strong in their consequence that playing with gender remains just that—elaboration, embroidery, variations on a theme of male dominance and female subordinance, male importance and female silence.

The seemingly trivial behaviors involved and the inner preoccupations of my gender have far deeper impact than perhaps they ought to. I speak here for acknowledging the importance of gender rather than succumbing to the confusion of it, and for trying to think about why the confusion so easily sets in. Anything that makes light of gender and understates the degree to which it is defining of people, and constraining for women, may have great appeal. Our social system depends on a female underclass, and attempts to disavow the importance of gender conveniently hide this dependence. The work women do is often invisible and takes many forms. One of these is that of maintaining a female gender role despite inner conflicts. This role, as I have learned it, does not offend and keeps much internal. In part for that reason, it is important, I think, to speak about the difficulties of female experience with as much candor as possible. It is important to make public more of what is usually hidden in individual female worlds.

Two

BECOMING A LESBIAN

TWENTY YEARS AGO, I first lived with another woman. This is a story about that experience, excerpted from a novel I later wrote. Although written in the third person, it is strictly autobiographical. To me, this story is not only about lesbians, but also about female-female relating and the challenge of intimacy between women. I call it "Becoming a Lesbian" because, for me, being a lesbian is an ongoing process of seeking intimacy, personal value, and happiness with another woman.[1] This process may have an initial stage, but it does not have an end. Often, I think, becoming a lesbian involves challenging basic assumptions about oneself. For me, it has required admitting my most basic needs of other women rather than walling these needs off, or denying them. It has required discarding some of my previous ways of being female, and finding new ones. As this story suggests, women often teach each other how to be lesbian. Fran, my lover, taught me, as she was taught by a previous lover.

I hope this tale indicates that I think lesbianism is a choice, rather than an inborn nature. At some point, I chose, for the first time with awareness, to meet my most intimate needs with other women. However, I think I did not become a lesbian suddenly, or as a result of any single cause, but rather as a result of many small experiences and invisible choices I had made along the way. Eventually I found myself living with another woman, sharing sexuality and interpersonal attentiveness, and feeling quite unprepared for it. I then had to learn a great deal about what was involved. I had to grow to appreciate the specific emotional contours of a lesbian relationship. I think that lesbian relationships touch the deepest emotions women have. They are important far beyond what one expects. A two-year lesbian relationship lasts for a century and leaves the parties to it forever changed. When a lesbian relationship ends, there is no overstating the heartbreak. In part to mend an early break, I wrote this story about a lesbian love.

FROM "JENNY'S WORLD"

I

Often these days Jenny thought about Fran, the first woman she had lived with. Fran was the first in a series of dreams that now haunted Jenny like broken glass. Jenny was younger then, although at the time she felt old, for she was in her late twenties. Fran was eleven years older. Fran was wiser, Jenny thought. She wore her graying hair short, her clothes tailored. She drank regularly, often heavily, chain-smoked, and spoke to Jenny with a tone of affection and of reason. Fran's father was a fundamentalist minister. Fran had therefore become a scientist. Each day she went to her lab. She knew how to tune her car and how to fix things around the house. Anything that moved she believed she could take apart and then put back together again. Her very way of speaking conveyed precision and depth. She was one kind of dream come true for Jenny.

Jenny had first met Fran at meetings of a lesbian group they both attended in which Jenny was outspoken, making more enemies, she felt, than friends. Fran came up to her after one of those meetings and asked for her phone number. Within a few days, Fran called to ask her for a date, her way of proposing it formal and somewhat nervous. When Jenny accepted, Fran had responded by saying "Nifty," which made Jenny wonder about her. The people Jenny knew did not say "nifty."

That night of their first date was as clear to Jenny now as if it had happened yesterday. She pulled her car up to the front of a large mock-Tudor style house in a section of town where the lawns were deep and the houses big, some of them huge as mansions. Fran had told her on the phone that a dirty white V W bus would be parked in front of the house where she lived, so Jenny could not miss it. As she drove up, Jenny saw the bus, but since it was dark out, she was not sure exactly how she was supposed to tell if it was clean or dirty. She did know, however, that she ought to be on time. That had seemed implied in Fran's tone of voice on the phone.

Jenny walked up to the house, crossing the damp front lawn to reach an entrance that reminded her of entrances to buildings at Ivy League colleges. Beside the heavy, dark-wooden doorway was a small, lit, yellow light. She rang the bell and Fran came immediately. Jenny looked at Fran, then quickly away and up at the high wooden ceiling of the large living room behind Fran. Elaborate wrought-iron lamps and ornamental ironwork hung down from it. Never before had Jenny been in a house like this. Fran invited her in, smiling, her intensity showing in a vague tremor in her lips and in a shaking in her hands as she reached to take Jenny's jacket, which Jenny would not let her take. Jenny wore wool shirts as jackets, then as now, and she liked to hold on to them.

In those first few moments, Fran, in her stance and bodily motions, seemed to Jenny like a woman poised on the verge of excitement. A highly refined and constrained excitement was the feeling she conveyed. She led Jenny to a seat on a couch in the living room and asked her if she would like a drink. Jenny did not drink much and could have cared less, but she said yes. Pointing to a glass on a table by her side, Fran said she was drinking scotch. Jenny said that would be fine for her too.

While Fran went off to the kitchen to get her drink, Jenny looked around the living room and thought about Fran and this house. The house seemed to be as mysterious and awesome as Fran was. Perhaps she had a husband who had left her, some children who were not there. Jenny did not find out until much later that night—after she and Fran had gone on their date to a harpsichord concert—that the house did not actually belong to Fran. She rented a room with a bath in the back of the house behind the kitchen. In the time since she had been living there, however, she had become friends with the owners, who were now away on vacation. She was taking care of the house for them while they were gone, using the whole of it as if it were hers. Although Jenny found out later that night that the house was not Fran's own—it was simply one of the shells she moved in and out of with seeming ease—the image of Fran in the big solemn structure stayed with Jenny and seemed to fit Fran more than many of the images that succeeded it.

After Jenny and Fran returned from the concert, they sat and talked in Fran's back room. Jenny sat on a couch at the opposite end of the room from Fran, who sat on a chair. Darkness from outside the room seemed to invade through side windows despite lights on within—two glowing lamps sitting on a large golden oak desk set against an inner wall. Jenny and Fran talked back and forth, getting to know one another. But the experience felt to Jenny more like an inquisition than a regular conversation. Fran asked her many questions about her life, leaving little space for Jenny to ask questions of her in turn. Jenny felt far away from Fran because she was sitting across the room from her. At the same time, she felt as if Fran's questions were opening her up and reaching deep inside her, exposing her to herself.

Jenny saw into her own feelings as a result of Fran's questions. She felt that Fran valued her, whether that was true or not. Jenny also decided then and there that she would end her marriage. She made that decision not in order to be with Fran, or because Fran said to do it, although Fran certainly seemed to imply that ending her marriage might follow logically from what Jenny told her. Rather, it was because, prior to this one night, Jenny had not felt that anyone else in the world other than the person she had married could get to her deep inside, could touch her with words or with insights. Here Fran was doing that, thus proving her wrong. She was showing Jenny that there were other possibilities, possibilities Jenny wanted very much.

When Fran was finished with her questions and with revealing what little she did about herself, Jenny felt very tired. She stood up to leave, carrying her glass of scotch to put it down on Fran's oak desk. The glass was nearly as full as it had been when Fran had handed it to her earlier. Fran, too, then stood and walked up to the desk. She offered to take Jenny's glass, to see her to the door. Jenny looked at Fran and saw that

Fran was going to let her go, was going to leave a wide swath around her, a distance between them, as she had done when they had sat and talked. Jenny said something then, from inside her, about these people like Fran who asked questions. "Could you touch them?" she asked. Fran nodded, or seemed to Jenny to nod, or at least not to say no. Jenny reached out her hand and touched Fran's arm. Fran moved closer to her. Jenny was surrounded by darkness and by Fran's subdued excitement, by an embrace and a kiss.

"Would you like to spend the night?" Fran asked. "The couch you were sitting on folds out into a double bed." Jenny turned to look back at the dark green couch behind her. She was afraid. Never before had she gone to bed with an actual lesbian. The women she had slept with before were straight women who were having brief flirtations with her, not women like Fran who had loved and lived exclusively with women for the past eighteen years. That much Jenny had managed to gain from Fran in their previous conversation.

After sitting down to give it thought, weighing her fear against her need, Jenny decided to stay. Then, before she went to sleep that night, she outdid herself in sexual performance. In no way did she want Fran to know the inexperience she felt, particularly since, when she had been talking with Fran earlier, she had implied that her prior sexual affairs with women were more fully developed and more numerous than they actually were. In bed with Fran, Jenny wanted Fran to feel that she had been made love to by an expert, not a novice. She also did not want Fran to sense her fear. Finally, very tired, although not before deciding in her mind that whether or not she saw Fran again, she would still end her marriage, Jenny fell asleep.

The next morning when she woke, Jenny had breakfast with a woman she did not know, a formal person larger than herself, dressed in a deep blue oriental silk robe, whose hands shook and who displayed an intensity when she spoke. At a table in a sunny alcove off the kitchen, Fran served them each a slice of cantaloupe with their breakfast. Jenny did not like cantaloupe, it made her burp, but she thought she had best be proper and eat it. She looked over at Fran and felt like running away and also that she was one of the luckiest people in the world. Later that morning, Jenny went home, promising to come back at dinner time.

Fran stood in her blue robe in the front doorway of the house and asked Jenny to come back as she said goodbye to her. Fran stood erect and looked calm, yet the lift of one eyebrow, the break in her voice, her way of simply standing there, suggested that she feared that Jenny would not return. Jenny did return that night and slept with Fran. She also returned the next night and the next night and the next. For roughly two years after their first date, Jenny came back each night to sleep with Fran, except on those occasions when either one of them was out of town.

On the second night Jenny spent with Fran, they went out to dinner at a Middle Eastern restaurant where a belly dancer performed near their table. Jenny felt disturbed by the performance. Fran found it entertaining. Jenny drove them to the restaurant, parked a few blocks away, and walked with Fran up the street. As they walked, she looked over at Fran, who seemed preoccupied and intent, her gaze straight ahead. Fran was wearing a bulky-knit Scandinavian sweater her mother had made for her. The sweater, with its black and white design, brought out the silver in her gray hair. Jenny looked at Fran and thought that she was positively handsome. Never had Jenny been with such a handsome woman. She reached her arm around Fran's shoulder to show Fran, to show the street, that she was not scared. Fran's generation, Jenny felt, would not do such a thing in public. Jenny therefore would.

At dinner, Jenny found it hard to talk, given the noise of the restaurant, so mostly she caught glimpses of Fran when she thought Fran was not looking. Jenny also tried to eat. Fran asked her many questions. Yet the questions were either too serious or too pointed for Jenny to answer them well. Fran, however, answered directly the questions Jenny asked of her. Most of Fran's answers were short, her comments casual, almost flip. There was a tone of sarcasm beneath the surface in Fran's voice and beneath that, Jenny felt, a layer of hurt. Jenny also felt she was hearing Fran's story in bits and pieces that were not entirely connected. Names and years seemed jumbled together. Jenny hoped her confusion about who Fran had been lovers with, when, and for how long, or when Fran had moved here or there, did not show too plainly.

In the next few weeks, Jenny gained a more solid sense of Fran. It came in small increments, usually at those moments when Fran, a drink in her hand in the evening, was willing to sit back on her couch, or on a chair, and to tell a long story, her dark eyes taking both of them back to another time or place. Fran's past seemed to Jenny to be another life, perhaps because Fran presented it as such. She suggested that her other life was over, and that now she was a different person, someone who had emerged with great difficulty and as a result of much learning.

The sense of Fran's need to break with her past bothered Jenny, who kept searching for regularity and for a sense of the sameness about a person. Jenny wanted the security of knowing what Fran was like now from these stories Fran told about herself before. The woman Fran had lived with for eleven years sounded a lot like Jenny. She had similar fears. Fran had left her. The woman Fran became involved with next was different, more outgoing, more in command. She had rejected Fran. Coming back from a camping trip one night, she told Fran she wanted their relationship to be over. Fran had cried for hours in the back of her VW bus trying to get this woman to change her mind. Jenny felt that Fran's telling her about this breakup made Fran seem more human. There was something about Fran that was so remote, so permanently under control, held down by the alcohol, the smoking, the focused intensity of Fran's way of being, that Jenny, even from the beginning, looked constantly for breakthroughs—for moments when a more vulnerable, accessible woman would appear.

Fran gave Jenny one of those moments by surprise one afternoon on the second weekend of their knowing each other when Fran got very upset with her. Jenny had called earlier in the day to say she would be late in coming over and to ask Fran if she should come at all. When she finally arrived, Fran was agitated. Jenny sat on a window seat in the wood-paneled den located near the front of the house, in the one part of that room that was not dark. The sun came in through the window behind her and warmed her. Fran sat on a chair across from her, then stood, sat again, then stood, speaking with difficulty. There were "demands" she had of another person, she said. Over the years she had come to know them. She had not always. She had stayed in her eleven-year relationship and not known her needs until the end, she told Jenny, until that relationship became so painful that she felt like she was bleeding inside. That was when she left. She took off in her bus and traveled around the state for a year, sitting on rocks, thinking, and learning to like herself. She quit her job, gave away most of what she owned, and rebuilt the inside of her bus so that it could be a moving home for her. Never again, she told Jenny, would she let what had occurred back then happen to her.

"I want you to know from the start," Fran said, standing, looking across at Jenny. "I have a list of needs, expectations. I want to be absolutely clear about them."

Jenny heard and did not hear. She heard Fran saying she needed another person to be there for her, to be responsive to her. Fran then listed her needs: one, two, three, four. Jenny remembered the formality of their presentation more than what they were specifically. She felt all this must be occurring because Fran had sensed in her a desire to run away. It was more than a desire; it was a reflex actually. Fran must have sensed it immediately, just as Jenny had sensed Fran's hunger, her need for someone else's emotions to fill her. Jenny was not used to opening herself to another person, but she nonetheless felt it not beyond her to be with Fran. She told Fran she wanted to measure up, to respond. Fran said that was good enough. "Well met," she told Jenny moments later, lifting her glass in a toast.

Already in their first few weeks, a pattern had begun to emerge in Jenny's relationship with Fran, a pattern not easily broken, one that had its own challenge, its own tenderness and fear. Jenny would come each night to the big house where Fran lived. Occasionally, Fran came to Jenny's house, but because it was a small apartment with little furniture—a place whose emptiness was not apparent to Jenny until Fran commented on it—it seemed to offer them less. Fran soon decided that she and Jenny should use the master bedroom upstairs in the big house. "After all," she told Jenny, "it's sitting there empty, why not use it?" So that was where they slept. Jenny would arrive at Fran's in the evening, usually after dinner, and leave in the morning before breakfast to go back to her own house to work. Sometimes she would bring with her the notebooks in which she was writing, carrying them, a change of underpants, and a toothbrush in a red canvas bookbag. Most people had green bookbags at the time, or had had them several years earlier. Jenny's, therefore, was deliberately red.

When at one point Fran suggested that she leave her toothbrush, Jenny refused to do it. She might need it later in the day, she told Fran. "You could buy another toothbrush," Fran added. It was not about toothbrushes, however, Jenny knew. What if she did not come back? Then there would be this remnant of her in someone else's house. Also, she was very attached to her things. Even her toothbrush was important to her—the bristles were worn in just the right way. She preferred to keep it with her.

One quiet evening when Jenny arrived at Fran's house, Fran showed her slides of trips she had taken into wilderness areas. They sat at a large polished mahogany table in the darkened dining room. Fran projected her slides on a far wall. With enthusiasm, her kind of contained, deliberate, almost planned enthusiasm, Fran told Jenny about the beauty of the places she had visited and proudly showed her the pictures so that Jenny could see for herself. Fran had mentioned her wilderness trips to Jenny before. She had told Jenny about her backpacking equipment and how she had converted her bus, and she had shown Jenny her well-worn hiking boots. Jenny had kept a distance from it. This time, though, with the slides large and bright on the wall, Jenny could not keep her distance and felt scared. After Fran was through showing her slides, she turned on the lights in the room and smiled over at Jenny, awaiting her response.

Jenny, not big on tact, told Fran immediately that the pictures had scared her. The wilderness did not seem friendly to her. The marshy bogs were not friendly, nor were the stony mountains. She needed the security of a house, she told Fran. She needed her own schedule, her routine, her familiar protections. She needed to be inside. That was true for right now. It might always be true. She felt she risked losing Fran to say it. To her relief, Fran said that was all right. Jenny need not go backpacking with her. There were other people she could go with. The woman who owned this house was one. Fran then took Jenny upstairs to the master bedroom and showed her the woman's well-worn hiking boots in the walk-in closet.

The next morning when Jenny woke, as on many of those mornings of the first weeks she stayed with Fran, while Jenny showered, Fran went downstairs and made coffee. She brought it up in two large earthenware mugs and sat on a small couch in the bedroom, listening to classical music on her portable radio, reading from a book, and occasionally looking up to watch Jenny dress. Often at that time of day, the music the radio station played was Bach. Jenny previously had not heard much Bach, but she began to like it. Fran would sit on the couch in her robe listening to her radio. She would put down her book when she saw Jenny was done dressing. Before Jenny picked up her bag to leave, Fran would stop her and ask her to sit beside her or on her lap. Fran then would look directly at Jenny close up. "Je t'adore," she said once, translating when Jenny asked. Jenny was moved, yet found it odd. She felt that she did not deserve such attention from a woman of the stature of Fran, and also that she had to leave to go home to do her work.

Much as she pushed them aside at the time, impatient to get on with her day, those early mornings of Jenny's first few weeks with Fran were important to her. The sweetness of Fran's stopping her before she left and holding her, stroking her, clasping her close, meant more to Jenny than the nights that came before them. Jenny knew that, for she remembered the mornings when the nights had long since faded. There was the sound of Bach, the morning sun entering gently through a recessed upper-story window, Fran sitting there waiting, looking over at Jenny and sipping her coffee slowly. Then Fran would get up to see her to the door, Jenny like a kid going off to school, bookbag in her hand, although she did not have a lunch.

The nights that Jenny spent with Fran came to matter more to her later, after Fran moved to another house and as Jenny gradually joined her there and eventually moved in with her. That other house was smaller and much more theirs than the house in which they first met. It was set back in green hills at the end of a canyon, removed, surrounded by bushes and high trees, and visited by birds and by deer more than by people. In that house and in another near it, Jenny had experiences with Fran that marked her and touched her deeply, so deeply that by now they were like grounding. Like bedrock, they were what the rest was built on. If it had not been for Fran, Jenny thought, much that had occurred next in her life would not have happened as it did. Fran had taught her about living in other people's houses, and appreciating the outdoors, and feeling special about herself. At the same time, Fran had hurt her. Fran had left her. She drove off one day from the second house they lived in and then did not speak to Jenny for three years. Something broke inside Jenny then and never got repaired. As a result, it was now hard for her to remember back. Her past with Fran, the good parts of it, seemed hidden beneath trappings. The trappings were tough. They were Jenny's anger. Back in the beginning, however, Jenny could not predict such a break. She was very slowly entering a new world.

II

One afternoon during her first month of knowing Fran, Jenny arrived at Fran's big house to take a drive with her up into the hills. Fran had told her there was a small house about half an hour outside of town that belonged to some friends of hers, a retired couple now traveling around the country in their camper. They had asked her if she would live there and take care of the house for them while they were away for a year. Fran knew the house, she told Jenny, because ten years earlier, before this couple bought it, she had lived there with her lover. Back then, the house was no more than a cottage, very rustic, poorly insulated, and without heat. Patty and Bob, when they bought the place, had fixed it up so that now it was a very comfortable small home.

As Fran drove her bus up into the hills, Jenny sat beside her. She looked out the window, listening as Fran spoke, and thought about how people trusted Fran with their homes. The road up to the house wound through thick green trees and had views of wild brush and of orange poppies blowing in the wind. As they climbed, the air got quieter and the drops on the edges of the road became steeper. They seemed to be going much farther than half an hour away.

Jenny liked sitting up high beside Fran in her bus. She had never before known anyone with a VW bus, and it felt exotic to her to be riding in one. Jenny had never been up this particular road and she did not know where she was going. She was used to being in town, used to city streets. Jenny was, after all, a Brooklyn girl, although Brooklyn was very far behind her. She had a fear of heights and of strange places and people. Fran sat calmly next to her, looking out through the top of the front windshield of her van at the sky or at the high limbs of trees. She looked up at them as often as she looked down at the road, Jenny thought. Fran also occasionally looked over at Jenny with affection. She was enjoying the ride, enjoying Jenny, pleased to be showing her someplace new, to be taking Jenny away with her.

Not wanting to reveal fully her fear, Jenny asked Fran cautiously about the road at night and the safety of it in the rain. Fran assured her there was nothing to worry about. There was another way to come if a storm got bad or if Jenny became afraid. That way, however, took longer. Jenny did not feel reassured. She held on to her seat, held her breath, and decided that Fran was a perfect person to die with should the bus careen over the edge of the road after hitting a pothole at a bad angle. She could not know, just then, that only months later she would grow to love that road, to trust it, to speed on its curves with a daredevil's ease, or that she would copy Fran's way of looking up and out, whether she was driving Fran's bus or her own car. She could not guess that years later she would dream of that silly road and miss it with a pain longer than any trip, a pain that contained all the places it had led to and all her own needs to turn from them and move on.

After climbing and taking a sharp turn down and weaving back into a canyon, Fran and Jenny finally reached the house Fran had described. Fran drove her bus up a graveled driveway and pulled into a dusty lot by its side. She and Jenny got out and Jenny looked at the small white house before them, unpretentious, set into the hillside, its shutters neatly closed. Jenny helped Fran unload belongings from the back of her bus and carry them into a storage shed across the way. Then she went with Fran into the house. The space inside felt close to her. The rooms opened directly onto one another. There was a comfortable small living room in which a soft couch sat in front of a broad bay window. A television set sat opposite the couch. Two chairs were by the fireplace; a thick goldish-green rug lay on the floor. To the left of the living room was a dining area and behind that a long narrow kitchen. Down a hallway leading back from the living room, past a bath, were two bedrooms—a smaller one that had belonged to Patty and Bob's daughter, and the larger master bedroom farther back.

Jenny caught up with Fran at the entrance to the master bedroom. Fran was looking around, thinking, Jenny suspected, of what the room had been like when she had lived there before, when it was half the size it was now and not a bedroom at all but a drafty storage space. At present, in the middle of the room, a very broad double bed took up most of the space available. That bed looked so large that it seemed to Jenny to be the room. Fran told her it had been made by pushing two single beds together and laying a mat over them, which would give Patty and Bob plenty of space to be apart. Jenny, looking at the wide bed, imagined the older couple there more easily than she imagined herself and Fran. The bed was covered with a bold, white, tufted spread.

After checking through the house one last time for improvements and finding that Patty and Bob had left her a bottle of her favorite scotch in a kitchen cabinet, Fran led Jenny outside. Taking Jenny by the hand, she walked with her around the house, pointing out a workshop in back and flowers and young trees Patty had planted all around. Fran then gestured to the hillside across the way and told Jenny that deer were all over these hills. Jenny would hear coyotes and she might even see foxes, "if you'll be coming to visit, that is, like you did when I lived in town."

Fran offered that last line cautiously, as if expecting the hesitation that followed in Jenny's answer.

"Yeah, maybe I'll see," Jenny said.

They drove back to town quietly, Jenny thinking about the dangers of the road, Fran looking up through the top of her windshield and whistling, now and then, to the classical music that was playing on her car radio.

Two days before Thanksgiving, a month and a half after she and Jenny had gone on their first date, Fran moved into her house in the hills. Although she had her fears, Jenny continued to visit her as she had done while Fran lived in town. She came back each night to sleep with Fran and often to have dinner with her, as well, no matter how uneasy she felt about the road. She came, as she had to the house down below, with her bookbag and notebooks and a change of underwear, although Fran finally did convince her to leave her toothbrush in the bathroom and, ultimately, after a month or so, to leave a couple of shirts and a change of jeans in the bedroom closet. As before, Jenny left each morning, except on weekends, to go back to her own house in town to work. As time went on, she also went home to pack.

Two and a half months later, in the middle of the winter, Jenny moved most of her belongings to a garage of a friend of Fran's in town. The garage felt special to her because it stood beneath a tree that bore bright orange persimmons, Jenny's favorite fruit. Jenny then formally moved in with Fran. With her, she brought her clothes, her typewriter, her work (a nearly finished dissertation), her radio, her hair dryer, some pills for sleeping, and her car. The first night she came to Fran in this way, shorn of the place she used to go to, she felt exposed, unprotected, and terrified, and as if she were young and new.

In coming to Fran, Jenny was leaving behind not only an apartment but also a marriage. The man she had been married to had left to take a job in the Midwest the previous summer and Jenny had not followed him. She had been married for four years, but marriage had never been a form that fit her well. She rebelled against it. While married, she wore her wedding band proudly, since it meant to her that she was normal, but at the same time she made nasty comments when people noticed the ring or acted as if marriage made a difference.

As might be suspected, Jenny never was the wife her husband Steven wanted her to be. She never was anyone's wife really, except that she did do the grocery shopping and cooked. She was, then as now, Jenny, who was very young and who fought a lot with Steven and with anyone who came near her, which not many people did. She let Steven get close to her and marry her because he was smart. He could see into her, Jenny felt. Also, he challenged much of what her parents had taught her. By her early twenties, as a result of her parents' training, Jenny felt like a moral-political machine. She felt mechanistic inside. She knew how to act according to values she had been taught, but she did not know what to do with her feelings. Steven insisted that she follow her feelings and treat herself like a person, not a machine.

"Don't tell me why you want to do something," he would say. "Just tell me that you want to. That's enough. I don't need a reason. I hate your reasons. They have nothing to do with anything."

Jenny would feel hurt and confused. Yet she knew he was trying to touch her. Unlike her parents, Steven would not have political arguments with her over the newspaper at breakfast or while they were walking down the street. "What is really going on?" he would ask her. "What are you upset about?" He would also hold Jenny when she cried. He so much preferred her crying to her angry armor and her striking out, the way she broke things and sent cups, plates, and furniture crashing against the walls of the places where they lived. Steven often got mad back at Jenny when she did that, but he would hold her, and even when the sex between them was not right, he would sense, as with an extra antenna, what Jenny needed. Then he would cradle her in his arms and rock her.

Before she moved in with Fran, Jenny had to pack up all her belongings from her life with Steven. When she went back to her apartment each day that last month before she moved, she would work for a while, then pack and pack. Between boxes, she would lie on the floor and cry. She would also eat handfuls of sourdough bread, which was a comfort food for her. Then at night she would return to Fran, unable to explain fully what had happened to her, but explaining as much as she could in answer to Fran's many questions.

By now, Jenny had grown used to Fran's questions. She knew that Fran would ask and ask until she became frustrated by Jenny's difficulty in answering. Jenny was not used to being on center stage, even the center stage of a discussion between two at a dining table. She tried, because she wanted to please Fran, but she felt she was not the kind of person who could normally spill out everything. Fran, however, seemed to need that, and Jenny wished to bask in the attention Fran offered. Jenny therefore answered, although usually the outcome was that she would start to say things and then not finish her sentences, which irritated Fran. "If I am sitting here giving you all my attention," Fran would say, "the least you could do is to finish your sentences for me."

Jenny felt Fran was right, but she also felt that it was impossible for her to fill the void she sensed in Fran. Furthermore, she feared Fran's judgments of her answers as she might the judgments her mother would give at the dinner table. She feared Fran would be critical and verbally lash out at her. Jenny did not like eating at tables. She also did not like or trust other people's questions. She would speak in her own time, in her own way.

What she wanted and did like was the quieter attention that Fran gave her, the attention that seemed to ask less of her. Fran gave it in the way she looked at Jenny when Fran was raking leaves on a weekend or pulling weeds in the garden. Fran would stop when Jenny came near her and look up at her with affection. She would smile at Jenny, who would feel warmed. Or in the early months, when Jenny would clearly and definitely leave no more than one extra shirt in Fran's closet, Fran would open the closet door, look at the shirt, then at Jenny, and smile. Jenny felt understood, if not accepted. She knew Fran wanted her to leave more of her clothes.

There were also those times when Jenny was riding in Fran's bus or sitting in the evening talking on the living room couch, and Fran would abruptly stop and stare at her, Fran's eyes soft, the conversation between them suddenly interrupted. When Jenny asked her, "What?" Fran would say simply that she was glad Jenny was there with her. Or in bed, in that big white bed that both lured and frightened Jenny, where Jenny sometimes tried to hide to escape the inevitable, Fran would catch her at it. She would remove the pillow from over Jenny's head, look at her sideways, lift one eyebrow, and smile. It was as if Fran knew and also as if she was determined to overcome.

Jenny felt both Fran's warmth and her distance. She felt extremely lucky to be with Fran. Here was this impressive, knowledgeable woman, self-contained in her intense focused way, with a set of very evident moral standards, dignified in how she presented herself to the world, superior even in her stance, and deep in emotional possibilities, bestowing some small bit of her noble countenance upon Jenny. Fran, of course, did not see herself as superior or judgmental. She spoke to Jenny of equality, acceptance, and growth and said that she wished, for the two of them, that their relationship would be one of development and change. She hoped that neither she nor Jenny would ever take the other person for granted. They should never assume that either one could not change.

Jenny heard Fran's words and wished to believe them, especially since the more she was with Fran, the more she began to feel that she was becoming small again and beginning, under Fran's watchful eye, to grow. Fran would say the growth words, the caring words, when Jenny sat with her on the couch in the evening recounting to her the experiences of her day. Fran would listen, reassure her, and give her advice, telling Jenny, for instance, about how the inside of her car worked, how diseases spread, or how a person could learn to feel good about herself. At the same time, Fran would keep the emotional distance she had shown early on to be her way, ever since that first night when she and Jenny had sat opposite each other in Fran's back room. Jenny was not entirely comfortable with Fran's distance, but she thought it benign, that it freed her. Oh, how lucky she was!

Here was this patient figure there for her, not demanding of her other than that she share her life. Jenny felt very special. She carried with her everywhere a note from Fran that said, "I love you." A month after she moved into their house in the hills, Jenny wrote to her parents that she was happy. She was living with a woman and was happy. There were deer outside that came right up to the doors of the house. Some of them had fawns following them—spotted, awkward babies. The almond tree out in front of the house was in bloom, its delicate white petals falling to the ground like snow. "Imagine that, Mother," Jenny wrote, "an almond tree in our front yard! I am very happy!"

Jenny knew that she was happy because she felt like a cared-for child, whether child again, child for the first time, or for the first time in a long time, it did not matter which. Jenny looked at Fran's full woman's body, the age clear in Fran's face, and felt surprisingly content, as she had never felt in her whole life. "Happy." It was a word that had not before had meaning for her. Once, Jenny remembered, she had argued with a friend of Steven's when he asked if she was happy: "Happy? I don't know what it means. I'm not one way or the other. It's irrelevant for me."

Now, one morning after she had moved in her things and no longer ran off to her other house each day to pack or to work, Jenny was sitting on the couch in the living room of her new home in the woods. It was early. The bay window behind her was lit with a misty morning light. Jenny had been drinking coffee, eating toast, and writing, looking down at the papers spread out before her on the long coffee table in front of the couch. Then she heard Fran and looked up. Fran was standing directly across from her in the short narrow hall that led to the back bedrooms. She was wearing a deep rose-colored robe but the buttons were undone. The robe hung open in front so that Jenny could see clearly the flesh of Fran's body, her hips, the curve of her waist up to her breasts. Fran's eyes were sleepy. She rubbed them as she stood there, looking over at Jenny. "Morning," she said.

Jenny, nodding back, noticed that Fran's short hair stood on end on one side. She knew Fran did not like that, but she herself loved it. Fran's body emerging from her robe, however, was what caught Jenny, riveted her gaze until she quickly looked away and up, instead, to Fran's sleepy face.

Jenny wanted, right then, to go to Fran, to kneel before her and kiss her belly, to rise and be held, her head between Fran's breasts, to touch Fran, to make love to her on the soft gold rug by the bathroom door. But something in Fran would not have it, Jenny felt. Fran projected an early morning discomfort. Or else it was something in Jenny that would not have it; for Jenny, at that moment when she first caught sight of Fran's body, had thought of her own mother and her mother's body. Jenny's mother and Fran were about the same height, both of them a few inches taller than Jenny. Both were heavier, both similarly solid and similarly inexplicable in Jenny's eyes, placed there before her as if to represent something she could only yearn after. So, of course, she did not go to Fran, only marveled at her and remembered forever after the sleepy shape that had moved her.

When Fran crossed the hall to turn on her morning music before washing up, Jenny watched her turn away and felt ashamed. She was ashamed of the origin of her desire. She was sure Fran would not feel pleased to be told that the mother-child core of their relationship was what was most compelling to her. Fran would rather understand their tie in terms of mutuality, pleasure, and growth. Jenny, however, felt that somewhere, even if it was where it could not be spoken, Fran knew Jenny's truth to be so. Fran knew that Jenny basked in Fran's mothering and that Fran herself was nourished by it. Probably, however, she did not know how guilty Jenny felt, as if this mothering she received was something she stole from Fran and hid from the world. Jenny was angry.

Here they were, the two of them, in a house at the end of a wooded canyon road with Jenny coming home each night to a comfort that could neither be acknowledged nor discussed. It was obvious, it had to be obvious to everyone, but Jenny felt she alone bore the weight of it.

She also bore another kind of weight, that of responding as Fran would like, of "being there," as Fran would say. When with Fran, more often than not, Jenny would tend to take off, to go somewhere else in her mind where Fran could not follow, where she could be alone. Jenny did not feel such behavior peculiar. She had done it all her life. But Fran challenged it in her and, in doing so, challenged something fundamental to her. Nowhere did Fran present her challenge more directly than when she and Jenny were in bed. There, from the very beginning, it was as if the scene had been set, the expectations made plain. There were lessons to be learned.

It started as a test of wills. That was how Jenny felt on one of her first nights in their house in the hills. The bed in the back bedroom glowed white, the spread and sheets reflecting moonlight coming in through small high windows across the room. That night, Fran got into bed before Jenny, which was unusual, since ordinarily Jenny curled up earlier alone, resting, trying to feel safe, waiting for Fran to finish watching television and finally come in and join her. Tonight, however, Fran already lay in bed, waiting, watching as Jenny self-consciously, trying to hide her naked body, slipped in beside her. The bed was warm. Fran had turned the electric blanket to its highest setting. "I turned it all the way up to Mother," Fran said. She had also turned on the heat, Jenny noticed. The small electric wall heater in the room was set so that it would warm them later. Then they would be free not only to lie under the covers but also to emerge and play on top of them, to "fully enjoy one another," Fran proposed.

Jenny, however, had other things than enjoyment on her mind, as she always did. She wished tonight to get into bed and to lie there quietly and cry herself to sleep, to be comforted by Fran but mostly to be in her own world of crying. She wished to think about Steven and his being gone. He was precious to her, like a possession she had once had and protected and thought was delicate. She had thought she was special because of him. Jenny wanted to think about that feeling, hold on to it, and get lost in a sense of being lost with Steven gone. It did not matter that she had broken their relationship, Jenny did not like to lose her things. She did not like to lose anything she had ever chosen.

She looked up. Fran was looking down at her, a bemused, questioning expression on her face. It was an expression Jenny often saw in Fran at other times when she wondered, as she did now, about what was real. Why was Fran so persistent, so interested in her? Why didn't she just give up?

"What's happening?" Fran asked.

"Nothing," Jenny answered.

"Be here," Fran said.

Then Fran gently prodded until Jenny rolled over fully on her back. Jenny resisted enough to feel Fran's opposing force, Fran's determination set against her own. Then she let Fran lay her back, pin her arms to the bed, and hold her shoulders down. She let Fran and, at the same time, struggled against her, trying to wrestle herself free. Jenny soon put all she had into the struggle so that she was finally fighting, sweating, pushing her strongest, but pushing more inside than outside. She was simultaneously containing herself and trying to break free. She was pushing against Fran not with all her might, but with all her psychic might.

Then something changed and Jenny started really to try to break loose from Fran's hold. Forget the restraints, she told herself. She had always been able to be free. She had this basic faith that she always could find a way out, a way to bite or scratch. She could make a quick turn with her body, evade a captor out of sheer struggle, the sheer stubbornness and the quick shifts of her moves. So she lashed out at Fran, looking for loopholes, seeking to dig her nails deep into Fran's arm, or into whatever she would get hold of. Jenny wanted to go for Fran's eyes but could not reach them. She was struggling now for real and she knew it. Fran must have known it, too, the way she skillfully avoided Jenny's attempts to bite her, to claw at her. Fran stayed there leaning the weight of her body over Jenny's, keeping Jenny's arms pinned beneath her, Jenny's legs locked under her own.

Fran had wrestled her almost without moving, Jenny felt, simply by staying on top of her, by persevering, by looking down intently, holding firmly to the bed those points of Jenny's body on which she counted to keep Jenny still. At last, Jenny gave up. She relaxed back quietly on the bed.

"You win," she said to Fran.

"No," Fran shook her head. "It's not a matter of win or lose."

Did Fran know? Jenny wondered. Did she know what the fight was about? She looked up and searched Fran's eyes for an answer, asking with her own but without using words. Jenny moved her eyes about, trying to have them speak for her, darted them, raised and lowered them quickly. She was asking if Fran understood and telling her about it at the same time. She was telling Fran how she both wanted, and did not want, what Fran offered her and about how Fran had to be able to handle her, to counter her fears, to keep her from running away. Fran had to be good enough, big enough. She had to be Jenny's equal, or to be better than Jenny. She had to know more about what Jenny needed than perhaps Jenny knew herself. For when Jenny wrestled with Fran, she was very small—a baby in a crib asking her mother to take care of her. Her eyes had to speak for her because she did not yet have words.

Fran's eyes reflected back to Jenny a partial understanding. They reflected an attitude of seriousness and of mild but not superficial amusement. Jenny felt that Fran had probably missed the child part of what she wished to tell her.

Jenny also felt mastered, yet Fran still held her pinned tightly to the bed, as if she awaited a signal not yet given, an outright permission. If Jenny were to struggle against her again, Fran was saying, if Jenny were to try to break free once more, Fran would not let her. Fran knew her role; she knew what she was supposed to do. She was not to let Jenny trick her, even at the last minute.

"Okay," Jenny finally said. "It's over. I'm done. Let me go."

"Are you sure?" Fran asked.

"Yes," said Jenny, rolling away as Fran gradually eased up and slowly lifted her hands from where they had been locking Jenny's arms to the bed. Then Fran moved her legs to the side and sat down beside Jenny, facing her. "I want a drink and a cigarette," she said, letting out a deep breath.

When Fran came back to the bedroom with her drink and her package of Salem menthol cigarettes, she sat up against the headboard behind the bed, slowly sipping her scotch and smoking. Jenny sat next to her, resting. The smoke from Fran's cigarette reassured her, as did Fran's deliberate, careful sipping of her scotch. Fran dipped her finger into her musty golden drink and held it out to Jenny. "Unblended," she said. "It has a smoky taste." That kind of scotch, Jenny knew, was Fran's favorite, as it eventually was to become her own.

Jenny opened her mouth to suck on Fran's finger, once, then again and again. As she sucked, she was drawn closer to Fran, her body seeking to curl around Fran's body as her mouth did around the smoky tasting finger Fran extended to her. Although Jenny moved closer, Fran continued her ritual of smoking then taking a sip or two of scotch. Then, seeming to have taken the time that she needed, she stubbed out her last cigarette in a small black ashtray on the headboard behind her, a cast-iron ashtray in the shape of a lady sea nymph that was a present from a previous lover. She put down her drink on the headboard and turned her attention once again to Jenny.

Moving her hand down the length of Jenny's body, she let it come to rest between Jenny's legs. Then she moved her own body so that she was sitting opposite Jenny at the foot of the bed, her legs crossed beneath her. She looked over at Jenny, watching, waiting, until Jenny lay back, giving in. Jenny lowered her body and put her head down slowly on the pillow behind her, but she did not feel relaxed. She felt on edge, uncertain of what Fran would do next and of whether she should let her. What was happening did not seem mutual, and these things, Jenny thought, were supposed to be mutual. Jenny lay back as if steeled for an assault. Fran's hand remained in place. She stroked Jenny carefully, then bent over her and, with her tongue, found Jenny's point of need, began to lick it, raising Jenny toward her.

"No," Jenny let out a cry. "Stop!"

Fran stopped, sat up, placed her finger back where her tongue had been, and continued as she had begun before. She was taking her time now, moving slowly, not probing but, rather, stroking, watching all the while for Jenny's response. Jenny felt a response but did not want to show it, was afraid to move her hips as she had seen Fran do many times, up and down, up and down, as if in tune with inner music. Rising and falling rhythmically, Fran would absorb a small touch with her whole body, then yield, letting herself spread out.

Jenny, however, would not do that. Yet now she had to move. She turned so that, at last, her head was in Fran's lap. Then she could look up into Fran's eyes as Fran touched her. She needed to see the acceptance in Fran's eyes, the encouragement, the connection. Without it, Fran's finger, that touch that aroused her, was foreign and to be feared.

Now Fran held Jenny, cradling her as she touched her. "Close your eyes," Fran suggested. But Jenny would not do it. She needed to check constantly the gaze that looked down at her. Only in this way could she let herself be touched until a feeling rose inside her, a feeling that made the nerves of her legs seem like hollow cores and that traveled to her feet and made her curl up her toes, curl them up and bend her knees so she could feel it all the more. That feeling, Jenny later told Fran, was like gold. It was like a vein of gold ore being tapped, tapped and tapped inside her until it ran. Jenny felt like a baby cradled in her mother's arms, held and cradled and given gold.

Then suddenly, as suddenly as she had relaxed, Jenny stiffened and pulled back. "Enough," she told Fran.

"Why?" Fran asked. "Where did you go?"

Jenny shook her head. She did not want to say. Fran tried again several times to touch her, to bring her back, calling after her each time she went away, "Where are you? Where did you go?" and most importantly, she told her, "Be here. Concentrate on right where you are. Don't pay attention to me. Focus on yourself. Feel all you can."

Jenny tried for what seemed a long time, but after a while Fran's touch began to hurt her, to scrape against her. An inner defense she had long ago built up was now back in place, making her feel alone. Fran seemed far away, a woman she almost did not know. Jenny reached down her hand to touch Fran's arm, to draw it up, to tell Fran to stop.

That part was over now, but Jenny could not explain to Fran why. She could not tell Fran where she went when she left her, that she went to Steven, to her work, to sentences she had been writing earlier in the day, to a picture of the absurdity of herself and Fran in this bed. She went to her own selfishness, to the wrongness of Fran's attentiveness to her, and then to the center of her need, which was far, far away—wrapped up with herself as a tiny child and her urge to cry out with pain, to say no. She went also to how foreign Fran was to her, to how Fran held her own body when naked, how upright, poised, and unashamed she seemed. Fran had told Jenny she had not always been proud of her body, but that when she was young, twenty years ago, a woman fifteen years older had taught her, by making love to her, to love herself, to cherish her body, to take pleasure in its movements. That woman, named Stella, was a hard drinker, smoked like Fran did, had a husky voice, and now lived with a young lover and a miniature poodle in an apartment in Los Angeles. Jenny thought of Stella teaching Fran and of Fran now teaching her. She then thought of her own sentences, her sheets of yellow writing paper.

"Be here," Fran said. But Jenny was too tired. She could, however, draw Fran up and have Fran lie back beside her. She knew that Fran would respond and almost exactly how she would respond. She kissed Fran's breasts, then touched her, following the directions Fran gave, the directions Fran had been giving implicitly, yet clearly, since their first night in Fran's back room when Jenny had worried about being a good enough lover. Jenny knew, by now, how, gradually, to build up Fran's feeling so that Fran's body would rise beneath her hand like a giant ocean wave, cresting and falling back. She kissed Fran, touched her, watched her. There seemed little for her to do but to ride Fran out, lying beside her, stroking her, following.

Fran's eyes, Jenny noticed, were closed. She did not curl up her toes. She did not, as Jenny did, shake unrhythmically, her body unleashing small tremulous sobs. No, Fran in bed was a careful study of the evenly paced, full female response, or so Jenny thought. Fran seemed focused on herself, just as she had told Jenny to be. She was as controlled and as self-contained as she was in real life, which made Jenny feel left out. In the end, though, after Fran had worked up a sweat and Jenny knew it was coming, Fran reached for her and drew her close. She clasped Jenny to her at that exact moment when it counted, her sighs letting Jenny know, her smile afterward, her kisses, her saying Jenny's name, making up for the time they had been apart.

Jenny felt rewarded and taken in. She felt she had served, paid something back. She watched Fran drift off to sleep, then rolled over by herself and lay thinking. She thought about how Fran had said there would be other nights, nights when Jenny might even let Fran take her all the way. She might come to trust Fran that much.

Indeed there were other nights. They came one on another like parts of a process building. Jenny let Fran touch her more and more, let herself make sounds that Fran could hear. Fran had said she wanted to share it, she wanted to share everything. Jenny worked at concentrating, at responding to Fran's commands. She did not fight with Fran again as she had done that first night when she had struggled against her to be free. Yet she often thought about that night and about how Fran's opposing force had pleased her. Then, too, Jenny thought about the gold, the feeling of the hollow core. She kept striving for it and was disappointed if her efforts of an evening or an afternoon did not yield it.

One weekend, Fran told Jenny she had a fantasy of their spending a full day, or an entire weekend, in bed. They could have a special meal, eat cracked crab and French bread, and drink white wine right there, which once they finally did. They ate the meal, that is, naked, surrounded by white sheets and the vast white spread. Jenny would not spend the whole day, though. She needed to get up and leave.

Especially on weekends, when both she and Fran were at home, Jenny felt she needed to run away, to leave not only the bedroom but the entire house. There was something about being with Fran without a break that made Jenny tense, made her bowels stiffen and her head begin to ache. Then she would devise to go into town, to do the laundry, or to buy a paper, then to stop at the local library where, among the many different books, she would begin to feel better. Why looking at books would make her relax, Jenny never altogether understood, but standing there looking at the titles of the books, the many subjects and worlds they represented, the promises, the thought of her own work and of new knowledge, it was like adventure opened up for her. Jenny's interest in the world opened up and she was free again. Then she would be ready to return to Fran.

Jenny discussed with Fran the fact that she felt constrained when she and Fran were alone together at the house for long. Yet her tenseness around Fran did not change. It did not change until the following year, the next fall, when she and Fran moved to their second house in the hills. In that house, located not far from the first, Jenny felt more isolated in her own world and her own work, and her aloneness seemed to make her feel easier.

III

The second house Jenny and Fran moved to was set farther back in the hills than their first at the end of a narrow private road in a very quiet canyon. Its yard was the steep side of a cliff. Oak trees towered above it. Like their first house, this one, too, was small and cottagelike and came furnished, its owner temporarily away. At the center of the house was a broad open living room with a soft white rug and white couch across from high bookshelves and windows looking out. Here Jenny felt protected. Soon after she and Fran moved in, Fran told Jenny she had decided to quit her job. She needed to think about whether to continue her work as a scientist. There were ethical problems with it, she said. Fran then stayed home more of the time than she had before. She would read for long stretches and repair things around the house.

One afternoon, she helped Jenny unload into a storage shed across the way the belongings Jenny had previously kept in the garage beneath the persimmon tree in town. As they carried in Jenny's possessions, Fran said she felt Jenny should at least unpack some of them into drawers and cabinets in the house. Jenny, however, refused, as she had once refused to leave her toothbrush.

Although eventually Jenny did unpack and bring inside some of her things—her dishes, her wedding dress, a peasant blouse her mother once gave her, other pieces of clothing and special material she felt might get mildewed if left outside—she was uneasy about it. She felt that most of her possessions did not belong in the house. She still did not believe her stay with Fran would be permanent. She did not believe it even though one morning as she stood with Fran by the long soft sofa in the living room, and looked out at a neighboring hillside, Fran held her hand and sought to reassure her. "We can be together forever," Fran said, "for as long as we want to. You can unpack."

Jenny looked back at Fran suspiciously. Such thinking was not realistic, she felt. She also felt there was no arguing with Fran when Fran sought to reassure them with her dreams. Jenny now knew much more about Fran than she had at first. She also knew more about herself. She knew that she valued highly the slow, careful lovemaking Fran had taught her. She valued looking up at Fran as Fran held her, looking down as Fran moved beneath her. She valued simply watching Fran from across a room, prizing her, enjoying her handsomeness, feeling for the deep discomfort Fran took care of with her alcohol and cigarettes. Jenny valued, too, the changes she felt that Fran had encouraged her to make. No longer, for instance, did Jenny set her hair; she let it stand free, a great lion's mane of curls. No longer did she wear a bra. "To hold up what?" Fran once asked. Nor did she take contraceptive pills anymore, or wear women's pants or shoes. She wore boots. She also drank wine, the good, thick red wine called zinfandel.

In the evenings, Jenny would sit on the couch in the living room of their new house in the hills, sipping her wine while Fran drank her scotch. From the start, Fran had been concerned to educate Jenny's palate. Her first Valentine's Day gift to Jenny had been a bottle of fine red wine, which she told Jenny was hers to drink all by herself. At times, Fran would bring home unusual wines, or encourage Jenny to taste them when they were out. Jenny felt that the wine was a way that Fran instructed her more broadly about life—that there was an activity called "enjoyment," you could sit back and do it. There were finer things. One deserved them; that tasting came slowly. Life, like wine, was to be savored.

Fran took Jenny, too, on several camping trips in her bus. She showed Jenny how to look around, how to stop and appreciate the countryside. Although afraid of the strange open places they went to and eager always to get home, Jenny did begin to understand, to learn. She wanted very much to be like Fran, to live in a world where her home was transportable, where stopping and looking outside herself did not mean she would be overcome by fears. She wanted to sit, as Fran did, and read by the side of the road, to do nothing and seem to enjoy it, even to backpack someday, forgetting the troubles of her life. She wished to act like Fran, self-contained and self-assured, to let things pass her by.

Yet Jenny was not like Fran. On their trips, Jenny wrote while Fran read. It was not enough for her to see the flowers in bloom in the desert where she and Fran went on their first long trip, Jenny had to write down exactly what the flowers looked like and what it had meant for her to see them. Her writing kept her from feeling too alone while Fran drank her scotch, smoked, and read. It soothed her, calmed her, taught her. Jenny felt she was learning—the goals of a good life were becoming clearer to her—but she was not often happy. She felt she was not learning quickly enough how to be the person Fran wished her to be.

At home in their new house, Fran acted increasingly inward and depressed. She would sit at the dinner table and look hurt when Jenny refused to answer her many questions; or she would sit reading on the couch, sipping her scotch, and looking sad. Jenny continued to work first thing in the mornings. Later each day, she would go off to look for jobs, and eventually she took one, then another. She did not think Fran would mind. She did not know that Fran minded. Yet in their new house, Fran was not sexual with her often. Fran said that was because she felt bad about herself. She asked Jenny to have patience.

Jenny heard coyotes crying outside in the woods at night. She started writing a novel. She started to live more in a world of her own. Fran complained, at times, about that world, about Jenny's self-absorption, calling it selfish, stinging Jenny with her words. Nonetheless, once when Jenny got very sick, stomach sick with an intestinal flu so that she lay in bed with a fever, Fran came into the bedroom and sat beside her. She drew down the covers and touched Jenny gently, feeding the dream Jenny still had that Fran cared for her tenderly and deeply. For several days, Fran sat nearby reading in the living room until she was sure Jenny was well. Jenny could not remember anyone before sitting near her and waiting like that while she was sick, although perhaps they had.

The rest of it she preferred not to remember. Fran soon found someone else. Fran denied it. She spoke simply of a friend, another couple she wanted Jenny and herself to know. With this couple, Fran felt, she and Jenny could expand their concept of love. Jenny, however, knew that something was wrong, was over, a trust had been broken. Fran's intense, total caring no longer was there only for her. One night when Fran did not come home, Jenny got angry and broke a set of wine glasses Fran's new friends had given to them. Fran felt gravely justified in being angry back at her from then on.

In the midst of this, Jenny's father died. Jenny went back East twice to visit him in the hospital. Then she went back for the funeral. From the time she left on her funeral trip, she could not reach Fran by phone. Fran was off camping with her new friends. Jenny called the house and listened to the phone ringing, called back, listened again, and cried. She cried for the loss of her relationship with Fran instead of for the loss of her father. When she came home, Fran was not there to meet her at the airport. Instead, Fran sent her new friend.

It was Fran, however, who finally declared that their relationship was over. She and Jenny had taken one last camping trip during which, at night in the back of Fran's bus, Jenny lay with her legs apart and let Fran touch her. She hoped to feel the old caring, the sweet hollow veins of gold. Instead, she felt Fran's steadfast attempt, her coldness, the harshness of Fran's touch as Fran sat beside her dressed in a gray plaid woodsman's shirt. Fran looked stern more than gentle, intent on a task. Jenny rolled over and cried in gasping breaths, ashamed that she had asked, that she had thought she could recreate, recapture what they had had, that she had thought she could offer herself in the end and save them. When she and Fran took a hike the next morning, Fran told her she wished that Jenny were stronger and had fewer troubles. She wished that the world would not always look black to her and that Jenny would come out of herself more. Jenny asked for time, said she would try, that she was willing to learn. But there was no time. Fran's patience was up. Whatever Fran needed, Jenny no longer offered it.

Perhaps it was Jenny who seemed to promise too much, Jenny who misled Fran. However, Jenny did not feel that way. She felt that Fran had failed her.

The day they parted—not weeks, but months later, after going back and forth far too many times—the morning when, before going off to work, Jenny left Fran standing in the soft, white living room of their home in the woods, Jenny looked at Fran's eyes for a sign, searched her face for softness. Fran was hard, as perhaps she had to be, her face unreadable except for a veneer of cool disdain. Jenny sensed that Fran's disdain was not only for the housecleaning she was about to do, but also for Jenny's having brought them to this parting because of her lack of trust. Nonetheless, before she walked away, Jenny saw one long heavy tear roll down from beneath Fran's left eye. That tear pleased her, as if it said Fran still loved her, and that Fran found her special and would miss her.

That night, Jenny returned to the house to do her part of the cleaning and to pack. She was angry at Fran for leaving her alone in the empty dark house at night, so she cleaned less thoroughly than she might have otherwise. She packed up her balalaika, a small Russian stringed instrument like a guitar, that she had smashed in a prior moment of her anger, and placed it on the front seat of her car. Her balalaika was her most treasured possession, yet she had banged it and banged it on the floor one night when Fran did not come home. Then she had sat with it and cried before gathering it up in her arms like a broken doll.

Jenny looked at the house one last time before she left. Fran was gone and she could not believe it. Nor could she know that in subsequent years, she herself would seek to be Fran—she would buy a tent, a backpack, and sturdy boots, go off alone into the woods and the desert, prefer scotch to wine, plan to buy a bus, learn to tune her car and to fix things around the house. She would live in back rooms off other people's houses and seek out places far away, reached by back roads, that felt special to her, like when she had lived with Fran. Years later, after she had made these attempts, she would look back at them and see Fran, not herself, and feel suddenly bare, without comfort, without home. She would come back to the hills, those same hills where she and Fran had lived, only to find other people in their houses. She would be alive but with a sadness that she could not forget. Fran was gone but not the memory of the time that Jenny had been with her, the soft spot Fran had helped her to open up.

Fran had loved Jenny. She had made her feel the center of the world, a person deserving of attention. She had adored Jenny, hard as that always was for Jenny to believe. Fran had challenged Jenny to relax. She had made her want to have good times. She had opened new worlds for her, both outside and within herself. In the beginning, Fran had seemed so frightened that Jenny would leave her, and now Jenny was sad and frightened in leaving Fran. Fran had held Jenny, had given her the gift of her full woman's body. She had let Jenny feel like a child in bed with her, a small child seeking contact with her mother and seeking to grow.

Fran had given Jenny a sense of her own inner possibilities. She had made her feel sensitive and special and like her dreams could come true. In the beginning, Jenny had not understood how this marvel of a true-lesbian-older-woman with a body so like her mother's could be so ready to embrace her, and now she could not understand where that readiness had gone.

Why a relationship of only two years' duration—a match with a woman so different, so little inclined to be content with her, who did not finally value Jenny enough to stay with her—should be so important to her, and cause her so much sadness and prompt so much new direction, was a mystery at once hard for Jenny to understand and yet simple. Fran had touched deep needs in her. Jenny would forever after be marked by Fran's way of being a lesbian. In bed with other women, she would wait for them to be like Fran and try to teach them what Fran had encouraged in her—particularly about being there, and trusting, and trying to feel good. In future years, Jenny would learn new lessons, have new experiences, and her time with Fran would move farther into the background, but it would still be there, reminding her of her needs. At times, Jenny would look at that relationship of her youth and find it wanting. She would feel that Fran had not really cared, and that Fran had not deserved her affections. But that was because Fran was no longer with her. Jenny's loss was real, but so too was the longing she had felt, her need of another woman, the sweetness of the relationship she and Fran had shared.

Three

THE FAMILY SILVER

I HAVE JUST COME BACK from a trip to Florida to settle the affairs of my lover's aunt, who died suddenly at the age of seventy. She was carrying her groceries up the stairs to her apartment when she dropped dead of a heart attack. A neighbor found her. When we arrived several weeks later, we found her grocery list and the cash register receipt itemizing what she had bought—lettuce, tomatoes, salad dressing, breakfast cereal, milk, tuna fish. It was an otherworldly experience: going to Florida, where I had not been before, to clean out the house of a woman I did not know—sorting through her clothes and jewelry, finding snapshots she recently took, using her bathroom, meeting her friends, literally stepping into her life, not the life of someone still with us, but a vacated life.

We were there for a week, closing out the small business Aunt Maxine ran out of her home, disposing of her possessions, and looking for vital documents, like the title to her car—a long white Cadillac with a red carriage roof and matching deep-red leather seats. Maxine was a short, buxom woman with bleached blond hair. She had dropped ten years from her age when she moved to Florida. Her closest friends knew her as sixty at her death. She dressed dramatically in bright colors and bold prints and wore her best jewelry daily, her gold chains and diamonds. Her apartment had not been cleaned in five years. The living and dining rooms, full of cartons and paper goods, were devoted to her small business. She sold rubber self-inking stamps of the kind that says "Jane O'Hara, 48 Front Street," or "First Class," or the date. She played golf and was a supporter of the local theater group, and the best way I can put it is that she collected clothes. I emptied her closets, putting her clothes in large plastic bags to give away to charity, counting, as I bagged them, for tax purposes. There were 419 shirts, including gold lamé and sequinned shirts and golf shirts, 275 pairs of pants, 7 leather jackets, 162 pairs of shoes, 16 jumpsuits, 83 handbags. Stacked beside her bathroom sink were hundreds of old lipstick tubes that she never was able to throw out.

Maxine was acquisitive and materialistic. When she felt in need, she bought something, usually clothes, preferably on sale. She liked large earrings and large beaded necklaces and had forty pounds of costume jewelry in, and on, her dresser in the end. She had married three times and received a significant diamond ring from each husband. The husbands, however, did not amount to much and she divorced them, preferring the life of a bachelor girl. She liked going out with others, and having a good time, and making money, although she only began making money on her own after she gave up on husbands and the myth that they would take care of her. She worked long hours, both to have the money to buy things she wanted and because she was constantly afraid her money would run out. When younger, she had gone to art school. The paintings we found in her apartment showed that she had talent. She also could sew and had a fully equipped sewing machine in her bedroom, but she preferred playing golf and being taken to dinner. She did not believe in doctors and saw them as a self-indulgence, which is one reason she had not been aware of her heart condition. She was a big talker and could fill up a room with talk. Her friends said she lit up any room she entered. They also said she was always an "up person," which to me meant she had no tolerance for depression and that she would not have understood or liked me.

She was a woman whose values I have little respect for in the abstract, but there I was sorting through her clothes and the odds and ends on her bedside table, becoming intimate with her. After a few days of doing this, I knew exactly how she dressed and that her style of dressing was not mine. However, occasionally I would still take a shirt of hers that seemed tailored in cut and large enough to fit me, and carry it over to the bathroom mirror to try it on. One look would reveal it was a shade of pink that she could wear and I could not. She liked gathers in her clothing, bows, bright purple colors, large oval earrings. She liked over-statement as a form of self-expression, while I like understatement. Despite such differences, however, I finally came to think that if I had met her in person, I would have liked her, although only if our meeting was brief and if I had no expectations that she would meet my needs, for responsiveness of a subtle sort was not her style.

Aunt Maxine seemed well suited to Florida. Florida is a peculiar place —home of the sun loving, of those who seek life without winters or who want to start a new life, home of the elderly, the Los Angeles-style glitzy rich, the poor. It is part of the South, yet there in South Florida people spoke like they do in New York City. The people who came in and out of Maxine's apartment while we were working there, and those at the supermarket in the nearby shopping center, were upwards of sixty-five and mostly women. Maxine's closest friend was a gay man, but her other friends were small, square-shaped Jewish women like herself who wore heavy makeup and colored their hair, usually bleaching it blond. These women were eager to clear out Maxine's closets, look around her apartment, see what her niece was doing, and either give an opinion, or announce very clearly that they were keeping their opinions to themselves. They spoke in loud voices and carried out garbage and books and moved furniture. The few men who came, although bigger and taller than the women, were slower, and they looked fearfully at the physical work, as if it might give them a heart attack. The women took charge and got bossy. The men waited to be told what to do. This was reminiscent, for me, of the types of families I have known, where, around a house, women are useful and men are not, unless told by the women what to do.

While clearing out Maxine's apartment, the physical activity of sorting and bagging and carrying out trash occupied me, and the people coming and going and working in the apartment made my life seem full. At the heart of my experience, however, was an emptiness. My life stopped during that week and for several weeks afterward, because I wished not to feel and because this was a death. Now at home, I keep trying to fill in the empty space. I keep thinking back to Maxine's bedroom, probably because I spent so much time there taking her clothes out of her closets and looking around the room at the dusty empty beds and the closed shades. For entertainment and for a break, I would repeatedly go over to her dresser and sort through her jewelry, looking, each time, for something I could take home and feel was mine. Yet there was nothing there for me. This was jewelry that belonged to a woman who carried her golf clubs in a pink leather golf bag. I have spent much time in the past few weeks seeing, in my mind, images of a woman who played golf, ate out, bought clothes on sale at Marshalls, and worked long hours driving around in a red and white Cadillac selling rubber stamps.

One night as we drove back from Maxine's apartment to our hotel, Judith asked me, "What is family silver," and "Why do people make such a big deal of it?" Her mother had advised her to save any family silver she found at her aunt's home, and she wondered why it mattered. Not knowing, I tried to explain anyway—that it is what women have of material value in a family. Most things women have wear out, like bedsheets, or even beds or furniture, or clothes for themselves or the children. Silver is more like a durable good because of the value of the metal. However, you have to keep it up by polishing it, and eventually it wears out too, or the plate does. All women's things wear out. Silver also has social value. It brings people together for special occasions and dinners. Using it is a way women run things.

As we spoke, I kept thinking back to things my mother has said about her mother's silver. Her mother had two sets—a daily set which got more wear, and a better set for holidays. Often I have been told about my grandmother's silver. A few months ago when speaking with my mother on the phone, I told her I had just polished the two silver candlesticks of my grandmother's that my mother gave me several years ago. I was unable to get all the black out. My mother said that was the way old silver was and then gave me detailed instructions on how to clean a set of silver flatware. She advised immersing it in a solution of Soilax and warm water, and then adding crumpled up aluminum foil to create an electrolytic process that cleans the flatware but also takes off a little of the plate. She then mentioned some frightful things that eat silver, like vinegar and eggs.

In our conversation, my mother told me again, as she has several times, that she wanted to give her silver, actually my father's mother's silver, to my sister. (My mother's sister has their mother's.) However, she did not want to do this until my sister's children were more grown because, in my sister's house, they threw away silverware. They threw it out with the garbage, either by accident or because they were not paying attention. Better they should throw away stainless steel, my mother said. She then concluded by asking me about my stainless. How many settings did I have? I said six. She said that was not enough, I needed twelve. What pattern did I have? I should check to see if they still made that pattern and get more. You cannot have just six.

My mother had told me previously that I would be getting my father's sister's silver, which is less ornate and desirable than my father's mother's but comes in a special chest. My father's sister's silver, my mother said, has her initials engraved on it, although unfortunately they are her married initials. My father's sister, Aunt Jessie, went into a nursing home earlier this year and so would no longer be needing her silver. My mother said she was keeping it for me in her basement on the condition that I come back East and visit her in order to get it. After all, you can't just send it.

From these conversations with my mother, I learned that, more than for its use in eating, and more than because of its value as a precious metal, family silver is a big deal because it provides lessons in cleaning, sibling rivalry, childrearing, and proper behavior. It links the generations and makes people come home to claim it.

On our last full day in Florida, I found Maxine's silver flatware in a back corner of one of her high kitchen cabinets behind a box of recipes. I had gone into the kitchen to inventory the contents to decide what we were giving away. The kitchen was so greasy that none of us had used it during the week. When I reached back in the cabinet, I found an accordion case with felt linings and, within it, a full set of National Sterling flatware. The imprint "sterling" on the flatware, I was later to learn, meant each piece was made of solid silver (92.5 percent pure), as distinguished from being silver plate upon a baser metal. Maxine's silver was untarnished and seemed never used. The pieces had a plain pattern around their edges, with space left for initials, but no initials were engraved on them. Because of its plainness and lack of use, Maxine's silver seemed to me not really valuable, not really "family silver." The family silver we might have found was Maxine's mother's set, but that, along with her mother's china, had been stolen from the storage room of Maxine's apartment complex years ago. To replace it, Maxine had bought this silver and a set of china with a floral pattern on it. She kept the china, a Japanese copy of an old English style, in a living room cabinet next to her television, where we also found several pieces of tarnished silver holloware (bowls and salt and pepper shakers) that may have belonged to Maxine's mother. Before we left, we mailed Maxine's silver home to us, probably to sell it, and we gave away most of her other things.

That week we spent in Florida was very much about material things for me, which is often, I suppose, how people deal with death and with the questions it raises about living, questions such as, Why golf? Why rubber stamps? Why take home the silver? Some of the answers are obvious—because that is the business her third husband got into after they were divorced, and she learned about it from him; because that is what people do, you don't just leave the silver. Yet the harder questions to answer, for me, concern value: what value playing golf or selling stamps? What determines this value? Is the value different if one is a woman? How separate the person from what she does, or sells, from the clothes she wears, the things she keeps, the friends she does or does not have?

MY AUNT JESSIE

My aunt Jessie sold ladies' underwear for a long time at a department store in New York City. She is eighty-three now, and since she has moved into the nursing home, she is walking again and is less depressed than when she was living alone. Jessie is more direct in her statements than other members of my family. "I love you," she says to me frequently on the phone, even when I cannot say it back. I spoke with her on the Fourth of July, and after telling me that the weather was disgusting, meaning hot, she said, "You know, after the Fourth of July, you think Christmas. I guess that comes from twenty years in a department store." I remembered back to when I worked in a bookstore, in order to grasp the truth of her statement, but mostly I liked the implication. It was, to me, a statement about a world of artificiality, a constructed world, a commercial season, about a logic that ran contrary to what is viewed as natural (in nature, Christmas does not begin in July), yet it is how we live. I also felt my aunt was saying to me, "It's a long way to Christmas. It's a long way to anywhere from here. When are you coming to visit?"

Perhaps she was only talking about the store. I easily feel guilt with my relatives. Thus, I try to avoid saying anything that will provoke them to ask me when I am coming to see them, for the chief thing I need in relation to them is distance. Since emotionally, I have none, I have put much physical distance between us. I live on the West Coast, my family lives in the East. I visit them as infrequently as possible. My most immediate relatives are Jessie, my mother, and my sister and her family. Recently, Jessie and my mother have been talking about my coming back to visit them. My mother says, "I'm retiring." Jessie says, "Are you coming in July?" Both mean, as I hear it, "I'm going to die soon. I am elderly. I'm frail. Why aren't you here?"

Although I knew in advance I was going to Florida, I was reluctant to tell either Jessie or my mother about it. I did not want to tell Jessie because of certain parallels—Jessie is my father's sister and Maxine was my lover's father's sister, and Jessie often wishes to be dead. When I thought of telling Jessie about the trip, in my mind I saw her threatening a funeral, standing by her grave, pointing at the tombstone, and looking over at me. I heard my mother asking, "Do I have to die? What about the living? You can go there to clear out someone else's, but you can't come here to help me." My mother, only months ago, cleaned out Jessie's apartment and settled her affairs when Jessie went into the nursing home.

Why I ever mentioned to my mother that I was going to Florida makes only a demented sense. It comes, I think, from my not wanting my mother to feel I am where I am not, and from a wish that she would decide I had done my part by cleaning the apartment of another aunt. That, however, is not the kind of logic that holds much sway with my mother. I had thought, too, that going to Florida to settle an in-law's affairs was a family matter and something one ought to tell one's mother about. The trip, and the unsettling event of Maxine's death, were a secret I had been keeping for over a month and I was eager to tell it. So just before I left, I told my mother I was going. She swore she would not tell Jessie. "Why tell her? She never needs to know," she said. But then, of course, "It slipped. I didn't know what I was saying."

My mother told me she had slipped and told Jessie when I called her one night from the hotel in Florida. I had, again, an inexcusable urge to be in touch with her. Specifically, I wanted to ask her what to do with Maxine's costume jewelry. "How do I tell the better from the worse? Who buys this?" I wanted to know. I thought she would know and that would help me decide what to give away and what to keep. My mother was of little help. She claimed to know nothing about costume jewelry, but she actually knew something. My mother, I have found, knows something about everything, although she claims not to—"You want to know where the scissors are? I have no idea, but you might look in the top left drawer of my desk." She said of the jewelry that unless it had a designer's name on it, it was worthless, but it might be interesting for me to look at. I told her about Maxine's apartment and about going to the lawyer and the sheriff, who gave us, in a brown paper shopping bag, Maxine's wallet and jewelry and the shoes she died in. The trip was like that, best discussed in terms of concrete, physical facts.

When I got back home, after putting it off for a week, I called Jessie to explain why I had gone to Florida and why I had not told her. She took it silently. Mostly, we discussed the tall buildings in Florida that were built right up to the beach and the mess Maxine's apartment was in. "My apartment was a mess too, you know. Your mother cleaned it," Jessie said. "Not as bad a mess as this." I told Jessie that my lover had not been close with her aunt, seeking to make the situation seem unemotional and not like the relationship between Jessie and me. "It was an obligation," she said, as if helping me out. We discussed the disposition of the Cadillac. "You should get what it's worth. Put an ad in the paper.

But if you can't, you can sell it to a dealer." I never mentioned Maxine's silver to Jessie. I felt it would hurt her feelings to know we had brought this silver back with us, even if I felt her set was better and I would prize it.

Soon after I got back, I received in the mail from my mother a letter in which she criticized Judith's Aunt Maxine for not cleaning her apartment, for playing golf, and generally for living the life she did. It felt like an attempt to destroy Maxine's character and meant, to me, that my mother was feeling jealous of my visit. In her letter, she also discussed her retirement, hinted at being at death's door, and suggested that perhaps she was losing her mind—how else explain that slip to Aunt Jessie? Finally, she announced a time the next month that I would have to come back to see her since she was going to have a retirement party and had suddenly set a date. I wrote her back telling her to stop threatening me with parties, or the loss of possessions from relatives, or I would not visit her at all. Along with the note, I sent selected pieces from Maxine's jewelry collection that I thought were in my mother's taste—a light green jade necklace, a silver Mexican ring, and a silver scarf holder.

There is something soothing about the luster of sterling silver, that metal that is not as valuable as gold. It has always seemed to me a second-class metal, so that what you do with it is what counts, the crafting of it into shapes and designs. Silver is the people's jewelry. It shines despite grim circumstance. It is soft for a metal and has, for me, a feeling of inevitability about it—you can always fall back on silver. Members of my family have favored silver, even when wearing gold. We tend to identify ourselves with silver, with being second best, not fitting in (like silver in a world of gold), and with liking handmade and imperfect arts. Silver is a private curiosity with us, something we look at on the sly and admire and gauge ourselves in relation to. We wonder, Do we look like this silver? Does it look like us? Are we brave enough to wear it? My sister and my mother and I each has a small collection of silver jewelry that we like.

I wish I could say that my family has the qualities of such well-wrought silver, but I cannot. I basically do not like families. I feel they are constraining. My family is something I have inherited, but that I wish I did not have, which is to say I wish to be free of my past.

Yet I know that to speak about family silver is to speak about connections within families and across generations, especially among women. In Florida, for example, a couple of Maxine's friends, two seventy-year-old women, tried to get me to carry several cartons of books down the stairs of Maxine's apartment building by doing it their way—using a shopping cart. I refused, wanting to carry the books in my arms, my way. They proceeded to use the shopping cart, and as we passed each other on the stairs, they would not let me hear the end of it. Like silver, this was a low level, low luster argument, not apparently about anything important, yet Maxine's friends had to insist that their way was best and I had to refuse, each of us with a passion. What gets passed down through the generations, I think, is this desire to do things one's own way. Thus one daughter no longer engraves her initials on a set of sterling, another does not have a set at all. Silver seems not functional, it takes so much cleaning, it is expensive. Then a relative dies or passes her silver on and there is a decision to be made: Do I use it, or sell it, or put it in the basement? Which generation am I?[1]

CURLY HAIR

Something else passed down through the generations in my family is curly hair, and, much like family silver, it is both gift and burden. My sister has curly hair, her three daughters do, and so do I. When my sister and I were growing up, having naturally curly hair was a chief fact of our lives. It was not the right kind of hair, not the desirable kind, not the hair most other people we knew had. It was not gold hair. It was the silver of hair and it was something we felt we alone had inherited, and that we constantly had to correct for. We had to overcome our hair—tie it down, grow into it, be better than it. It made us feel we stood out like sore thumbs. Much inner personal misery was tied to our hair, an outward manifestation that was easier to talk about than other difficulties, such as being a big child, in my case. I felt like a rounded mass of flesh with curls on top when I walked across the street to visit a neighbor, a small, thin girl with straight hair. She was Catholic and had told me that the Jews killed Christ. I assumed I did it. How could she like me, given how I looked, given who I was?

If only my hair would be straight, I used to feel, I would be like everyone else, I would be happy. I think people often have a feature, a skin color, a cultural heritage, a personal characteristic that makes them feel they stand out and for which they will be rejected, an outward sign that sums up all the inner pain and that they wish to hide or change. Women, who are so dependent on appearances, feel especially in these ways.

To the outer world, one's sensitive feature might seem no more than a curiosity. On one occasion when I was in high school, I went into a bathroom where a group of tough girls were smoking. One came over and asked to touch my hair and then said, startled, "Oh, it's soft. I thought it would feel like Brillo." I felt good that she thought that my hair was soft. I also felt let in on a reality—to the world, my hair looked like a steel soap pad. Once, growing up, my sister applied hair straightener to her hair, and the house smelled foul. My mother and I were horrified, feeling there were some ends to which one did not go. My sister's hair did not get altogether straight, but she was satisfied with the result, as if proud of having had the nerve to try. I remember, too, the nightly physical pain of wearing curlers and the trouble of turning my head on the pillow, the quest for the softest curlers (so they would not hurt) and the largest (so they would straighten as much as possible). I stopped using such curlers only when I began living with another woman for the first time, at age twenty-nine. The point here for me is that physical self-acceptance is not natural so much as learned. It takes a long time to come by even a small amount of it, and for a woman, self-acceptance may depend a great deal on intimate acceptance by other women.

My mother, much earlier, may have had the best idea about what to do with curly hair—cut the hair short so the curl will seem to go with the head. However, on the subject of hair, daughters tend not to listen to their mothers. In the process of growing up, I learned that hair is not a matter of appearance in an abstract aesthetic sense. Rather, it was about fitting in, being one of the people who counted for me, one of a majority. It was about being current and beautiful, like movie stars and others I wanted to escape from myself by being like. When I tried to change my hair, I was trying to be the more valuable metal, the more valuable person.

When I look back on pictures of my sister and myself as young girls, it is clear to me that, in some, my mother has wet our hair and then pinned it down with a barrette to make it look straight for the photograph. Thus we learned about how it was fit to be seen—in public, one's hair does not curl. Much later, I see my sister's daughters in photographs and notice their hair. My sister says it is a major preoccupation for them. I am aware that although in a photograph, my sister's girls look very cute—the three of them, since small, topped by furry-looking thick brown curls—in person, this mess of curls is a tangle for each of them. My sister says her oldest has told her next oldest that some people simply do not like you if you are Jewish and left-handed and have curly hair. I had not expected such things to be passed down.

My sister's two older girls have temporarily solved the problem of their hair by letting it grow long, and, as it grows, pulling it down to make it seem straight. The hair is still frizzy and it bushes out, but it looks as if it is flowing downward, and that general impression is important; the attempt to straighten their hair shows they are trying to blend in. My sister's youngest child, Annie, has not yet adopted this longer style, however. As if reacting to the anguish the other two express about their hair and to the attention they give it, beginning very young, she refused to brush her hair, or to have it combed or brushed by anyone else. She said brushing hurt her, which sometimes it did, although there may be more to it. Beyond physical pulling, I would guess, to comb or brush her hair was to pull her out of her childhood, and out of her self, out of her own world and into a world where hair, like the rest of the person, conforms; where, although harboring silver, one claims to value gold; where one passes for someone one is not—a straight woman, a Christian woman, a younger woman, a man—as women often do.

Although my sister's girls have many years of pulling down their hair to look forward to, for me, having curly hair is no longer a misery. I have grown up into an era where adults, at least, do not stigmatize curly hair. In fact, many women have permanents, which, at first, seemed backward to me. Why curl your hair when it is already straight, when it is already the way it is supposed to be? Straightening curly hair, on the other hand, has seemed not backward so much as necessary, perhaps because I am more familiar with the motivation for it. To see someone with a permanent feels disconcerting to me. This woman pulls her hair up to make it look right; I push mine down. She seems to get the benefit of curly hair without having gone through the suffering of it, although I know little of her suffering—much as a lesbian born after liberation knows little of the anguish of a lesbian born before, or a woman born after the washing machine knows little of the trials of a woman who lived earlier. A straight-haired woman's curled hair seems to me like new silver, acquired wealth, like getting to pick your pattern instead of inheriting your grandmother's, which is fine except that it does not answer the question that is so central to me—how can I feel good about, and value, what is mine? How can I accept what I have been given?

Hair, a woman's pride, like those other possessions that belong, if only momentarily, to us—those things by which we are marked, and that feel part of who we are—what do we do when these are lost? Such possessions are our wealth, our family silver. My aunt Jessie wore a wig for twenty-five years because her hair had thinned. She liked her wigs and felt unpresentable without them. When she moved into the nursing home, she stopped wearing a wig, and when my sister's girls first came to visit her, she was extremely worried they would be afraid when they saw her, as she put it, "with no hair." After their visit, my sister told me they had not been afraid. What they noticed and cared about was how Jessie acted toward them. She had not acted in a way that scared them. My sister felt Jessie looked fine without her wig. She looked like all the other women did in the nursing home, with thin gray hair. This was a world of silver. It did not have the same pretenses as elsewhere.

When I visited Jessie in the nursing home later, I noticed that all the women in the dining room had perfectly done white or gray hair, in sharp contrast to physical problems in their bodies. The room seemed beautifully aglow with their hair, and I wondered again about the relationship between a woman's appearance and her reality, her sense of self and her dignity. I wondered about what really matters in one's life and about my own concern with my appearance. I vowed never again to care about looking perfect, a hard promise to keep. But which of our promises are easy? Especially hard, I think, are those promises aimed at transcending the ways of one's gender, the old self-protections, the passed-on gifts.

Some gifts are subtle. When Judith and I went back to visit Jessie six years ago, while she was still living in her apartment, Jessie slipped onto Judith's finger a handsome, Indian-made silver ring. Jessie had gotten the ring many years before, when she used to take vacations in Arizona. I think she wanted to give her new in-law something and had decided on this ring. She found a finger where it fit and slipped it on. Judith liked the ring and decided to wear it all the time. She felt married into our family, or accepted in, by virtue of this gift. She made clear to me, too, that she liked silver and preferred it over gold. I knew that my parents' first wedding rings were silver bands, so I soon put on a silver ring myself, feeling that it was a fitting act. We never, of course, traded rings. That would be too heterosexual, too married, too coupled. We simply finished off something Jessie started with her gift.

WOMEN'S WEALTH

This discussion of gifts, family relationships, and family silver illustrates, for me, some characteristics of social patterns among women, at least among a few I know, with special attention to the concrete physical facts, and the details of information and concern, around which our lives sometimes interconnect. The circle of relationships between myself and the other women I speak of here opens outward and turns in on itself again. Before leaving for Florida, for instance, I called my sister to ask her husband, a lawyer whose mother lives in Florida, for the recommendation of a local lawyer to help settle Aunt Maxine's affairs. There is something here about a habit of turning first to one's women relatives, and about the probability of finding that one of them lives in Florida. But the main thing for me was that getting that lawyer's name required that I call my sister back, after I first talked with her, in order to say to her, "Don't tell mother." I explained that I feared she would tell Jessie. My sister greeted my request with a significant silence in which I heard, whether intended or not, my mother's refrain, "You can go there, but you can't come to see me."

Who said what? Who felt what? That the line between my sister and myself, and my sister and my mother, is blurred for me is significant, but no more so than the line from an old song—it is a song about who does right by who, whose suffering should not be in vain, who should be recognized, who should be heard, about attentions due one woman by another. It is about my needs of my mother, my mother's needs of me, my needs of my sister, and hers of me.

Women are said to be open, soft, expressive. Silver is known for its white color and said, because of its softness, to be fairly useless structurally, so ornamentation was made with it. Social patterns among women are, to some extent, in the eye of the beholder—my world of women is soft; it is also frightening and full of invaders. Yet, to some extent, each woman's mind's eye grasps outer realities. The outer world of women is soft, I think, because it is an underworld that yields to dominance, that provides indirect routes to get things done (a web of telephone connections, for example), and that takes very seriously the appearances of things (for instance, clothes, those signs of social place, and hair). This is a world that relies on ephemeral strategies, of being here one minute and gone the next, and of shifting one's position. Direct routes, anything very visible, would be interrupted, or the resources would not be available to women.

A world of women is frightening, I think, because it is unfamiliar—without power, without hierarchy, without order as order is normally understood, not described well by the words we know. Further, such a world is different for different women. Not every woman has relatives in Florida, not every woman's family has silver tableware. In fact, few do, but what counts is the idea of a woman having something of value—inner lasting value even when a thing wears out—the idea of use, of crafting, of making it your own, of not fitting in, not being what is valued most, not being gold.

In a world of gold, the silver is kept secret, locked in a box and wrapped in silvercloth to keep it from tarnishing. It is taken out for family and social use—to celebrate an occasion or keep the children in line. Silver tableware was once a possibility for only the wealthy, but aspired to by the middle classes. Acquired by them when production processes changed, and considered wealth, it was passed down in families, among women, and it fell to collectors—men appropriating women's wealth. Now, when most tableware is stainless steel, silver is largely unnecessary, archaic, mostly nostalgic. Initially silver had a functional advantage in that it did not interact with foods as much as prior metals—iron or pewter, for instance. But silver was never very practical. Its uses were more ornamental, ceremonial, social, and to do with status. Further, it could be sold for money. It had that larger material value.

The questions silver raises concern value, and I am saying that I think the value problem is central to understanding relationships among women. To know these relationships one must, first, think it worthwhile to see that they exist. Relationships among women are often hard to see because they are camouflaged and devalued; they look like something else and fade into the background and are characterized by invisibility. Had I not pointed it out, for instance, no one but those close to me would know about my female relatives or about the particular web I make of them. Our relationships are interstitial, unremarkable on the surface. They are like Maxine's empty apartment, one among many that look like it. In my mind, there is an image of a woman on a phone in a nursing home in Connecticut talking with her niece in California about her woman lover's father's sister who died two months ago in Florida. The niece is seeking to repair damage done when her mother, somewhat vengefully, spilled the beans and told her aunt about it. Meanwhile, in another state, three curly-haired nieces of the niece are considered by their grandmother to be not yet ready for her husband's mother's silver flatware. She fears they will, by accident, throw it out. Suggestive, interconnected, understated, loaded with emotion, and with a rushed sense about it, plotless, fading away just beyond reach, this is a woman's world.

When women hold on to silver in their worlds—their mother's, or their mother's mother's, somebody else's, or their own—when they pass it on, whether the silver is used or kept in a bottom drawer, whether it is a single piece or a set, something is being said. When the silver must be sold for money because the woman is poor, or needs the money, or no longer wants or can keep it, when a woman takes out her silver and asks her daughter, "Do you like my pattern? Would you like to have it?" and the daughter, uncomprehending, tries to tell her, "I don't know how to answer your question," something more than silver is in the air. Sometimes the silver is not silver at all. It is a piece of cloth, an old dress, a head of curly hair, a memory, a belief, a sense conveyed that we are this kind of people. What will the next generation make of the wealth of the generation before? What is one woman to make of her own wealth? Why is it so easy to lose family silver? It can be stolen, melted down, destroyed by fire, misplaced, thrown out. When the silver is lost, what else is lost? What does this silver represent—the kept female past, the precariousness of the female present, the need to guard what is women's? In some sense, this silver is an inner core, something too good to discard. "I keep my grandmother's family silver in a bottom drawer," says one woman. "Of course, I don't use it. There are not enough settings, and, anyway, it's too good."

Four

THE PASSING DOWN OF SORROW

My mother has always seemed big to me. I used to think she looked like Marilyn Monroe. As I got older, I thought she looked more like Ingrid Bergman, which means that I thought my mother was the most beautiful woman in the world. When I was growing up, we would ask my mother why we had to do something. "Because I am your mother," she would say, and I would think she must not feel she was our mother if she had to say this. My mother seemed to me a person who felt absent apart from the role she played, or from the reasons she gave for things. These were not her reasons, or her wishes, but something outside herself—"Because it needs doing . . . Because it needs taking out . . . Because that's the way we do things in this family."

Of my two parents, my mother was the more volatile. My father expressed his emotions in a subdued way and seemed to me more rational, more simple, more obvious. He was slow and general compared with my mother. He did things with persistence, guided by principles. He was more directly affectionate, while my mother had a harder time expressing her positive feelings for others. My father loved my mother and felt she was wonderful. I think he steadied her emotionally while he was alive. My mother moved abruptly and was quick and smart. She seemed to know about everything and to be good at all she did, but she felt inadequate. She repeatedly told me that "Nothing happens for anyone in our family without their working to make it happen," and she seemed to be referring especially to herself when she said this. I could hear the hurt in her voice, as if she felt the nothings she had to work for should have come to her without work. There was the implication in her tone that she was not born lucky, or favored, as was her older brother, a first-born Jewish son. My younger brother, like her brother, she used to say, was born lucky. He had mazel. That was something never said of my sister or me, or of anyone else in our family.

My mother's feelings of inadequacy, like her feelings of sadness, were beneath the surface and not immediately apparent to others. Her surface behavior was often a display of just the opposite of what she felt. She would get proud or angry when she felt scared or hurt, and she would push people away when she wanted them close. I think my mother wished to be above having frailties and needs and to be knowledgeable and respected, and she wanted her children to be that way too. I also think that my mother felt, and still feels, very much alone, and that a person who feels alone acts differently than someone who trusts others.

My mother often speaks as if she is lecturing, rather than in an interactive way. I think I learned, as a child, to be silent when she spoke, or to fight with her in order to have a connection with her. I also learned that my mother might cut off contact with me suddenly. Something I might say would scare her and she would get quiet and withdraw. As an adult, I find I often say goodbye to people several times in order to check that they have not yet left me. I also need to get very close to people because my mother was so distant. Only by getting close do I feel that I exist and that others, and myself, are not the same as my mother.

I am the oldest of three children. My sister is three years younger. My brother, who was seven years younger than me, killed himself as an adult. My sister and I suppress our emotions and dampen our affect when we speak, wishing to escape being emotional like our mother, or being hurt by her or someone like her. My sister was the quiet one in our family. My brother was the baby. I was the one who fought back more. I always felt that my family was unusual because of the socialist political beliefs my parents taught us, and because my father was a writer. Otherwise, it seemed traditional. My father had his world, my mother hers, and as children we moved between the two, learning about male ways of being from my father, about female concerns from my mother. There was much distance surrounding each person in our family. We discussed things intellectually, rather than speaking of our personal feelings. Much that was important was said indirectly, or left unsaid. Much about my mother's moods was not explained. Growing up, I reacted to my mother's surface behaviors and I often did not know what she really felt. Now I am drawn to speak specifically about my mother—from out of my family constellation—because, for a long time, I have been unwilling to do so. I have feared that to speak of my mother would be to speak badly of her, and I have wanted not to hurt her.

I am sure I do not have a proper perspective on my mother. In my mind, she is either too bad, or not bad enough at all, and the issues are very much of good and bad—was she good or bad to me? I usually think about my relationship with my mother in order to explain inner difficulties I have, why my life is not easy for me—a version, perhaps, of my mother's complaint, "Why was I not born the lucky son?" I do blame my mother for my troubles in this way. Not to do so would be to grant her less importance than she really has had for me, and to grant inflated importance to others—my father and the rest of the world—to imagine others have enabled me to escape my femaleness. That growing up female is, for me, largely about growing up my mother's daughter makes a surprising sense, and one that I did not, at first, expect to see. That what has been handed down to me—as well as how to set a table, clean a house, or not lose the family silver—is an inner trouble of an entrenched and depressed sort also makes sense to me. Not that I think that only mothers, or women, hand down emotional troubles to their children, and especially to their daughters. But I do think that women internalize much emotional pain and that mothers pass this pain on to their daughters. I think that the passing down of inner sorrow is an important strand in the persistence of female gender. This essay is about sorrow, about expectations of irrationality among women, and about how internalizing trouble is part of femaleness.

That my mother was hurt long before I came into the world is hard for me to comprehend. She once wrote to me, "I have known few moments of true happiness in my life—once when you were born, and several times as you were growing." I liked especially being told that my mother was glad when I was born. I usually feel I cause her nothing but unhappiness. Yet my mother's comment has a mixed meaning for me. On the one hand, it makes things seem normal and glowing: here is a mother happy to have a child. On the other hand, it says my mother rarely feels this way. She goes on in her letter to tell me that she does not value happiness. Other things are more important to her, such as working for progressive causes. I am left feeling that, for my mother, something that I have learned is good and normal—happiness—is not so for her.

The mental image I have of my mother is of a woman brooding. She is sad and about to cry. She is sad because I am not there, and because my father and brother are gone and no one cares about her in the right way. She is also sullen, which means there is anger in her sadness.

My mother used to tell us that the point of seeing a good movie was so we could have a good cry. Often, when there was a conflict in our family, my mother cried. I grew up feeling that being sad was more real than any other emotion because, for my mother, that was so. Not long ago when I visited my mother, I disagreed with her in a conversation and she responded by feeling hurt and crying. When I asked her not to cry, she insisted she preferred to cry. I felt miserable for making her so miserable. Our disagreement was over the fact that she thought being a lesbian ought to be kept private and in the bedroom, while I felt it should be talked about. She also thought a single woman who purposefully got pregnant to have a child was a whore, and I felt differently. My sister says my mother has a hard time agreeing with me, as I do with her, and that when I contradict my mother, she gets unusually upset. I feel awful for contradicting her, and I wonder why I do it.

I have, all my life, tried not to be like my mother, probably because she was not a man. I wanted to be like my father. I felt he had more admirable personal qualities—rationality, an even temper, an ability to feel content—qualities I did not then associate with his gender. In many ways, I have been successful in being like my father, doing the same kind of work he did, adopting his habits of gentleness. But the ways I am like my mother feel more at the center of me. They are more internal and they seem to have happened without my knowing.

When last I went back to visit my mother, things flared up between us, not atypically, but to a greater extreme than usual. My lover, Judith, had come with me to buffer the effects of my family on me and to place my life with my family in the context of our life together. Along with visiting, we planned to pack up my aunt Jessie's silverware and a decorative chest it was stored in and ship these back to our home in California. When Jessie, my father's sister, moved into the nursing home, my mother had stored the silver for me in her basement. Part of the difficulty of this visit was that my mother felt I kept leaving her to go off to see my aunt, and she did not understand what I was doing in the basement when I was packing up the silver.

The day on which most of the trouble occurred was tumultuous from the beginning. My mother had stored others of my aunt's possessions in her basement—clothes Aunt Jessie no longer needed, old medicines, miscellaneous photographs. My mother wanted me to go down to the basement with her and sort through Jessie's things and decide what to give away and what to keep, and then load the giveaways into her car and take them with her to a thrift shop. That morning, I was slower to get up than my mother wanted, or she had extra energy. I remember she left hurriedly in her car to mail a package right after the post office opened. This was the day before I was to leave to return to California.

When Judith and I went down to the basement later that morning to sort through Aunt Jessie's things, my mother was already fired up, like a brew in a cauldron ready to boil over. We descended a set of stairs off the kitchen to the basement—a large, semifinished room with walls on three sides, a white composition ceiling, a white linoleum floor. There were two guest beds, bookshelves against the walls, a small desk of my mother's, some file cabinets, and a closet in which my mother keeps her out-of-season clothes. Behind doors lay a furnace, washer and dryer, and storage shelves. But the main feature of the basement for me is that all around are reminders of my family's past and especially of my father—pictures of him, one of his father, paintings by him, books he wrote and collected, and copies of advertisements he designed for the Ladies' Garment Workers Union, one of them framed on a wall. This is the house my mother moved to after my father died and the basement seems to me full of all the items too weighted with emotion to keep upstairs.

When I visit my mother and sleep in her basement, it is hard for me to get ready for bed—to place my flashlight above my head at night in a bookcase I know only too well from its placement in my father's study over many years. In my mind, this is the original bookcase, the one all others are deviations from. On the top shelves are now books of my mother's and, above them, a soft-looking photograph of my mother's younger sister when she was in college. This basement is, at once, familiar and foreign to me. It is familiar because it reminds me of my father, and foreign because my mother's things are now in places where my father's once were, and because my mother has decided where to put his things—down in the basement in exactly this way, some placed carefully on the walls, others not carefully stored, like drawings by my father that are mildewing in a large accordion envelope near the furnace. The thought of these pictures poorly kept always bothers me. Why does my mother not take better care of them? I feel. I do not feel, Why does my mother not take better care of me? Life in our family is indirect. Worries about oneself are expressed as concern for other people and for things.

Upstairs, my mother's house is more fully hers—more tied to her present life—than the basement. There, too, it is full of reminders of my family's past, but these are more specifically my mother's surroundings—her dining room table, her pots and pans, her white glass lamp throwing a soft light opposite the front door. The house upstairs reflects my mother's way of organizing external space. She leaves clear surfaces and makes rooms feel restful. It does not reflect the inner turbulence I associate with my mother.

When Judith and I arrived downstairs, my mother began taking out large plastic bags and several suitcases that had Aunt Jessie's clothing in them, tossing these containers abruptly onto the beds or asking me to lift them. Then she lit into the contents, pulling out the garments with rough motions and coming to sudden decisions about whether to give away a sweater, or pair of slacks, or hold on to an item and send it to Jessie for reconsideration. The vengeance with which my mother attacked the bags was very familiar to me. I had seen it in action many times before when she would march into my sister's or my room, or my brother's room, and decide it needed to be cleaned up, the closets and dressers sorted through and anything extra tossed out. She would attack as if suddenly the confusion of the room, or of someone else's sense of order, had become too much for her, or as if suddenly she needed a target. She needed to be rid of something. Cleaning out a linen closet was a similar experience, although the object of attack was less tied to an individual person's things than to more generalized towels and sheets. Still, her movements frightened me. I hated those attacks. Once when I was already grown, I remember feeling like crying for my brother when his orderly, but jam-packed, teenager's room was suddenly torn apart by my mother. My father stayed in his study, keeping out of my mother's realm, and only I seemed to feel like interfering, as if it was wrong for my brother to be unprotected. In my family, I usually feel hurt for someone else—for my mother, or father, or brother, and less often for my sister, perhaps because she is closer to me.

When my mother attacked Aunt Jessie's things, I felt hurt for my mother, because she was upset, and for Aunt Jessie, whose belongings were thrown around. I also felt hurt because it felt tragic to me. I felt this was not supposed to be happening. These tirades and launchings into other people's things were supposed to be in my past, in my childhood. My mother was supposed to be better now, to have grown out of it, to be less angry, not more so, to be more happy, more restrained, not less controlled. Further, I felt that I was no longer supposed to be treated as an object of her attacks. Even if I only looked on, I felt attacked by my mother because I knew she was angry at me. If she felt burdened by having to take care of Jessie, and thus struck out at Jessie's things, she was also including me in her striking out. She was telling me she felt I was not doing enough for her. Often, my mother strikes out at absent people to make statements to those present. When hurt, she identifies all of us as sources of her pain. She feels we have wronged her, or let her down.

Judith and I tried to cooperate with my mother in sorting through the clothes. We wished not to anger her further, nor to come into conflict with her, and we wanted to get this over with soon. I felt embarrassed that Judith was witnessing my mother acting in an aggressive way. While as a private event, my mother's attacks on objects and people seem undesirable to me, they do seem normal in terms of my mother. To an outsider, however, I felt her actions would not seem acceptable.

I describe my mother's physical actions rather than her words here because, for me, they summarize her way of relating and give a graphic image of it. Her words have a more painful feel and are harder for me to remember. Although some of my mother's speech sounds beautifully musical to me, her words are often harsh, critical, or ridiculing of other people. Growing up, I learned what my mother felt were desirable, and undesirable, characteristics of people from hearing her sharp comments about others. I wanted never to be the person who had such a fault as my mother would see in others and comment on sarcastically. My mother felt that Jessie, for instance, was at fault for feeling uncomfortable about wearing certain clothes and thus rejecting them. My father was at fault for thinking his work had value when the world might not. Children were at fault for being crybabies and wanting their needs met right away, adults for being upset, or anxious, or for having specific desires, or for having fears. My mother often ridiculed people for worrying. I think she experienced most human vulnerabilities as faults, perhaps because they left another person exposed in a way she did not want to be exposed herself.

She wanted to be strong, impervious, above it all, and, to some extent, she was. When I think of my mother, I do not see a small, weak woman but a big, strong one, a proud woman concerned about her dignity. I think my mother covered her troubles with pride and with an affect of superior intelligence. Yet her habit of striking out at people has made my own inner world harsh. My mother's criticisms of others are often ways I accuse myself. Her tone of ridicule is the tone I most fear from the world at large. I expect that world to tear me up, as my mother tore into things verbally and physically. I have learned only slowly, over time, that it is not wrong to say what I want, or to care about particular things, or have needs.

I helped my mother put into the trunk of her car the clothes she decided to give away. She took them by herself to the thrift shop. While she was gone, I returned to the basement to pack up Aunt Jessie's silverware and to measure the decorative chest. While downstairs, I also looked around for other mementos of my family I might like to take. This, to me, is a sign that I am more willing than I once was to include evidence of my past life in my present one, to admit that I did not emerge fully grown as myself, but came from this particular family, these parents, whom I have often wished away. In recent years when I have visited my mother, I have usually taken back with me a painting by my father. This time, I had in mind a drawing of a baseball player he did in pastels; two brown bowls, now gathering dust in the basement, that my sister once gave my mother; and a blue and white bowl of my mother's that she thought she had already given me.

When I visit her, my mother is always telling me to take something, anything. She says she wants to simplify her life, that she is going to move into a smaller house soon and she does not need all these things. On this visit, she made her moving seem more imminent than usual. She said she needed to clear out the basement. I should take what I wanted and my sister would rent a truck and take the rest. Therefore, I now considered the bookcases lining the basement walls. All around in the shelves, sticking out from the books, were little white labels I wrote the last time I visited my mother, when she asked me to go through the books and advise her about what to give away and what to keep. Most of these books had been my father's. Many were old books he had bought at flea markets and in used bookstores—labor histories and biographies of American reformers. Some were picture books about artists. There were several nature books, a couple of books about how to raise a dog, two copies of my father's high school yearbook, and a couple of my old college textbooks. My mother had not given away any of the books yet. I thought I would ask the shipper, who would be coming that afternoon, what it would cost to ship the empty bookcases after the books were gone. I was interested in four of the broad sturdy ones.

When my mother came back from her errands, I planned to borrow her car to visit Jessie in the nursing home and say goodbye to her. My mother objected, as she had each time I had gone to see Jessie during this visit. She looked hurt and angry and conveyed to me that she felt my leaving her was wrong. She was my mother. Who was Jessie? Who comes first? she implied. "You don't have to see Jessie," she said. "She calls me about every little thing. She will have you wrapped around her little finger." Since my father died, whenever I have visited my mother, I have also gone to see Jessie, and my mother has never felt comfortable about it. I think that Jessie is a continuation of my father for me. She is also herself and is more direct than my mother, and seeing her is thus a less emotionally fraught experience for me. I am always surprised when other women, like Jessie, are not like my mother. I usually feel something is missing inside of them. I wait for the anger and the hidden meanings that I look for when I am with my mother.

I came back from Jessie's in time to meet with the shipper in the basement to weigh, and get prices on, the items to be sent. I told my mother not to come downstairs. I did not want her to confuse me about my decisions and I felt she should not have to be bothered with this. I then sent off the silver, the chest (which was the size of a small dresser), the baseball player picture, the various bowls, and two small woven rugs that my mother wanted me to take—one my sister had brought back from Mexico, and one that I had previously given my mother. "They will just get worn out if I keep them," she said. I did not entirely understand her comment. Why would the rugs get more worn out in her house than mine? I wondered. Did my mother fear seeing the rugs wear out if she kept them? Were they too delicate for her, or just something extra to worry about? Would she rather I have something special like this? Why waste it on her? I often do not know which of her many possible meanings to pick in interpreting my mother's statements. I do not really know what motivates my mother. To understand her, I have to put much effort into deciphering her actions.

I also got an estimate for shipping the bookcases, along with a small, honey-colored wood desk of my mother's. Rarely used and now in the basement, this desk reminds me very much of my mother because, to me, she has always had it. Wherever we lived, there would be a corner with her desk in it. My mother would sit there, paying bills or writing a letter, occupied in a way that felt safe to me. She was doing something during which she would not strike out at me, or indicate her unhappiness. Over the years, I have repeatedly asked my mother to hold on to her desk for me and not give it away, but she has never once indicated she comprehends that I might value it because it is hers. She simply says the desk is junk and not worth shipping—that it did not cost much to begin with and the wood and glue are dried out. But I associate it sentimentally with her as I associate the bookshelves with my father.

It seems to me that, in my mother's view, whatever I want to take from her house is the wrong thing. When I ask her for something, as I recently did for a labor movement drawing of my father's, she is suddenly not ready to part with it, although she cannot say so directly. She simply pauses and looks for a long time at the drawing and comments on the trunk it was in and the set of pictures it is part of. When I took the blue and white bowl, she let me know that she really wanted me to take some glass plates that had belonged to my father's mother. When I asked for a silver ring she had offered me years before, she wanted, this time, to keep it where it was, in a flour canister in a kitchen cabinet, along with other pieces of jewelry she values but does not usually wear. In this canister are the jewelry her mother, and my father's mother, once wore, kept safe in this woman's version of a vault.

When I take things from my mother's house, I have to expect that although she has told me to take anything, she will not want to part with her belongings, and she will be unsatisfied with my choices—as if they indicate I am valuing the wrong kinds of things about her. I am speaking not only of taking physical items from my mother's house, of course, but of all the takings—the modelings of oneself after, the ways I have chosen, or not exactly chosen but learned, to be like my mother. There is, I think, an admonition in every exchange between us: "Be like me in this way. Value me for this, but not for that. Do not take my diseases, my woman's ways, but my strengths. Don't take my troubles. Above all, do not take my unhappiness." I have long noticed that my mother never wants to hear that I have troubles, especially emotional troubles. She needs to be the only one to have a problem, or if I have a difficulty, even a cold, she has to have a worse one. I have assumed this is because she must always be the focus of attention, but it is possible she simply does not want to see her problems reproduced in me.

When I thought about my mother's comments about her desk, I thought about how often when I value something and tell my mother so, she is quick to attack it and devalue it. I usually try to keep what is special to me away from her, and not tell her about it, for fear its special-ness will be destroyed by her. It may seem odd, or wrong, that I grant to my mother the power to destroy what is mine. But I think she actually has such power. She has an instinct for the kill. What is odd, it seems to me, is that I keep telling her what matters to me, that I do not keep myself altogether hidden from her. I think that my mother strikes out at things I care about when she feels she is losing me, or losing my at-tention to her needs—when something else seems to claim me. She also threatens to disappear at those times if she feels I am going to strike back at her and hurt her. I will look into her eyes and feel she is threat-ening to break up inside and no longer be there. This is camouflage, like animals use in the jungle. I often wonder why my mother is so attack-ing. I think maybe she feels herself under attack in an inner way and is striking back at those inner forces.

INNER STRUGGLES

My mother often speaks of her mother with love and reverence. I re-member after her mother died, she took her mother's bathrobe and kept it in her closet without washing it, so it would still have her mother's smell on it, the gentle scent of her mother's body and of the toiletries she used. Eventually, I got that light blue bathrobe and used it until it wore out. I remember my grandmother as small, lovely, and calm, and as hav-ing her own very definite mind. My mother was proud of the distances her mother swam in the ocean during the summers. When I visit my mother, she still takes me back out to the shore to look at the big rock out in the water that her mother used to swim to. We pull up the car and sit and look across the water at the rock and watch as if her mother is still out there swimming.

My sister remembers my grandmother as cold, which, to me, means distant. I know she was strict in terms of household order, like keeping a clean house and keeping things in their place. I think my mother felt her own mother was highly competent, and that she felt incompetent by comparison, or perhaps because of things her mother said to her. I think my mother wanted to be like her mother and that it was hard for her to be different and, especially, to be less even tempered. I have an image of my mother, when small, being alone with her feelings. Whatever she felt inside may have attacked her, or confused her, and it still does. That is why she attacks and confuses me.

I often think of my mother and me as chicken and egg. I see us in the hospital right after I was born. My mother, then twenty-three years old, is looking at me. She fears being rejected by me, and so she pushes me away, or holds me at a distance, as she was held at a distance. It is not clear to me if she rejects me first, or if I reject her first. I suppose a baby is mostly reacting to her mother, but the infant can be a bundle who evokes fear in the mother. I think my mother was afraid of my needs. She needed someone to take care of her needs. She may have been at a loss when confronted with me, and she may have resented me. This image of me as a baby in the hospital is not just about being an infant, for me, but it summarizes my relationship with my mother over all time. To me, everything in those first few minutes, the pattern, is as it has always been. A central theme of my relationship with my mother is that I feel responsible for her. If she rejects me, I think it is because I have rejected her. Whatever is wrong with her, I feel I have caused it, and that is why she is so angry at me. Maybe some people have a relationship with their mother that changes a great deal over time, but mine has not. I feel there is a force within me that is my mother and has a life of its own and is never resting and often rejecting of me. I talk back to this force to get it to stop attacking me, as my mother, perhaps, talks back to her inner forces.

I think my mother repeatedly tells her internal forces that she is not a bad person, that her actions are justified, that someone else is at fault, that she has been sorely deprived and is frightened, and that she is trying to gain control. I tell my forces, too, that I am not bad, and that I am doing the best I can, against inner odds, to maintain the ways of a normal person, that I am not to be ridiculed or torn into, that it is all right to be vulnerable. In having inner forces to contend with, my mother and I are alike. In how we deal with these forces, we are different. My mother's solutions to her problems are often external; mine are internal. It seems to me as if my mother lives amidst much self-protective external scaffolding. I have spent much of my life trying to find her inside that scaffolding, which is one reason I am so internal—I keep looking for my missing mother.

I think my mother is missing for me because she deliberately pulls away. She has often told me she thinks it is best not to respond to a child when she calls, or cries, because then the child will always expect you to respond, and you will be controlled by the child and not be free. As an adult, I consciously tell myself to respond as requested, and right away, when others ask something of me, so deeply learned is that other instruction not to respond. My mother often responded differently from what children wanted. She would give a different present, serve a different food, tuck the blanket in a different way than a child asked for, or she would strike out verbally, or with a sudden gesture, or by hitting. I think she wanted to make the difficult need go away. She also wanted us to know who was who—who was the mother, who was the child, who was in charge. I think that a child calling for her mother, or asking her for specific things, or getting upset (I learned to cry and throw tantrums) is trying to take care of her own needs. I know my mother fed and clothed me well. She overfed and overclothed me as the first child. She sang to me in bed at night when I was sick, explained things to me, took me places, made sure I got the kinds of things children need. Yet because she saw my needs as threatening to hers—and, therefore, pulled back or struck out at me—and because she saw herself as less competent than she wished to be, I felt in danger. I still have that sense of being in danger—a sense of terror that I will be hurt by others, or by myself, when I am in need—although I have learned to take care of myself quite well.

My mother seems pained when she tells me about how I learned to tie my own shoes early on, saying to her, "Mommy, let me do it myself." I think she felt pained because I was taking myself away from her. One of my father's paintings shows a mother bending down, encircling a child, tying the child's shoes. When we look at it, my mother tells me I was not like that. She views my father's paintings of mothers holding infants with a similar discomfort. She has often told me she did not like that early period of dependency of child on mother—and, I think, mother on child—and so she does not like those pictures. I think such a dislike is not unique to her. Many mothers may not like that early period. What is unusual is that my mother says so. In addition to her feelings about dependence, I know my mother did not like being locked into stereotypical ways women were supposed to act and be. She did not want to be a frilly, sweet, little woman who had less stature than others and stayed home and raised kids without going out to work. She was raising children at a time when the women around her were staying home, influenced by a Freudian psychology that my mother did not like, that held mothers responsible for their children's ills and made women feel guilty for their own wants. My mother wanted to go out and work with kids in nursery schools and do creative things with them. That type of work made her happy. I think she was best when she was not around us all the time. The problem was not that she was absent when she was gone, but what happened when she was there.

As much as I have had troubles with my mother, I want the world to be sympathetic to her. My mother's younger sister views my mother kindly. She sees her as a daughter of immigrants who has pulled herself up by her bootstraps and improved herself with formal education, self-education, and an interest in arts and reading. My mother's mother came from Russia, her father from Poland. He was a wholesale fruit dealer. My grandmother took care of the house and children and members of her extended family, was active in a Jewish women's organization, kept kosher, and, unusual for a woman at that time, drove her own car. I sometimes think my mother has traditional expectations about how children should behave toward their parents because of her past. She grew up in a house where her maternal grandmother, who spoke only Russian and Yiddish, lived on the third floor, and in a town where members of her mother's extended family had settled and lived all around. She feels children should still make a place in their homes for their parents and not go too far away from them. I think it is hard for her to experience my living far away, and my not getting along well with her, not only because she worries about what will happen to her when she gets older, but because this is not how it is supposed to be. I sometimes think she feels disgraced by me because the children of other members of her extended family visit their parents more often and get along better with them.

When my mother's expectations of normal family life are broken, I think she feels lost and unprotected. I know her mother did not live with her, but her mother died in her arms in the bedroom in the house where my mother grew up. When my mother worries about my getting serious physical diseases, it is her mother's diseases she expects I will get. Thus, I expect that too. When I think of my own death, I see my mother's mother dying. I may, indeed, be the mother she once had, who did not help her enough, and who might yet do so. Such expectations of who is supposed to be who, and how we are supposed to act—expectations of continuity—layer over every visit between my mother and me, although we speak of other things, such as what to have for dinner and what to do with items in the basement.

LEAVING MY MOTHER'S HOUSE

After the shipper left, I went with Judith to the grocery store to get supplies for dinner and to the liquor store to get a bottle of wine as a present for my mother. This would be our last dinner together and I wanted it to be special. I also wanted to get cartons from the stores to pack up the books in the basement—to make it easier for my mother to dispose of the books and ship the shelves, since she has bad knees and has trouble bending. When I got back, I unloaded the groceries and went downstairs. For the next hour, Judith and I packed up the books, attaching the labels to the boxes, while my mother prepared dinner. For dinner, we were going to have rice, shrimp, and green peas, and we were all looking forward to it. When the packing was done, I came up to tell my mother we were through. The shrimp was simmering in a frying pan on the stove and smelled good to me. Even the rice smelled good. It was invitingly warm upstairs.

But my mother suddenly became angry. She had been having a drink and reading a newspaper in the living room, but when I entered she stood up, looking at me incredulously. She quickly became enraged, irrational, livid, full of tears, full of sentences no one could talk back to, speaking her own kind of sense that I am slow at understanding. Who did we think we were? she asked. What were we doing down there? All day, we had been going off by ourselves and telling secrets where she could not hear us. We were plotting to keep her from finding out that we were taking the books off the shelves. Now no one could see them. What if someone wanted to buy the books, how could they know what was there? I only gradually grasped that my mother thought I was taking her books, that I had packed them up to take some of them with me. "But I told you what I was doing," I said. "How can anyone see them if they're in boxes?" Our conversations are often like that. My mother speaks in a rush that keeps me from speaking, and when I speak, she says something seemingly unrelated, and implicitly hostile to me, which is an indirect way of asserting what she needs.

Judith and I went back to the basement and put the books back on the shelves. There were seventeen cartons of them. We put them in their original groupings along with their labels—"Okay to give away." "Save for Mother." "Save for Susan." When I came up to tell my mother the books were now back on the shelves, I expected her to be relieved, but she was tearful and still incensed. She had a martini in her hand—it was not her first—and in the hallway off the living room, she tossed what was left of it at me. Instead, it hit Judith in the face and on the front of her sweater. Judith felt the alcohol sting her face. She turned to me and announced, "I am not staying here tonight."

I went into my mother's study and started packing our suitcases. Judith called a friend of hers who lived nearby to see if we could stay there overnight. We would leave directly for the airport in the morning. My mother became more agitated. She said Judith should not feel offended because the drink was meant for me, and it was almost finished anyway and mostly water. Finally, why didn't I grow up? She said many things I do not remember because she said them sarcastically. I think sarcasm is one way she strikes out. She also cried and wanted me to feel sorry for her, which was painful for me. I know that when her words got to be too much for me, I stood in the corner of her study and put my hands over my ears. Twice, I tried to get out of her study and my mother stood in the doorway, angrily barricading me inside. That was the most disturbing part for me. I was surprised when I tried to go by her the first time and she did not yield to let me through. I felt that if I had pushed her to make my way out, she would have pushed me back and we would have had a physical fight. I have never bodily fought with my mother or anyone else, and I did not want to start. I saw images of women in movies fighting with each other and I did not want to be like that. I also felt that if it came to a fight, my mother would win. She is bigger than I am, but more importantly, she would fight harder.

I was frightened, both by a past—when my mother was, indeed, much bigger than I was and physically struck out at me—and by the present. I felt held by force, as if I might soon be in physical jeopardy from my mother. I considered calling the police. I felt there was a point beyond which my mother should not go in her actions toward me. But I did not think she had reached that point yet. More than frightened, I was horrified that my mother would be doing this, that we had an audience, that things had gotten this much worse.

I think that my mother barricaded me into her study, and became so desperate, not only because I was leaving her, but also because of all the other people who had previously left—my father, my brother, her mother. A close friend of hers had died recently. That day was, in fact, the anniversary of my father's death. In retrospect, it should not seem strange to me that my mother barricaded me into a room, or that she threw a drink at me. With the drink, I think she wanted to startle me, to wake me up, as from a nightmare. She had to wake someone. Why not me, her oldest daughter, upon whom so much has always rested, so much that is conflictual? If she could not wake me, then at least she could keep me. That my mother did this in the presence of Judith was hard for me to experience. It made it seem especially crazy and definitely wrong. Judith's presence was supposed to keep my mother within bounds, to keep exchanges between us semiformal. But my mother was disregarding Judith. She was treating her as if she was of no value, and as another person to be struck out at. I could not help thinking this disregard had to do with the fact that Judith was a woman. My mother would not have thrown a drink at my sister in the presence of her husband. But then, she would not have thrown a drink at my sister, period.

Still, I think a woman does not provide as strict a sense of personal boundary as a man does. More emotions come out in the presence of women only, flowing across the boundaries.

It seemed to me we were arguing in my mother's study and in the hallway outside it for a long time. I did not want to be hysterical like my mother. I did not want to be saying how awful I felt, and crying, and accusing other people of not growing up. Earlier, when I was in the basement, putting the books back on the shelves, I had heard my mother on the phone talking with the man she is close to about what a terrible thing I had done. She was crying and hysterical. When my mother gets hysterical, I get stoic. I become withdrawn and deliberate. I speak with little affect. I am guarded. I try not to feel. I think a lot. Sometimes my mother has accused me of being cold and calculating, which hurts me because I know I have feelings.

I left my mother's house wishing not to go. I faced a dilemma. On the one hand, I felt I had to leave because Judith, who had had her fill, would not stay, and because my mother had thrown a drink at her. On the other hand, it did not seem right to me to leave my mother prematurely, to hurt her the night before I would be leaving town. I knew that in my experience with my mother, this scene was not unusual. However, my mother did not usually throw her drinks (I did not remember her ever having done so before); she had not barricaded me into a room before; and her disturbances did not normally last this long in such an active way. By now, she usually would have become withdrawn. She would be back into herself, unhappy but no longer striking out. I kept telling myself that people who are victims of violence stay with their attackers when they should not. But I was not sure if I was one of those people, or if I was simply a woman with an upset mother, and this was what happened in families, and you did not just leave.

While I felt that Judith should not have to stay in a house with a woman who had just thrown a drink at her, it was harder for me to see that logic applied to myself. Would I be leaving if my mother had thrown her drink and it had hit only me? I was not sure. I thought my mother might settle down in time and become more peaceful. But what if we stayed, and after we went to sleep, something else happened and I woke up and my mother was like this again? I thought I should not stay around and find out. Thus, I left without being sure I was right to go, but feeling afraid and that I had no other choice.

I felt terrible leaving my mother. I picked up my suitcase to go out in front of the house and wait for Judith's friend, who was coming to pick us up. As I walked though the living room toward the front door, I passed my mother sitting on the couch. Her male friend had come and was sitting with her, his arm around her. She was crying. He looked at me and said in a tone aimed at shaming me, "How could you." I felt my father would not have said that. He would not have wanted to divide my mother and me further, and although angry, he would have tried to get me to stay. I felt I just had to walk out. It was one of the hardest things I have ever done. I have left my mother many times, sometimes quietly, sometimes in tears and conflict, but this would be the first time I would leave her in quite this way, so alone, so distressed. Yet always when I leave my mother, it feels like this. Each leaving feels like new, and each is hard for me. Each time, I feel I am not supposed to leave, and that I am making my mother unbearably sad. I feel I will never see her again and that I take her sadness with me and it will haunt me later.

It was dark outside as Judith's friend drove us away. The other houses and the streets outside seemed harsh and cold to me. I felt there was no reason for me to be anywhere else but in my mother's house. Only once before when I visited my mother did I not stay in her house. I stayed in a motel because the house was too full with my sister's family. Given how Judith felt, I feared I might never stay in my mother's house again. I knew I would leave in the morning without calling to say goodbye to my mother.

The saddest thing I felt as I left, however, was that I was leaving, un-eaten, the food my mother had prepared for us. The shrimp, rice, and peas were still in their pots on the stove when I walked out the front door. I feared my mother would get mad at them later and throw them out, feeling in them the pain of my going. But perhaps she would put them quietly away, as a normal person might—a person without the kinds of feelings we have, my mother and me. It is hard for me to say that I myself missed not having had that dinner, harder yet to say I miss not having had a relationship with my mother in which she could have made me happy. I usually think of what my mother misses, not what I miss. I think it is my mother who is most hurt, whose life is most tragic, whom I am most sad for. I do not usually think I miss my mother, but that I miss other women—friends and intimates I know in the present, whom I did not grow up with, who give me a cleaner slate than my mother ever did. These are women who do not respond to me in my mother's hostile ways. Through my relationships with them, I try to find for myself much that was missing in my relationship with my mother. Still, I miss my mother with a sadness that is hard for me to comprehend because my mother's goodness—her generosity, her giving—was so mixed with rage. It is hard to miss someone who hurts you, but I do.

Maybe those mothers exist who serve cookies and are sickeningly sweet to their kids, the good mothers, and the good enough mothers. I had primarily a real mother. I think she gave to me as best she could and that female giving is a complex experience. My mother gave me sorrow and trouble and, eventually, her silver ring. She gave me more anger than I have often known what to do with, and a sense that the world will slight me, and that no one can be trusted, and that something is wrong with me. She taught me how to keep house and to cook, and told me to do the dishes as you go along, and never to leave a milk carton on the table. I learned, from her, to wear sturdy clothes, to be bigger than all the pettiness around me, and to fight back—to be resilient. I learned to be resilient because my mother was, and because she needed me to be that way in relation to her.

My mother, like me, likes to go to the ocean. I like to go because the sea is rough and raging. The turbulence out there is like the turbulence in me, and it reminds me of my mother. She is like that, and she often took us to the shore, as her mother took her and as my sister now takes her three girls. I know some people look at the ocean and see peace and enjoy basking in the sun. I fear the sun. It is too still for me. I like watching a storm and watching the clouds changing. I know that when I meet a woman who hurts me in my mother's familiar ways, I wish to jump in and change, or save, her, and turn her into the mother who loves me unequivocally. I have to remind myself to hold back, to avoid this woman like the plague.

What makes the sorrow my mother has passed down to me peculiarly female? What makes it not unique to my mother and me? When I came home from that visit with my mother, I stopped to pick up my cats from the woman who was taking care of them. I told her about my experience back East and she told me about recently seeing, on a street corner near her, a mother fighting with her daughter. The mother was swinging her cane at the daughter and yelling at her. The daughter was wrestling with her mother to get the cane away. The daughter, it seemed, had come back to help her mother pack up her furniture and possessions so she could move to a different house. After they had done most of the packing, the mother decided that the daughter was there to steal her things, not to help her. Out on the street, she was swinging her cane and yelling at her daughter that she was a thief. The daughter was trying to stop her mother by wrestling the cane away and arguing with her.

At least we don't fight like that, I thought upon hearing this story. I would rather have my mother throw a drink at me. Nonetheless, I was struck by the fact that I did not have to go very far to find an experience similar to my own, and I was shocked that I had found one so similar. I was also reassured because this other mother and daughter seemed much worse than my mother and me. We would never fight physically and never out on the street. My mother might think I was taking her books, but she would not be as deluded as to think I was stealing all her things. However, I knew she probably had felt I was, and that our situation was much the same as that of the mother and daughter in the street.

In a similar manner, I think that others might view my story of my mother and me with a desire to distance themselves from it. By my story, I mean my tale not only of my mother throwing her drink, or of my taking things from her basement and leaving her, and of her leaving me, but also my general story of the extremeness of my mother's sadness and hostility and my own vulnerability to her, my story of the effects of my mother's inner life on me. This story is more extreme than some others. It is, I think, an illustration of what happens to women in situations of unusual grief and stress, but it is also an illustration of how female gender may be centered in grief. One of the most difficult things for me about my mother is that, at first glance, and even later, she appears normal, or like others, and like the image of a well-adjusted, congenial woman. She does not speak an unintelligible language, or dress oddly, or look bad, or cry all the time, or swing objects in the air threatening people with them. She is pleasant in appearance, perceptive, emotionally appealing, highly knowledgeable in conversation, dutiful, hardworking, and self-sacrificing for others. She speaks about her good times and suppresses her unhappiness and considers herself lucky compared with others less fortunate—all of which hides, if thinly, the extent to which she is inwardly angry and hurt.

Similarly, I think, women generally hide the extent to which they are different from a happy or well-adjusted image. Women internalize a great deal. I think this is because much of the labor that women do is emotional and because of the subordinate position of women. Women have traditionally had few important external resources (such as armies and brute power), and so we have learned to use internal resources well. We learn to be valuable by taking outer world conditions into ourselves and converting, or improving upon, those conditions. As caretakers of others, for instance, we absorb the hurt and misery others feel and convert these internally into the strength needed to help others. As teachers and as raisers of children, and as intimates of men who die before we do, we invest a great deal of ourselves in others, only to see those others leave us. We are hurt by the world both because we are not men, and thus are viewed as second best, and because we are women, and thus vulnerable. We are hurt because we are an underclass and are exploited without regard for who we are, and because we are expected to be accessible and thus do not develop barriers against being hurt. Often, women are viewed as responsible both for what is wrong with others and for fixing it. On the outside, we often maintain a facade that is reassuring to others who depend on us. Part of being female, I think, is to weather adversity, to persevere despite what is asked of one, because one must. The expectation that women will be strong and will carry a great burden, but not show it, is one reason why a woman who strikes out, like my mother, is so unsettling. She is showing the strain of what she feels.

Yet I am sure my mother is not alone in her ability to bear a great deal of pain. Women often learn to absorb the injuries, the many small humiliations, the violence against others and themselves that they experience and to ignore these and carry on. We learn not even to realize our discontents with our subordinate status, which is why there is no female revolution. I think that the sadness women feel is often so deep, and its source seemingly so inexplicable, because the injuries done to women are minimized, or are invisible, and because the strength women develop in order to survive obscures the extent of our troubles. When a woman is made fun of as a child because she is a girl (as I know I was), when she learns to view herself as not smart enough or not good enough (as my mother learned), when she must look over her shoulder and see herself as an object to be attacked, when she is addressed disrespectfully, when she must dress like a plaything or a decoration, when she cannot get a job because she is a woman, when her anger is ridiculed and she is not paid for her work, when she hurts for her mother and fears for her daughter—these are only the more visible slights in a long string of experiences in which the subtlest glance of deprecation is extremely hurtful. Women are often depicted as weak when just the opposite is so. I think only very strong individuals could absorb as much pain as women do.[1]

In this vein, I think there was no one life event that caused my mother's sadness, but that her trouble was internal to begin with, and compounded by her experiences, and that her very strength caused confusion. Because she could endure so much, she felt she could bear anything, which was not so. When she broke down, she was disappointed, as was I. She blamed her disappointment on forces outside herself. Yet I felt not that the outer world had let me down, but that my mother had.

I think that women are often like my mother in that we are sad inside beyond telling, hurt beyond consolation, and driven out of our minds. We do not know our own needs and limits, and we are often strong enough to persevere despite much self-denial. We feel alone and deprived, yet we still do the emotional work expected of us, especially that of caring for others. I think that the pain women feel gets hidden in different ways in each woman. No woman entirely avoids this pain, and women pass it on to each other. It gets passed down especially to girls, who learn to be women in important inner ways from their mothers and from other women. It gets passed on among women each time we teach, and help, one another to bear our respective pains. My mother may have had less protection against her inner sadness than some other women do, and more of a desire for freedom from it, which was why she raged. Her rage has made it hard for me to proceed on the surface as if nothing were wrong with her, or with me, or with a world that looks at both of us and tells us to keep our pain hidden.

With an intensity that I rarely notice because it is second nature to me, my mother has taught me lessons she did not wish to teach about how pernicious, brooding, resentful, and persistent inner female struggles are. I cannot see my mother and not see the female condition. If ever I thought I could overcome what is female in my mother, or in myself, a glance at my relationship with my mother reminds me I cannot. My mother wounded me deeply. I daresay that is what mothers do to their daughters more generally. Such wounding is unavoidable in a world that devalues women, and it is why girls often so need to leave their mothers, which then produces pain for both. Yet oddly, there is nothing sought after more by mother and daughter than to relieve the other of her pain.

I never took the desk or the bookcases from my mother's house. I did not want to take any material item from her that she did not wish me to have. But the items of real value are not material. As I hope my discussion has shown, I think that the very commonplace things in a woman's house are part of a language in which mothers talk to their daughters and let them know about what is important in their lives. I learned from my mother that happiness is a rare experience. I learned from my mother that there is a great deal of pain involved in being female.

PART TWO

Academic Settings

Five

HURTS OF THE SYSTEM

IN THIS ESSAY, I SPEAK of how I have been hurt by institutional rejections. My purpose is to make my own reality visible and to see how my individual experience is a female experience. I also wish to identify how faults of an institution are felt as the faults of an individual. Speaking of discontent with institutional arrangements seems to me particularly important for women, for too often the failures of the outer world to respond to us are internalized and felt as an inner failure. When I acknowledge my own pain and its sources, I feel relief. I also feel dissatisfaction and wish the academic world were more accepting of a wider variety of people. My tone in this essay is often acutely sad, for I speak from a great depth of feeling. I wish to acknowledge hurt and something wrong in academic institutions. I wish to speak of the inner emotional costs of being overlooked, being devalued, being a woman in a male setting.

INNER HURTS, OUTER WORLD

The teaching position I have had for the past six years has been eliminated. Next year, I will be paid just a small amount and will teach only one of my courses. I will teach not so much for the money—I would do it for almost nothing—but for the continuity. I want no one to know there is a change in my institutional status. I want not to feel that change myself. I feel stripped of protection upon losing my position. I feel that what I teach is not valued and that I am not valued. I find it hard facing my classes this year knowing that only one of them will be there next year. In that course, Women and Organizations, I ask the students to speak about their experiences of refusing to play by men's rules—the frustrations and lack of rewards that occur when they act, instead, like women. When I speak of my own experiences of this sort—of not reproducing a male academic style, for instance, and not seeking career advancement in the usual manner—I fear the students will view me as a failure.

In my second course, Feminist Methodology, I encourage the students to do social science as I do—in a personal and idiosyncratic way—knowing that a consequence of being like me is to be unemployed. I do not want the students to be without jobs, but I do want them to assert different values in their work and to require the academic world to change so that it accommodates them. I want them to be aware of being women and of how that affects their perspectives. I would like a university to be a different sort of environment than it is. I know too well, however, the difficulties involved in asserting a more individual and female orientation, especially the internal problems of self-worth that arise.

A few weeks ago, I finished teaching a brief version of my Women and Organizations course in a graduate program at a nearby women's college. The students appreciated the course. Then, in the last class session, they asked me, "Exactly what is your position at the university?" I did not want to tell them. One of these students said she felt encouraged because this course showed her it was possible not to be like the men. Since I was doing differently and I had arrived, maybe she could too. "But I haven't arrived," I told her, looking across the table at her through a sudden rush of inner tears. "Well, you're teaching at X University. To me, you've arrived." What if these students truly knew? I thought. What if I no longer had a status in what they felt was a prestigious university? Would they value me then, or want to follow my example? Do they know that there are costs to my choices, and that the important thing is the nature of my choices, not the nature of my gains? I, myself, find that hard to remember and keep clear.

For twenty years, I have worked to have privileges of the academic system—a stable source of income, library use, a position higher than the lowest, a place in a university at all. The highest I have ever been appointed is as a visiting assistant professor. Mostly I have been a lecturer. Often I have been unemployed. Yet teaching is the way I earn my living most of the time. It is preferable, for me, to being a secretary or working in a store, which I used to do sometimes when I was unable to find an academic job.

I work all the time. I work most seriously at writing. I have had three books published and I write papers and articles, but, more often, autobiographical stories. In recent years, my autobiographical writing has become part of my social science. I have been learning how to experiment with the personal essay in order to make broader statements. I have been lucky to have developed, through my writing, a reputation for innovative work in sociology. Yet beyond that reputation, I have difficulty. All of my academic jobs have been temporary, and when one of these jobs terminates for me now, it is as if all my work means nothing. I am back to zero in terms of income and any idea of what my future holds, much as I was upon completing my Ph.D.

My Ph.D. was in communication research, an interdisciplinary social science field that focuses on the processes through which people convey meaning. However, I am a sociologist in the nature of my work. At the time I chose a doctoral field, I had no idea that selecting an interdisciplinary field, rather than a traditional discipline, would later become a problem for me. I did not anticipate that people would later exclude me from employment, on the one hand, because I did not have a degree in the field of sociology, and, on the other, because I had done work that outstretched the field of my degree, communication. I thought, in fact, the opposite, that crossing fields would enable me to have more opportunities. However, I was considering these things in a time of greater expansiveness in the academic world than has occurred since. In general, I have made my decisions about my work optimistically, assuming that things will work out for the best.

My academic work has always had a dual purpose. I have sought to make an outward contribution, certainly, but, at the same time, to do work that responds to my own inner emotional needs, for my work is a central way that I nourish myself. Perhaps more than some other people, I seek personal definition, freedom, and emotional grounding in my work. Whether I am writing a study or a story, I try to get close to emotional realities of others and of myself. In describing these realities, I am always struggling against the conventions of expression—already formed words, ideas, and structures of representation. I think that my struggle to be unconventional has centrally affected both the appreciation my work has received from others and the disregard, and occasional hostility, it has also received.

For example, *The Mirror Dance: Identity in a Women's Community,* my second book—a sociological study of a midwestern lesbian community—described interpersonal dynamics in the community using the multiple voices of seventy-eight community members and associates whom I interviewed. I presented this work as a traditional sociological case study and also as an experiment with social science narrative form. Reviews and articles about *The Mirror Dance* grasped the way it was different in style from a conventional study. "*The Mirror Dance* presents complexity without telling the reader how to sort through it," explained one sociologist. Another wrote that "The data are presented and analyzed through a distinctively feminist methodology" that "merges fiction with social science methods."[1] A text on feminist methods in social research understood the project this way:

> Deliberately working toward a perspective-free voice, Krieger forces readers to recognize that what is conventionally called an objective social science stance is actually a particular view from a particular standpoint. . . . This innovation sets most mainstream definitions of social research on their heads.[2]

I experimented further with narrative form in *Social Science and the Self: Personal Essays on an Art Form,* this time using my own individual voice to argue for viewing the social scientific observer not as a contaminant whose subjective perspective will bias a study, but as a source of knowledge whose more full self-expression will make a study more true. In *Social Science and the Self,* I drew on ideas from the painter Georgia O'Keeffe and from Pueblo Indian women potters to talk about the involvement of the self in creating knowledge, and especially about the involvement of the female self. Reviews of this study by feminist scholars pointed out the unconventional nature of the work and, interestingly, often expressed an identification with what I was attempting. "Krieger's struggles with alienation, belonging, community, vulnerability, and courage have been mine, too," wrote one reviewer. "She is providing a strategy for the near-simultaneous representation of *social science* and the *self.* " In her review, this sociologist used the first person "deliberately and brazenly as a sign of solidarity with Krieger. I would like to see *Social Science and the Self* required in all our graduate programs. I would like to see a lot of 'I's' respected and nourished." Another reviewer offered a personal story in keeping with the nature of the study:

> One night when I was in the throes of finishing my Ph.D. dissertation, I dreamed that I was in a line of people slowly marching towards a guillotine wielded by my adviser. As he chopped off each head, he declared, "I pronounce you my colleague." Just before it was my turn, I jolted out of the dream. It left me with disturbing thoughts about professional socialization as loss, conformity, even as a kind of violence to the learner. That long-ago dream suggests a kind of underlife that *Social Science and the Self* brings into full view. How, Susan Krieger asks in a series of thoughtful essays, does the individual self of the researcher and writer affect the doing of social science?[3]

I have also been moved very often by private correspondence from people who tell me about what my work means to them. Recently, members of an ethnography seminar wrote to me, each on a different sheet of colored paper: "I thought I'd write on bright yellow because your book let in a lot of light for me." "Thank you for sharing your experiences. You give me hope."

These appreciative responses have been deeply important and encouraging for me and have helped me to feel less alone. Yet despite such appreciation in both feminist and sociological circles, I have not advanced up an academic ladder, as many of my friends have, and as I would have liked for myself. In fact, I have done just the opposite. As I have accumulated more publications and teaching jobs, and as I have become more defined by my work, the starting assistant professor positions have become inappropriate for me. I would not turn one down, but I would no longer be offered such a job. I am no longer any senior faculty member's fantasy of a woman who will give her all for a department and, at the same time, advance in a field according to others' expectations. I am not an undefined woman who could become someone else's dream. I am defined, and defined more clearly, by each of my accomplishments. Further, I seem to have made a place for myself so apart from things, or from the way academics usually make a place, that the criteria for inclusion get called into question each time I apply for a job. "But she doesn't have a Ph.D. in sociology," they say. "She doesn't do quantitative work." "I don't know her." "I don't think it's science." "If they took her courses, how would our students get jobs?" "Where is her theory?"

I think no one feels obliged to include me anymore, if they ever did. I seem to have proven myself, but in the wrong way. When I apply for higher level positions, associate professor, for instance, the question cannot help but arise, Why reward me for not having done what others have felt required to do? Why reward me for making different choices? I seem to have gotten away with something. I think I am responded to as if I were a threat to other people's ways of doing things. I do not feel like a threat. I feel I am being punished for my choices. I feel hurt and saddened because I believed it would all work out better for me.

There is more to my dilemma than individual hurt. I think that my predicament is related to my being a woman, and to my holding on to certain female values in a male world.[4] It is related to how women are rewarded for their work in universities and elsewhere. Women are often rewarded with intangibles for doing women's work. Women's work is the informal work required to sustain social life, and sometimes to change it—the low-class work, the housework, the cleaning up after, the work that fills in the gaps men leave and that takes care of emotions and the personal dimension. To some extent, women are rewarded in-tangibly—with praise and admiration and with statements of how in-dispensable we are—because the work we do is beyond value, or price-less. Childbearing, for instance—there is no way really to pay for it. Women's work is also rewarded intangibly because it is valueless. It is not valued officially, or in formal currencies such as money and posi-tion. The self-sacrifice involved in caring for others is often valueless, for instance, as is the status-enhancement work women do, the work of reflecting positively on others. Often, simply because one is a woman, one's work is treated as valueless. Often women's work is thankless, it goes without reward.

In the academic world, I have been appreciated but I have not been formally valued much, and that has been a problem for me. I have re-cently thought I will probably die before getting what in academic cir-cles is called a "regular job," which is to say, a tenured position, or a ten-ure track one. Maybe on my deathbed, as they did with Ruth Benedict, they will make me a full professor. But I do not really believe that. I imagine myself forever stepping carefully onto college campuses, feel-ing illegitimate, staying only temporarily, teaching a course or two, not counting for much.

An internal sense of not counting and of being illegitimate haunts me and separates me from others who are more connected to academic life. Last spring, for example, I received a letter of invitation to contrib-ute to a volume of autobiographical essays by feminist sociologists. The letter stated the purpose of the volume:

> We're asking people who've been involved in the last two dec-ades of feminist sociology to write essays about their own biog-raphies as they bear on feminist presences, and absences, in contemporary sociology. . . . In particular, we're interested in how gender relations, emotion, and sexuality—elements of what is usually thought of as a "private sphere"—are related to institutional developments.[5]

This description seemed to fit me. However, after reading it, I looked quickly down to the bottom of the page at a list of the other partici-pants, a dozen sociologists, mostly women, who all, it seemed to me, had regular jobs. I then felt I was being asked to contribute not because of the nature of my work, but because they needed a token lesbian. "If you feel comfortable writing about the experiences of lesbian and gay sociologists in relation to the field and its ideas, that would add an important dimension," the editors said. If I had worth, it must be for this, I thought, because I was a member of a minority. Such are the effects of injured self-esteem.

I felt complimented to be asked, to be included with the women listed, to have something of mine published along with theirs. At the same time, I felt hurt and angry. To contribute, I would have to write an essay at my own expense and on my own time. No institutional structure supported me beyond my occasional teaching. But I was supposed to act just like those who had such support, with the same in-group academic manners. In the next few days, I often felt like crying. Or I felt angry, which is what I feel when I do not wish to cry. A week later, when calmer, I wrote back to the women who had invited me. "Yes," I said, "I'll be glad to do it."

To say yes, I had to have a plan. I decided I would write an essay that would be short, in plain language, and that would stand out from the other essays in the collection like a sore thumb. My essay would be like a thorn on a rose stem, pricking the other participants, and other potential readers of the volume, so they would feel my pain—the pain of having no job or protective status, of far too many rejections and too many experiences of being cast out from universities. I thought the other women would write about how they had succeeded in academic institutions, maybe not at first, and not without difficulties, but eventually. I thought they would justify the system because it had rewarded them, and because they had accepted many of its values in order to get ahead. To me, there was no justification for what had happened to me, no justification for a system that gave me so little. I had not been let in, and I wanted my essay not to fit in.

In the end, I did not do what I had planned. When I drafted my essay, I wrote about my experience as a lesbian in academia. I felt that was what was wanted of me. I also felt safer discussing being a lesbian than discussing inner resentments and pain I have felt because I do not have a full-time job. My essay described how being a lesbian had cost me jobs at universities, and how it continues to affect my day-to-day life in the classroom. Nonetheless, I wished the story of my lesbian experiences to stand for my more general story of being rejected by academic institutions for reasons that are far less clear to me, and for which I feel more at fault. I do not, for instance, feel at fault for being a lesbian, or studying lesbians, or not sleeping with male faculty (either literally or in the more general sense of falling in with them), all of which have had negative consequences for my employment status.

What I do feel at fault for is somehow, namelessly, not doing "what it takes" in more usual ways that are expected of everyone. I feel at fault for not moving anywhere, at any time, for a job. That is the big one for me—that I have not continued to rupture my personal relationships for job success. Sometimes, I feel at fault for not lecturing and not teaching in a more conventional manner, and for becoming the object of controversy as a teacher even when I try to avoid controversy. I feel at fault for not dressing right and not being more sociable and political and on the make. I feel at fault for still being around, for still trying to get them to give me a job, and for not having given up and disappeared. I think people want me to disappear. Each time I have not gotten a job at a university, people have told me to move or to change my occupation. I think they want me to leave so they will not be reminded that I am in need, or that they have something I do not have, or that something is wrong. I have found not disappearing to be the hardest thing I do.

When I wrote about being a lesbian in academia, I partly appeared. I wrote about a graspable component of my experience. I did not write about other choices I have made that are so essential to me that I cannot summarize them with a label. I cannot blame the outside world for costs I have incurred because of these choices, at least not in a way that convinces me. It is compelling and, I think, true to say that I have been denied privileges (and it is really more than privileges, it is life support) in academic institutions because I am a lesbian, and because I am a woman. To say so is also to be protected by an external identity from saying, "This occurs because I am me." Yet "because I am me" is at the heart of my difficulty. My lesbianism does not experience failure, I do. My being a woman affects inextricably all the decisions I make and the work that I do, but when I am rejected, the judgment of undesirability falls not on some other woman, but on me. A door to a library is closed, an office, a telephone, an address is denied, a group of people who might know me, to whom I might be of use, all are denied not to someone else, but to me. What's wrong with me? I wonder. It is hard to understand being so chosen without feeling that, in some way, I deserve it.

One weekend, not long after I wrote "Lesbian in Academe," the feminist sociologists got together as a group to discuss our essay drafts. During the discussion of my essay, the other women spoke of feeling aware of how heterosexual they were, and of feeling moved by my essay. I like readers to be moved by what I write. I also knew that my essay was not, to me, primarily about my being a lesbian, although specifically it was. Not wanting others to miss my point, I finally told the women in the group about how I had felt upon receiving the letter of invitation to participate. I told them how I had wanted to write an essay that would be like a thorn on a rose stem and that would make them all feel the great hurt I have felt, yet I had been afraid to do that. I feared making them feel guilty for having jobs I did not have, and for having protections that come with higher status in a university. I told them I had feared writing my "thorn on the rose stem" essay because I thought it would make them strike out at me so that I would stop causing them to feel guilt or pain. I feared they would view me as a failure because of my lack of a job, and that they would blame me, and turn away from me.

In a way, they did. No one came up to me, after the discussion of my essay, to offer me a job, or to plot with me about how to get one. Then again, these women did not exactly have jobs to give. I think I had hoped they would help me because it is easier to feel that my situation can be changed than to feel that nothing can be done about it. Similarly, it is easier to feel that my institutional troubles are my fault, that I have caused them (and thus can uncause them), than to acknowledge how much this situation is beyond me.

"What can we do to help?" the women at the conference did ask during the discussion of my essay, aware of my employment troubles because these were discussed in the essay. "It helps me that you appreciate my work," I told them, and I knew I was agreeing, again, to walk on water, to get along without eating. "You're not responsible for my pain" was what I knew I had to say. Yet, I did not really believe that. I have walked away, so many times, from people who have positions of the sort I would like, wondering how they can watch me leave when they know I have nowhere to go but home. How do they expect me to survive? I wonder.

I left the gathering of feminist sociologists quickly after each day's meetings and did not stay for meals or for informal socializing. When people asked others for rides at night to where they had to go, I walked off by myself for a mile to where I had left my car. I did not want to seem as if I needed anybody. I told myself that I am not good at informal socializing, that I would make a bad impression, and that I would get hurt by the casual words others would say over lunch or dinner—"Why don't you move?" "Why didn't you?" "What will you do for money?" In formal settings, like seminars, I can structure conversations to avoid casual hurts. I can speak back to people and clarify my position. Informally, I try to fit in more and wish not to challenge other people's assumptions. Yet their assumptions about teaching, professional life, and language contain judgments that implicitly find me wanting: I do not lecture, or know what I will be doing next year. I do not normally go to conferences, or speak about the field, or use the most current academic language, or lead a life defined by the overwhelming demands of students and colleagues. Informally, when others speak of their lives, I feel inadequate by comparison because my life is different. I feel I have failed to live up to an implicit standard. Thus I limit my exposure.

Nonetheless, when I left the conference, I felt I was leaving much warmth among the women present. I felt they had included and appreciated me, and I was sad to go. My sadness became pain later each evening and at the end, when the conference was over. I was sad that I could not stay in that warmth. It is something like knowing not to stay where one does not belong, or like knowing one's place. I think I have a protective arrogance about the worth of my work and about some of my views of reality, but I do not have an arrogance about much else. I am like the poor girl staying over at the rich girl's house thinking it is her own, and wishing it were her own, but knowing it is not, and often feeling confused, and always fearing she will be told to leave, and eventually she is told. I am not poor. I only feel excluded from a certain kind of wealth, or perhaps better put, from certain types of institutional support. I feel excluded from a system that I serve.

In my work, I seek to describe the world truthfully. I would have thought my work would merit more of a home in a university than it does. I do sometimes think of giving up and of going away. I have, more than once, considered changing my occupation. I have thought of being a psychotherapist, a real estate appraiser, an auto mechanic. When I walk by store windows and see "Help Wanted" signs, I usually think I should apply. I do not like the question of why I stay with it because I feel the important thing is that I choose to stay. I have taken comfort when told that my pattern of earning a living is more like that of an artist than that of an academic. Probably true, this statement makes me feel less bad about my earning pattern, less like a failure, or like a woman who cannot take care of herself, or who is unworthy of respect. Yet even if I am an artist, I still want a place in a university. I want a reliable way to earn my living that is in keeping with my sense of myself. I have found that difficult to achieve. I am a writer, I am told, although, because my father was a writer, I keep wishing I were not one. In my mind, writers are people who can't make a living at it, and who try to do impossible things, and think they are better than they are, and are often misguided. Yet writing is the main way I create and think, despite my own self-doubts.

To me, the hardest part of all the figuring out that I do, and I do such figuring often—"What's wrong with me? Why don't I? If I only . . . ? Why not just . . . ? If it doesn't matter anyway. . . . Who cares what the students think!"—is coming to terms with the fact that I have been unwilling to continue to move for a job. It is as if somewhere in the middle of the country, where the landscape is rural and desertlike, there is a silo and a university that will employ me, and I should go there, and with that employment, I will be happy.

I have been told to move so often that I frequently believe in that advice myself, even though my past experiences tell me differently. I did move a few times for academic jobs, and I did not become happy. I became sad. I moved to the Midwest after getting my degree, to the Southwest after that, and then back to California. When I returned to California, nothing around me seemed good anymore. A despondency and resignation set in within me that lasted for many years. Wishing to explain my sorrowful feelings to myself, I kept coming up with explanations that did not seem dramatic enough to account for the degree of my unhappiness. I finally concluded that my unhappiness was the result of cumulative losses I might not have felt had I not moved three times for jobs. Of course, these losses may have tapped into a basic sadness in myself, but I think I would have had a less harsh path had I not uprooted several times and left attachments behind.

Each time I moved, I lost a place that was important to me, and a feeling about myself in that place—especially a feeling that I belonged, or had a right to be there. I lost people I was close to. I still wish I had not left New Mexico and not left California that first time. I have lived, for some years now, in San Francisco, yet I continue to feel temporary and out of place. Still, I have ties here. My lover has a good job in the area. I see a psychotherapist here who is central to my well-being and central in my heart, and I do not want to leave her. When people tell me to move to that part of the country with the silo and the university that will employ me, they say there are psychotherapists everywhere. I can have a job and see a therapist, too, and maybe I will not need therapy anymore if I move. But I know, by now, the costs of losing my attachments. I know I am not a person who is the better for accumulating losses.

My reluctance to move is, in part, traditionally female. Women have traditionally valued their attachments, especially their personal and sentimental attachments, because these are often all women have had —ties to children, a husband, a house, an extended family, an ailing relative. Women have sought not to rupture their attachments, but to build their worlds around them. Women have moved when their husbands have, to support the husband, or because he earned the income, but most of all to keep a family intact. Women have been the home others have come back to. In keeping and being home, we have been part of a different system than men have been part of, one with different primary devotions. When women say, "I need to be home for the kids," "I can't leave town because Aunt Jo is sick," "I have to be here," "You go," "I'm off to Kentucky to take care of my sister's children," "Remember to come back and see your mama," these phrases suggest a different world of mobility and attachment than that implied in the injunction to move for a job. This different world is often disrupted by such a move. It is a world built around relationships based on need—being needed by someone else, or needing them—as opposed to relationships based on gain, or getting ahead.

I know that women do rupture their relationships and move for jobs as men do, perhaps increasingly, and women take their relationships with them, and, to some extent, women have always moved for adventure and for individual freedom and for wages, leaving much behind. Nonetheless, I have a sense of other values that seem to me part of the female legacy from times when women were less mobile and more totally part of female worlds. This legacy is not entirely left behind even if a woman moves for a job, or acts, in other ways, to make gains in a male world. This female legacy may be felt, especially, when the search for gains is frustrated, or when the rewards, or ways, of a male world are felt to be unsatisfying.

If, for example, I do women's work in academic life, as I do, and if I am rewarded like a woman, which means I am given little and left alone and left out, and expected to give a great deal back, then in some ways I will act even more like a woman than I did before and than I might were I to be treated more like a man. I will value my domestic rhythms more and the home that I make on my own that does nurture me. I have often assumed that I prefer to work at home, creating my own world with my work, because my father did so, because he wrote at home and valued that, but it is also because I was raised as a girl and because I take after my mother. Although my mother always needed to work outside the home for her sanity, she still kept a home as her main activity. She passed on to her children ideas of how to do it. Thus I learned how to set a table, and rearrange the furniture, and cook, and wash the kitchen floor, how to talk about other members of the family when they were not listening, and wipe dirty handprints off the woodwork, and I learned to make sure there was always enough extra food in the refrigerator for guests. These details matter less than the idea that such activities are a way to make a home, a place where the work one does creates the home that is then there for you.

When I am rejected by a university, I retreat to a harboring, home-making, mothering world of my own design, and I protect that world. It needs protection. When people suggest, as they sometimes do, for instance, in a version of giving me advice to move, that I commute to Los Angeles several days a week and stay over and fly back for weekends, I refuse. Why have a home if you are not there? I think. Who will walk the dog? What is the point of living with someone if I cannot be with her each evening? How will I work? I do not write when not at home. What about the joy of waking up and having coffee while looking at how the sunlight shines through my living room window?

For me, perhaps, bureaucratic places can never comfortably be my places. I have a hard enough time making even what is close to me feel like mine. Only with the repeated motions characteristic of a person who cannot take for granted that the world is safe do I make my intimate surroundings—the rooms of my house, for example, or my relationships with other people—feel protective and not alien to me. My ties to a physical place, or a piece of geography, are extensions of my sense of personal place.

I have always thought I did not need a university to provide me with a home. I have thought that my friends, usually women, who expected a university to be nice to them misunderstood the situation. But it is as much a female desire to want a public home as to want a private one. It is, I think, often female to feel wronged when the larger world does not act toward you, as you, as a woman, have learned to act toward others. They say that women have unrealistic expectations of formal work organizations, that women are naive to expect to be rewarded for merit, treated with loyalty, and retained, that we are wrong to want the same in return as we give, that this is not the way the male world is. If women do, indeed, have higher and better expectations of the male world than it can live up to, that world is not harmed. It is improved. But the pain of carrying around such expectations is often great, as is the vulnerability felt in admitting to being disappointed. It would be easier if I could say that I do not care about rejection from academic institutions. It is harder to say that I care, even though I have different values than the mainstream.

A final set of experiences I wish to speak of concern my place in the status system of a university. While not the military, a university is hierarchical in many ways. Its hierarchy has less to do with following and giving orders than with following a protocol of deference—people higher up are deferred to more often and given more respect. They are valued more than people lower down. A great deal of the activity at a university involves marking one's place, or showing where one is in the status system. Because I am near the bottom of the ranking for people who teach, I often experience status injuries. People treat me as less good than themselves or someone else. When I step onto a university campus, in addition to feeling that I am not legitimate because I have no regular position, I immediately become aware of my low place. Nowhere is this more apparent than when I enter the library.

In the library on the campus where I have most recently taught, the status hierarchy of the university is displayed on the cards used for checking out books. The statuses are listed according to the differences in privileges granted to each. At the top of the list are faculty, and faculty proxies, followed by staff, then students (doctoral, graduate, and undergraduate), and then other categories (associates, student spouses, alumni, visitors). I was surprised, at first, to learn that as a lecturer I did not have faculty library privileges, since lecturers are considered to be staff. On several occasions, library administrators have pointed this out to me, unasked, and I have felt hurt. When I have inquired, I have been told the main difference between the two privileges is that faculty never pay fines. Thus, the difference is not much. Why this gratuitous need to make me feel inferior? I have wondered. Yet the university as a hierarchy encourages people to feel better than others by acting superior to them, or by denying them resources.

In general, because the library is the one place on the university campus where I have been able to go even when unemployed, the library has come to stand for my connection with the university. As with the larger institution, I always fear the library will not let me in—something will be wrong with my card or with me and I will be denied entrance—and I fear that, once in, I will not be allowed to take out books. I plan to go to the library often, but I only sometimes get there. When on the campus, I avoid the library building. Simply looking in its direction makes me anxious. Further, my library card is often a gift to me. Because I obtain it with help from friends when I am unemployed, or employed for short periods, I tend to feel illegitimate when using the library. I am grateful to use it, but I do not feel I am there on my own merits. I feel similarly about my teaching appointments, that these are a gift, or a courtesy, to me, and that I teach by chance and because of oversights in the system, not because of my merits. Thus I teach illegitimately.

My relationship with other symbols of the university suggests similar themes. When I arrive on the campus, for instance, I often fear that a police officer will tell me to leave, a parking administrator will refuse to grant me a permit to park, my key will no longer fit the lock on the door of the building in which I use an office. When I walk on the campus between classes, I am extremely self-conscious. Do I look like a graduate student, a visitor, a lesbian? I rarely think I look like a faculty member. I think that everyone who looks at me sees right through me; they see not me but my lack of status and my deliberate attempts to hide that lack—to wear protective clothes and a facial expression of impassivity and to act as if I belong there. In my interactions with others, I fear that if I do not seem busy, speak formally, and smile often, people will look at me strangely. Who is she? What is she doing here? Must be someone temporary who does not count.

In the office of the program in which I teach, I have watched an administrator pause on the phone while speaking with someone before referring to me as "Dr. Krieger." Her use of "Dr." is a shaded way of saying, "she's not a professor here." Students usually say "Professor" when addressing me, but that more complimentary title is incorrect for me. At this university, as at many others, the title "professor" is reserved for people with tenure-track appointments. Administrators and faculty members often take pains not to call a lower status person by a higher status name. I feel the slight each time they do so with respect to me. I wish everyone to call me by my first name so I can avoid such reminders. More than a name, the title attached to me is a statement about my place, and about my place by comparison. In a context in which others who do what I do are called professor, and in which professor is the fancy status, the high status, the male status, the symbolic head of the family status, I am the hired female help.

Before my years of teaching as a lecturer, I had not much awareness of the meaning behind the phrase, "knowing one's place." Now I do. I also have respect for the sense of oneself involved, a sense often had by women and by people of lower socioeconomic status, or those who do the more menial background work of an organization, perhaps because they speak another language. I have come to know the feeling of an uncrossable boundary between myself and others with a higher status. I have learned that I am supposed to act like a professor but not be one.

I have also learned to absorb certain status slights, as when a graduate student calls me "Dr." in a withholding manner, or a library administrator reminds me that I have lesser privileges, or when a faculty member speaks to me as if I were not there, and as if, since I have not passed the tests—I have not climbed a tenure ladder—I cannot join the club and I deserve what I get. Lecturers are not the only ones to experience status slights. Assistant professors, too, are treated as inferior, unimportant, and temporary until they get tenure, as are associate professors until they reach full professor. Women are slighted at all ranks. People who deviate from a male self-aggrandizing institutional style are slighted, as are minorities of many kinds, and people with unusual beliefs, and staff. A university is a system of many slights. Any opportunity to assert superiority over someone else is used in the status hierarchy, where superiority is often shown by judging others' work to be not good, by injuring another's self-esteem in the process of enlarging one's own.

I am not as sensitive to judgments about my work as I am to statements about my place in the university structure. These statements are hurtful to me because they imply an inferiority, not only of position but also of person. I know I do not easily separate the two; perhaps women often do not make such a separation. Having a fairly penetrable boundary between self and other, self and institution, women are often likely to feel external slights as internal hurts and as signs of our own failure, and these hurts and signs can be many. When a student tells me she is taking my methods course for her soul, but not for use in her dissertation, I am hurt, for instance. If, for a moment, I think I have a chance to mold her work, such a student will remind me of how sub rosa I am. She will tell me why she must do as she has learned in her required methods course to please the regular faculty members on her dissertation committee, and why it does not count to please me. I can sit on no committees and she knows this. I cannot help her get ahead in the way these people can.

When I am rejected as a friend by an untenured assistant professor who is afraid of taint by association with me—because of my lack of status and because my work is not approved of by those who will judge her work—I am hurt. When I become an object of controversy because, as a lecturer, I am easy to attack and easy to abandon, I am hurt. So, too, when I am snubbed by others—faculty, lecturers, students— because, having little rank, I am not considered a valuable person by them. Having had such experiences often, I have come to feel that if I do not know my place in a university, someone else will surely put me in it.

Women, I think, learn to know their place, often without realizing it. A woman learns to act small, to cover up, and not to invade male spheres in order not to become the victim of harassment. A woman learns to present herself as less good than someone else. To feel I am inferior in a university goes against my grain, which is to believe myself intellectually superior. However, in the past decade, I have had to pass as an inferior—as someone who is less important than a professor, less to be listened to or sympathized with, who is of less use, and who will receive less respect. I have learned that I should not complain, that I cannot really expect better, that I ought to keep to myself and guard what I have.

These self-diminishing acts are essentially female traits, although not learned as such. They form an orientation that has been useful to me because it reduces friction between myself and others (I am not challenging them to treat me differently) and it enables me not to be bitter about what others have and I do not. I can tell myself I am different. I am so different I do not even qualify in the same way. I am off the map, off the ranking chart. I am apart from what others are part of. I do not have the same wants. But there is a cost to this way of thinking, for I become passive, resigned, depressed, hurt. I live with a great deal of isolation. I believe that I am, in fact, less good, that I deserve what I get, and that nothing will change. Things may change but not for me, or for people truly like me. I am sad to be so overlooked.

I had thought it was more common in my mother's generation that a woman would be ignored and left out, caught between being devalued, as women traditionally have been, and becoming respected, struggling for support for her sense of her own competence. I had thought that one day I would not be year-to-year about jobs, that I would not always be writing application letters, that my problems of status and employment would eventually disappear. I had not thought earlier that I would be affected much, if at all, by the fact that I am a woman, or by what little difference there is between what I do and what others do. I had thought the academic system had more tolerance for deviance than it does.

If someday I can live with less pain because of the situation I reflect on here, I will be glad. I do not want ever to accept the rightness of this situation, nor do I feel I can become indifferent to it. At best, perhaps, I can see more clearly how the faults of an institution become the faults of an individual, become my faults. This linkage is often invisible. I think I am not alone in experiencing status injuries, in having things not work out as I had planned, in experiencing conflicts because I am a woman, and in feeling pain because of rejections. People often experience such difficulties, but they do not want to speak of them for fear of showing vulnerability, or seeming to be a failure, or, especially among women, for fear of seeming ungrateful. Yet, one cannot help but fail when success requires acting in ways that are not one's own, and why be grateful for being penalized for being different? The problem seems to me not that I fail, or have been hurt. The greater problem would be not to care about my own value. I struggle to keep reasserting that value in the face of a world that tells me I have little worth.

My experience with institutional rejection has fed my doubts about my worth. Yet it has also fed an alternate view of myself in which I feel special and of interest. This view has been encouraged by the appreciative responses to my work that I have received from others. I think that people who value me wish the academic situation not to be as closed or inhuman as it often is, and they wish the different sensibilities of women to be given voice.

Often, I think, the voice of a woman will contain much pain. It will speak of hurts of the system, most especially the hurt of struggling with rejection and limitation and the stigma of inferiority. The voice of a woman will also often speak of seeking something better, perhaps less as an endpoint than as a process. People sometimes say that speaking about inner pain catches one, all the more, in that pain. I think that to speak of such pain is to be real rather than invisible. For me, it is to be more free rather than less.

Six

A FEW DAYS AGO, I cleared the remaining syllabi, books, and student papers from my study so that I would not be reminded of classes and teaching and, especially, of certain troubles I had this past quarter. My course on women and organizations went extremely well, but my course on feminist methodology in the social sciences had difficulties. When I had taught this course previously, it had felt very special to the students and to me. This time, however, it felt like a nightmare. The trouble began when I refused to allow a third-year male graduate student to take the course. He had said he was opposed to doing woman-centered research: "I object against it," he wrote in his first paper. "I want to do research that is centered on humans, not on women." It took me a week and a half to recognize that this student's opposition to woman-centered research represented more than ignorance. Rather, it was a sign of his intention to assert a position of male dominance in relation to my course and to me.

When I started teaching courses on women several years ago, before my first class I had an anxiety that many teachers of courses on women probably share. I thought about how I would respond if a man belligerently challenged me from the back of the room, attacking the feminist nature of my course, filling the air with a bravado display, and generally being disruptive—a hostile male. It was clear to me immediately that I would not stand for this. I would take the hostile student aside or speak to him after class, tell him to drop the course, get him to psychological services if necessary, call the police. The main thing was to show no tolerance for his behavior. The problem with my hostile male this past quarter, however, was that he was not a two-hundred pound man with a beer belly and a brimmed canvas hat, gesturing toward me with an opened can of foam as he spoke. This fellow was introverted, thin, and balding, with glasses. He mostly wanted me to feel sorry for him and to engage him in a densely articulated argument about his need to reject a focus on women. I refused him the instructor permission necessary to take my Feminist Methodology course, a limited-enrollment seminar.

Last year, a man in Women and Organizations acted in a way that was offputting at first, but my sense was that he was unaware of alternative ways to behave; with a few cues and instructions from me, he caught on. My sense with the balding introvert this quarter was that in ten weeks' time, he would still be arguing with me, and although I could refuse to engage his challenges, students in my class, who would be trading weekly papers with him and meeting with him in small group sessions, would not have that distance. I felt protective of my class—a highly interactive seminar required for undergraduate feminist studies majors that focused on the emotional experiences of each student in doing research and writing. It did not seem to me that the students for whom Feminist Methodology was an advanced course should have to respond to someone repeatedly questioning the legitimacy of their subject.

Whatever the reason—protection of the students, of the woman-centered and personal nature of my class, protection of myself—I said no. The male graduate student, angry with me, wrote a letter of complaint to me, and when I said no a second time, he wrote to the chair of the Women's Studies program and then to the student newspaper. For weeks, the paper never published his letter. During that time, the letter hung over my head and also caused anxiety for members of my class and for the program chair, who defended my decision. The newspaper finally published an article, but the story, by then, was not the male student's gripe at being refused permission to take my course, but internal conflict among feminist faculty members. "The Women's Studies program is embroiled in controversy," the paper's lead sentence read. This was a student paper searching for a story, and pitting women against women has often made for a good one, but the fact was this story was also true. Had my male graduate student stood on his own, he would have faded away far more easily and caused me less trouble than he did. But he turned, cleverly, to a woman dean in his graduate program who quickly decided that the issue was academic repressiveness (mine of him), not to mention the unwomanliness of my saying no to a man, and possibly the issue of why a faculty member, indeed a lowly lecturer, should have the right to deny access to anyone.

This dean—who considered herself a feminist—was joined by only a few other women faculty, but they were prominent. They spoke to the student paper and convened meetings to talk about "creative ways" of dialoguing with problem students (meaning problem men), "stimulating controversy" in the classroom, and other things I do not often worry about. These women were not criticizing me, they said. However, they thought I had acted hastily and that students such as my hostile male should be viewed as a challenge. What we need are more imaginative solutions, they proposed in the one discussion meeting I attended. I thought, "It's about saying no and getting support for it." The ability to say no and receive support was not the main concern of the meeting, however. It seemed a minor issue even among the majority of feminist faculty present, who assumed that in my classroom situation, saying no had been a clear-cut and acceptable good choice. But, they asked, what about other situations—larger classes, for instance—in which the teacher could not say no? That possibility was what worried most of the faculty.

I felt that the student who was causing a disturbance should either shape up or ship out. I thought feminist courses, especially, should have a paragraph written on their syllabi warning students they ought to be on good behavior. These are vulnerable courses. People play things out on them, and women teachers are especially vulnerable—expected to serve everyone and to smile when walked upon. Students should know about this situation and be careful and respectful in the extreme, rather than expect feminist faculty to bend over backwards to take care of obstreperous men and to absorb the insecurities of the system.

Fortunately for me, at the time I was teaching Feminist Methodology, I was also teaching Women and Organizations, a course that discussed separatism and the rationale for women saying no to men, or denying men access to women. In that course, we explore how separate organizations enable women to have their own power and culture, and how women need to protect their organizations from disruptive male influences and not put men at the center of their attention, even when we do include men in our groups. The subject matter of my Women and Organizations course encourages an intellectual understanding that seemed to me absent from Feminist Methodology.

My methods course was about the same size and gender composition as Women and Organizations—there were fourteen women and one man in Methodology and sixteen women and three men in Organizations. I taught both courses by emphasizing the inner experiences of each student as a route to learning. Yet my methods class seemed, very soon after my denial of the male student, not to be developing as it should have: trust between the students and myself was not growing over time as I would have expected, and there were many silences I could not explain. I felt these difficulties had to be my fault, that I was not conducting classes well enough. Yet there were external factors that are easier to identify in retrospect than they were at the time. For example, eight women students enrolled in my methods course came from the same graduate program as the man to whom I had refused permission and they all knew each other. Nothing like this course was offered in their department and they thought it would be good for them, even if my approach would not be viewed positively by their own faculty. When I decided to refuse the hostile male student, I was afraid that the other graduate students who knew him would see my action as unnecessary, since they had already put up with this man in other classes. I was also concerned that some of the graduate students might experience my denial of the male student as a potential refusal, or negative judgment, of them—if he was unacceptable, maybe they would be too. None of the students ever said they felt this way, but it sits in my mind as a possibility.

A second external factor affecting the course was that during the entire quarter, four of these graduate students met with the hostile man in a weekly seminar held the night before my class at the home of the conservative woman dean, who was his advocate. She was a person far more important in these students' institutional lives than I. During the quarter, however, I did not know about the existence of this other seminar, nor about its influence on a core group of students in my class. I only knew that, from about the sixth week of the term—the week the newspaper article came out, the week after the first faculty meeting occurred—from that week on, the students in my methods class noticeably began to pull away from me. The graduate students began to withdraw first and the undergraduates followed. The students generally became quieter and more challenging of me in class, more brooding, more unwilling to answer my questions about their experiences, more desirous of addressing only each other in class discussions, even if they did not say much because everyone was scared. I noticed an unwillingness to respond to me with eye contact. I was lucky to get one smile per session. I felt the students were trying to take the class away from me; to have it be their class, not mine; to have it feel like a conventional readings course, like, I later felt, the seminar some of them were having over at the home of the woman dean.

Because of tensions in my class, on several occasions I spoke with the students about my decision to say no to the male graduate student and about each of their responses to it. This relieved the situation somewhat, but, by the next week, the controversy would be restimulated outside the class. For example, two weeks after the daily student newspaper ran its article, the right-wing student paper printed a front-page story. The woman dean spoke to the right-wing paper, as did the male student; both were quoted prominently. A second faculty meeting took place the week after the right-wing paper came out, raising the issue once again and providing a further platform for the woman dean. These external events had the effect of making persistent the difficulties of my class.

My class was perhaps especially sensitive to unsettling external influences because my approach in the course emphasized openness in discussing each student's feelings. A relatively stable and protective environment is necessary to make such discussion feel safe. The course required a relaxation of intellectual posturing and academic self-protectiveness, and, because it drew on my own work, it required a sense of identification with, rather than disassociation from, the teacher. It was exactly such identification, however, that the students, especially the graduate students, seemed increasingly unwilling to allow. I sensed their distance during the quarter, yet it was only after the last class session ended that I realized how much my Feminist Methodology course had been undermined. During the last class, in the last fifteen minutes, I found myself again bringing up the subject of my refusal of the male graduate student. The final class session was not going well—it held, for me, too many silences and not enough appreciation for the course, the teacher, or the students' own efforts. I felt that although the students had gained important research insights during the quarter, the course had become a problem in their minds, and not a normal problem, but something made into one. In the last session, a few of the students spoke of talking with others outside the class about difficulties with the course and criticisms of me. Hearing them speak, I felt, uncomfortably, that I had become a difficulty along with the course, indeed the source of the students' troubles—something was wrong and it was me.

THE FACULTY MEETING

I walked into the room where the Women's Studies faculty meeting would be held. My trouble with the hostile student was on the agenda. The chair had circulated two background papers to the faculty attending: a copy of the student's open letter of complaint to the campus newspaper, still unpublished, and a copy of a memo written by the chair defending and explaining my decision to an administrative dean. The chair felt that the feminist faculty might be receiving increasing hostility from antifeminist students, and she wanted the faculty to discuss the issue more generally.

I felt I had to be present at the meeting. However, I wanted to be invisible. I took a seat far away from the center table on a chair set against a back wall, with no one sitting beside me. About twenty-three people soon filled the room, forming a group much larger than the eight to twelve who usually attended these luncheon meetings. The first discussion item was gender bias against women faculty in student course evaluations. Some women spoke of changing their teaching behaviors in order to score well on the evaluation forms. I felt silent and uncomfortable. For me, the discussion was too much about success and advancing in the system. What if being a good teacher meant one would not score well on the forms? Two-thirds of the way through the discussion, a woman who announced she had to leave soon to get to a meeting somewhere else impatiently launched into the second item on the agenda, referring to it as "the case of student X." When the chair had introduced this item at the start of the meeting, she had called it "the case." I had been startled. The term sounded too big and legalistic to me and too much like the student had a case.

"What does 'woman-centered' mean?" the woman who had to be somewhere else began. She claimed to have no idea what this term meant and said that the chair's letter of explanation to the dean gave her no understanding of why the male student was denied permission to take my course. Surely, denying permission to this man because he was unprepared for an advanced course in feminist methodology could not be the real reason for refusing him. Again, what did woman-centered mean? she asked.

The chair, who sat at the head of the long center table, grasped the woman's question from out of midair and turned toward me. Could I please explain? she asked. It seemed to me her memo had already explained the grounds for my decision better than I could. I thought that the woman who had to be somewhere else was saying, with her questions, that she did not agree with me. She was challenging the acceptability of what I had done by claiming it was not intelligible. I had no desire to be on trial in this meeting, and suddenly I felt on trial, and I felt guilty.

"No," I said to the woman, I would not explain "woman-centered." The logic of my decision was presented very well in the chair's statement, I told her. Then I spoke to the group and told them it was painful for me to be at the meeting, to have my decision challenged, to have it become "the case of X." It had already been painful simply saying no to the male student. He was the one who had given me trouble, but I now felt I was the source of the trouble.

Here are some details I did not discuss at that meeting that nonetheless throw light on the issue: I did not deny permission to the male student after the first class session because I hoped he would drop the course. I hoped he would decide that since it was so difficult for him to grasp or accept woman-centered research, he ought not to be in my class. When he did not drop the course, and especially after I had read his first paper arguing against a focus on women, I felt I should make the decision to drop him and not expect him to make it for me. I should take very seriously his statement, "As a man, I see no way to do woman-centered research." He was not telling me he was open to learning, as I might have wished. He wanted me to hear he was closed to it.

I said no to him on the phone the day after the second class session, feeling a strain in my voice that made it hard for me to speak. Passive-aggressive in style, this man answered me with silence, then told me how surprised he was. He was speechless with hurt. I felt he was experiencing the pain of being rejected by a woman, by me. I wanted not to be rejecting. I tried to make it easier on him. I told him the reason for my denying him permission was that he was not prepared; he did not have the prior understanding necessary for this advanced-level feminist course. He had said he wanted a humanist, gender-free course, but this was a feminist course, heavily gendered in its approach. He wanted chemistry and this was physics. None of this made sense to him. Then I used the word "exploitation" and suddenly it made sense—that he would be exploiting the course for his own purposes and this might not be good for others in the class. As we ended our phone conversation, he said he felt I was trying to get him to agree with my decision, which I was, but I said no, I just wanted him to see the logic of it. "You don't have to agree. I'm denying you permission, even though you want to take the course," I finally told him.

He called me back two days later, at night. I got out of bed to answer the phone. As he spoke, I felt the disturbed, needful depths of his emotions. I felt, What if I was needful and had called, as I had sometimes called my therapist at night. I should not toss this fellow out simply because he was troubled and hard put for words and called me late at night for a conversation full of distressed silences. He finally said he had left me a letter asking me to reconsider my decision; would I answer it? At school the next day, I found his letter—an account of how all the faculty in his department had deserted him and would not work with him, except maybe the woman dean, but she did not have enough time. His one hope now was me and my Feminist Methodology course. I again refused him permission to take the course and suggested that he use the course reader on his own to develop further the kind of humanistic method he was seeking.

This student next wrote to my program chair and to the student newspaper, and called for a meeting with the chair to discuss my rejection of him. The chair and the woman dean from his department subsequently met with him and offered him a readings course with the two of them jointly, in an attempt to meet his needs. He could read on his own, he told them. He did not want the authority of faculty over him. What then had he wanted of me? I thought. He had told me he needed my help. Denying him that help had been painful for me. It felt like I was denying him myself. I had fallen for his line that he needed me, and that I was unfairly rejecting him, even after I had thought it through and decided that the help he wanted was either help I could not give, or that he could not take, or it was really another way of his saying that he wanted a convenient woman to respond to him. Perhaps I seemed not well defended to him and so was chosen for this role. I know I could not have been institutionally of much importance for him. I was emotionally important to him at the moment (I felt his "I need you, you have to help me" had some truth), but I was not important in any other sense I can think of. I had to say no, of course—I could not put myself in a position of being wrongfully used by him, or put my students, or women he might research, in that position—but it never seemed like "of course" to me. It always seemed like, "Oh my God. I am going to say no to him and I feel so poorly justified. I feel only that if I have so much doubt about this student's potential effect on my class, I have to pay attention to it now, or it will be too late."

I made my decision before I called him and I felt I was not going to change it. Mine was a decision based on scant evidence and on a feeling about the future; it was a judgment.

THE FACULTY MEETING CONTINUES

In the faculty meeting, they seemed to be looking for black and white, right or wrong, for a defense of what I had done. I felt terribly indefensible at that moment. The majority who spoke up in the meeting said I was right, that I had a clear case; they could certainly read between the lines in the two documents. By then, however, I had forgotten about the documents. I was focused on the experience of being cross-examined by a group of women and of not getting the immediate, unquestioning support that I did not know, before then, I needed from these other feminist faculty. I teach courses on women in a women's studies program, and most of the people important to me in the university are feminist women—faculty and students. In saying no to a man, I wanted to feel these women were behind me, that I had a mighty force behind me that understood the necessity of my action.

Therefore, I felt disproportionately upset by the woman who challenged me with her questions at the start of the discussion, by the few others who joined her, by the woman dean whose views seemed behind some of their criticisms (although she herself was absent from the meeting), and even by the program chair at certain times outside the meeting. A song written by the feminist singer Judy Small came to mind. It retells the case of an Australian woman who was tried and wrongfully convicted of killing her own child. The refrain goes, "It's everybody's nightmare to stand alone accused, to be thrown into a prison for a crime you didn't do."[1] That song rang inside my head for weeks. I would not have understood before the feelings attached to those words. Yet I now felt inside a prison, which was my pain, and I also felt that none of it should matter, that I should not let this incident affect me so. The male student had wanted to use me, I felt, and some of these women now wanted to use me—to take their ideological stands in relation to me, to show they got along with men, to pretend this was only about politics and not about me.

I think I spoke for fifteen minutes at the meeting, but I cannot remember much of it except that I often looked at the floor beneath the table or at various largely faceless people dressed in black and far away. I tried to connect my sentences by means of my emotions, sure that I would not have any sense of logic if I sought, instead, for well-formed thoughts. At the end of the meeting, after more discussion of the case and its implications, the subject was tabled until another meeting.

As the group was disbanding, I got up from my chair and was looking around the room at the people, mostly women, talking to one another. One of them was a woman with whom I had consulted when I made my decision to refuse the male student. She had concurred that she felt it was right for me to tell this student no. "It will only get worse," she had said, meaning he would only get more troublesome. I felt she knew this because in her own introductory course, she had suffered with hostile men, some of whom were clean-cut and would act nicely on the surface. "Have you thought about what if he does something?" she had asked me. "It crossed my mind," I said, "but I don't think he will, and I'd do it anyway. I can't not do it based on fear." I would still do it anyway, even after what happened.

Now the friend whom I had consulted came across the room and gave me a big hug. She was dressed in a long-skirted dark dress, and I was in pants, feeling oh so butch-dyke-out-of-place, as I had ever since the start of the meeting. I was stiff as a board as I accepted her hug, and I did not hug her back, but her gesture felt good and it surprised me. Then a woman I did not know, from some other part of the campus, came over and said something to me. I looked at her oddly, surprised again. I shook my head no, I did not think it took strength or courage. Why should she be getting that idea? I thought maybe she felt I looked unsteady emotionally and so anything I did took strength, or maybe I myself thought so, or perhaps she came over because I looked like I needed someone to be kind to me. No one else said anything to me. People got their lunch dishes and trash together and started to move out of the room. My Women and Organizations class was waiting in the hallway, ready to come in to use the same conference room for our class, scheduled next.

I helped clear off the food trays from the side table to get the faculty out so my class could come in. We began the class late, and our discussion seemed slow and hesitant to me. I thought I might as well tell the students about my saying no to the male student, about the meeting that had just gone on in the same room, and about the open letter to the student newspaper that might appear any day. The students listened and I do not remember how the class ended. I do remember I was surprised when one student told me later that I had seemed shaken, so it had helped the class to be told why. I had thought I was hiding my feelings. This same student then volunteered to write a letter to the student newspaper so they would have it ready to print as soon as the hostile man's letter came out. "Why wait?" she asked. "Thank you," I told her. "I'm trying not to feed the publicity." Yet her offer was good for me to hear. No one offered in my Feminist Methodology class, or anywhere else. Maybe people assumed I did not need them, or maybe they did not want to get involved or felt they did not know me. I assumed I was untouchable.

CONVERSATIONS WITH THE CHAIR

The phone rang later the same week I had said no to the male student. The chair of the Women's Studies program wanted to know what procedures I had followed to deny this student permission. I knew the chair of the program as a no-nonsense sort of woman and I liked her. She had recently tried to make my teaching appointment more permanent. Now, on the phone, she was concerned that there not be further trouble for the program as a result of my refusing the male student. She felt a controversy about my decision could easily sap the energy of the program. I had not been aware of following procedures, however. When the chair asked me about them, I felt as if she were asking if I had acted above reproach, and I was not sure I had. I groped around for words. The most direct way to explain it took two: "hostile male."

"You didn't tell him that, did you?" she asked.

"No," I said, remembering my phone conversation with the student and how I had sought for inoffensive words, all the while feeling what I wanted to say was, "It's because you are a hostile male." At the time, I blocked those two words from my mind, fearful that calling him a hostile male would get a hostile response from him. I also felt that giving a personality trait as a reason for rejection from a course would sound like inadequate grounds, even if "hostile maleness" was not really a personality trait, but rather a form of behavior. I had given the student the reasons that he was not advanced enough for the course, and that he wanted a different kind of course (a humanist, as opposed to a feminist, course). Yet this reasoning had not washed with him, nor later with the woman who challenged my logic in the feminist faculty meeting. I now thought it would have been better if I had said "hostile male," named the thing for what it was, because then others would have known what I meant. Still, the chair was saying it was good I had not used those words. This conclusion did not feel right to me, but I think she had a gut-level sense of what you do, and do not do, to protect yourself in a university. I had perhaps only a gut-level sense of what you do to stay true to yourself. This often left me without protection.

I was trying to find a way to tell the chair about what had happened with the male student without going into the details. My process had not been a procedure, and I was sure the details of it would make it seem that I had done something wrong. I also did not want to take up too much of the chair's time. In the end, however, there seemed no way to tell her other than to give her the details: he said, he did, I said, I did. "Yes, there is another man in the class. He is still in the class." "Good," she said, betraying, perhaps, her heterosexuality. For the chair, the issue was that this student was a man. She needed reassurance that other men were in the class to feel I was not rejecting men, that I was not thus making us both unsafe. For me, the issue was the student's hostility, his male hostility, to be sure, but it was not his being a man that caused me to reject him. My safety lay in my being able to say no to hostility directed against me, and my class, whatever the source of that hostility.

I had wanted to give the chair a well-grounded sense of what had happened in my conversations with the male student in the hope she could figure out what to do—that she would put the best face on it, see me in the right, understand. She took in what I told her. Yet after her call, I felt undone. Why did she have to question me? Why couldn't she have assumed I had acted acceptably? Perhaps she did assume that, but I am sensitive about whether others think I have acted conventionally enough in a university, or protected myself well enough. I worry about this because I myself fear that I will misstep, that I will do something wrong and be cast out, or cause trouble for others that they do not want.

A few days later, the chair called me again to ask if I would do an individual readings course with the male student. She was going to meet with him and wanted to offer him an alternative so that it would not look like the Women's Studies program had turned away an interested student. I felt he should be sent back to his home department since they were the ones who had failed him, but more than that, I felt hurt, surprised, and misunderstood by my chair. This man was intolerable to me or I would have accepted him into my course. How could she expect I would do an independent readings course with him? I found myself saying loudly and clearly, "No, I won't do that." I felt the male student had wished to force himself on me, and now my chair was trying to help him. I thought perhaps this was happening because I was a lecturer. Lecturers are expected to do almost anything in order to keep their jobs. Or perhaps the chair felt I had created the problem of this man's discontent, so I should take care of it.

"I won't," I told her. She then spoke of offering him a readings course herself. I thought maybe she felt obliged to help him because she was a heterosexual woman and thus had a harder time extricating herself from men. I thought lots of things. I was aware that I did not know the chair well personally. I knew her only formally as a result of an institutional relationship in which she had more middle-of-the-road responses than I did. We left it that she would meet with the male student, reaffirm my no, and offer him something else if she saw fit.

Two days later, I received a copy of the chair's memo to the program's administrative dean. She had defended me well, and I felt extremely grateful. Her letter presented a detailed argument for my denial of permission to the male student that made my decision seem more legitimate than I had ever thought it was: "Feminist Methodology in the Social Sciences is one of two courses in a three-course sequence required for majors," her letter began. "It functions as a senior seminar, a capstone experience for Women's Studies majors. In the first class session, X stated that he objected to undertaking a woman-centered research project." With such a letter, I felt, my troubles were over.

The faculty meeting occurred the next week. By this time, the chair stood publicly behind my saying no to the male student. Thus when I was criticized for denying him permission, she was criticized too. The woman who challenged my decision at the start of the meeting challenged us both, as did the male student in his letter to the press, and the woman dean when she spoke to the paper. When someone had to present a defense of my decision to the student paper, the chair did it. My decision was, by now, the position of the program.

The week after the faculty meeting, the chair phoned me again. Another student in my Feminist Methodology class, an undergraduate woman, had come to her with a complaint and was seeking to drop the course, she said. The chair wanted to advise me to work things out with this student, both for my own good and because it should not look like the Women's Studies program was discouraging students from taking its courses. She said she was going to meet with the student again and would encourage her to stay in the course. I could see the logic of being cautious when at the center of a controversy, but I felt this student needed permission to drop my course. She had trouble with the personal nature of the research approach and was unusually uncomfortable doing the assignments. I told the chair I would encourage her to stay in the course, but in the next class session when I spoke with the student and saw the pain in her face as she looked at me, I broke my word. I was not going to tell her to stay in my course when it was too painful for her. She dropped the course the next week, which was fine with me. The problem for me, by then, was not the student but the chair.

By now, I felt I was being told how to conduct my class. The chair's effort to tell me what to do with the undergraduate who sought to drop my course was but one instance of this. The second and more consequential instance occurred when the chair mentioned, in the same phone conversation, that yet another student, also an undergraduate, had spoken with her. I never learned the name of that other student, nor the specific nature of her complaint. The chair suggested the complaint was generally about class dynamics, and that the student felt she was not learning in the course. According to this student, others in the class felt as she did. The chair felt I ought to open up discussion in my next class session, ask the students what was wrong, and correct it.

I was shocked that the chair had so quickly decided something was wrong with my class. I told her, "Nothing is wrong with my class. It's a wonderful course." She said I was being defensive, and probably I was. I was responding as if accused of a crime, and responding to a feeling— that either she conveyed, or that I assumed had to be present—that if there was not something wrong with me (something out of tune, or out of step), I would not have said no to the male student, or not said it in a way that would bring on an openly hostile response from him. I must have been doing something wrong or the two additional students would not have complained about me, nor suggested that others also had complaints. To argue differently was to be defensive. I told the chair I would do as she requested and see what I could find out from my class about what was wrong.

In the next class session, I opened up the kind of discussion I hated— a critique of class dynamics. I hate such discussion because the students in my classes always find things wrong that I can do nothing about. Their discomforts have deeper sources, I always feel, but they come out as if they are dissatisfactions with the interpersonal dynamics of the class. When I opened up the discussion, the main thing the students said was they wanted to talk more with each other in class sessions, rather than looking at and addressing me. I never had a rule that they could not talk to each other, and it seemed to me not unusual, or terrible, to have the students say they wanted more connection with one another—it meant they valued learning from each other. Further, it seemed not odd to me that their other complaint was about grades— they would rather not have them in a course like this. What was unusual was something harder to pinpoint that I felt at that time and even at the quarter's end.

I never held my difficulty against the chair. I felt she was attacked for defending me, and that occasionally she turned the attack back on me, viewing me as the source of her trouble. I continue to feel so grateful for her defense of me that I tend to excuse as understandable those of her actions that undermined my self-confidence with my class and thus contributed to my feeling I was inadequate as a teacher. My refusal of permission to the male student had been an individual decision. Acceptance of it by others was supposed to hinge on an acceptance of my right as a professor, teacher, or woman to make a decision about who could take my course—who could use me and how. Acceptance of my decision was not supposed to hinge on anyone else's judgment of the adequacy of my reasons for it. Yet things are not really so separable, and my reasons were called into question, in part because I did not, in fact, fully have the right to say no, in part because I was vulnerable in the university. When my decision was challenged, I was scrutinized and my class was also put under the microscope—was something wrong there, too, larger than this one man?

CLASS DYNAMICS

A few nights ago, I had a nightmare in which I was sitting at a long seminar table in a room much like the one where I taught Feminist Methodology last spring. The students—about half a dozen seemed to be there—would not obey me. They kept moving around uncomfortably in their chairs, indicating with their body language they wished to be elsewhere. They were physically writhing away from me. I wanted their attention to focus on our topic of discussion, but that was impossible. Disrespect for me emanated from all their body motions, and I woke up in a sweat. That was how I felt in many of the classes during the second half of the quarter.

The day we discussed class dynamics, I took medication before the class session, as I had before my earlier class that day, not thinking much about it except that I wanted to avoid a migraine headache and I wanted not to be at a loss for words. I told the students that in light of recent events, I wanted to check on how they were feeling about our class. Yet as the discussion proceeded, I felt emotionally absent. I felt I was saying proper-sounding words and keeping up a good humor in response to the students' comments, but my medication had smoothed things out so I did not feel any pain, even when the discussion became difficult for me. I remember asking several students, at the break, whether they were learning enough, seeking to locate the undergraduate who had complained to the chair, but failing to find her. At the end of class, after the students had traded papers with each other and planned their subgroup meetings for the next week, they fled. I was suddenly in a startlingly empty classroom. I wished someone had stayed around to talk with me. I felt that none of the students wanted to be seen speaking with me. The one student who did want to talk came back into the building later, after the others had gone.

That was the sixth week of the term. The newspaper article had not yet appeared (it would come out the next day), but the students in my class knew about it. The male graduate student had consulted with some of them when he wrote his letter, and I had mentioned his letter in class to prepare them. The session during which we discussed our class dynamics merges in my mind with later sessions, all of them emotionally painful for me to recall. In those class meetings, I had difficulty speaking with the students. I felt, increasingly, that they did not want to hear from me and that what I would say to them would be wrong. In recalling the start of my discomfort that week, I can see the students who were sitting across the table from me. There was tension in their voices and I lost a sense of connection with them when they spoke. Something was amiss but I did not know what it was.

At the beginning of the discussion, one woman who sat across from me spoke in a friendly and reasonable-sounding way. She was one of the graduate students in the woman dean's seminar, although at the time I did not know that. She spoke as if trying to lead the discussion, or trying to be a peacemaker (yet where there is no war, one does not need to make peace; that was the level of subtlety involved). This woman proposed that the students talk to each other more, rather than addressing their comments to me. I could enter the discussion here and there, she said, so that I would not feel invisible, but the students should be responding to each other. I remember feeling grateful to her. Her statement was one of the few in the whole discussion that acknowledged that I had feelings.

After a while, one undergraduate said she felt frustrated. How could she, a middle-class white woman with no experience other than her own, do research about anyone else? I thought her problem might stem from her having anthropology as a major, because in that field, research was being criticized as an imposition of the powerful on the less powerful. It did not occur to me that her frustration might be related to my having said no to the male graduate student weeks earlier. Not much of what was said in the discussion of class dynamics that day seemed re-lated to my refusal of him. It seemed primarily about my interactions with my class. During that session, I remember feeling I had to be silent. Looking in the direction of the clock on the opposite wall, I thought, "All they are saying is they want to talk to each other. Why am I feeling there is something wrong with me, that they are telling me I cannot be trusted to teach them?"

I was hurt more by the students in my class who challenged my as-signments, wanted to ignore my presence, and increasingly protected themselves against me, than I was by any of the others—the faculty, the male graduate student, the press. I think this was because teaching, for me, is about being valued by students. It is about having whatever is me rub off on them. It is about being acceptable. Now, suddenly, the stu-dents were saying, "We don't want to have much to do with you. We will say we value the assignments you give us, and that we value each other, but we won't say we value you." I have never felt so tainted.

By the end of the quarter, my class seemed to be a headless monster—a group without a teacher, or with a teacher but no one much liked the idea of her. The students met in subgroups outside the class every two weeks. By the ninth week, some of them proposed they would rather have met mostly among themselves during the quarter and limited their time in the larger class with me. In the first half of the quarter, students had come to my office hours excited about what they might do in the course; in the second half, they stopped coming. Those who came—and only when I asked them to—seemed not to want to talk with me much. The graduate students responded warily when I asked them how they felt about course issues, or about how the course fit in their lives. In class, similarly, my questions aimed at helping the students speak about their emotional responses to the readings and research got guarded and limited answers from most. My questions about how the students felt about my own work also received limited answers. The stu-dents were reading a book manuscript I had just finished and I had told them I needed positive responses, but it seemed increasingly hard for them to give me any. At the start of the quarter, I had thought there were several lesbians in the class. One of them, who had proposed to do research on the subject of lesbianism, dropped it. Another never revealed her gay identity to me, even in private.

I think, over time, I became a symbol of something the students in my class wished to avoid, a woman they wished not to be like. When they turned in their final papers, several of the graduate students included a parting shot aimed at me: "I can't say I enjoyed the class sessions," one wrote. "I have never been in a class where the teacher talked so much about her feelings." Another said, "Although this has been a course about feminist methodology in research, I would not call our class feminist. There was no equality. The teacher had all the power." Such critical comments helped me to identify those graduate students who had taken the seminar with the woman dean. The judgmental tone used in their statements seemed to come from somewhere other than my course. I hated to read the negative comments in the students' final papers. However, I could not fail to notice that, for the first time, some of the students were speaking directly about what had gone wrong and telling me I was it. They were doing this in writing and at a time when they could expect not to see me again, but they were attempting an analysis and they were articulating a discomfort I also felt, although my explanation for why the discomfort occurred differed from theirs.

VULNERABILITY

I decided, in the end, that the key word that helped me understand the situation was "vulnerability." I tried to explain this to some of the students in comments on their final papers, hoping they would eventually understand. I still wanted to reach them, even when the class was over. I wanted them to see that they had been unfair to me and, more importantly, to understand why. I wanted to offer an explanation other than one that found me faulty as a teacher, or that saw our class dynamics as flawed because of my personality, lack of self-confidence, focus on feelings, or whatever traits the criticisms pointed to. My own explanation was more contextual.

First, I think I was vulnerable because I was a lesbian. When a lesbian says no to a man, even if in a public situation (she does not want him in her class), the question is raised in people's minds: is she doing this because she hates men and does not want them in her bed, or is there a good reason for it? Thus her motives are suspect more than is usual. A lesbian is also vulnerable because when she says no publicly to a single man, she dramatizes her lack of solidarity with all men, a facet of her experience normally hidden in her private life. Saying no to men, or showing disregard for the importance of her ties with men, the lesbian seems alone and unprotected. It is expected that men will take offense at her and that she will not get the support she needs—the support necessary to advance in a university, for instance. A lesbian is vulnerable, in addition, because when people say or think "lesbian," they think "sex" and they think "woman," and suddenly they have, in their minds, undressed the individual and become intimate with her. Being a lesbian thus calls attention to one's female vulnerability. Acting butch, or acting like a man—as some lesbians do and as I, in part, do—is a way a woman can cover her vulnerability, thus making it harder for the outside world to invade, or to take advantage of her.

I think I was also vulnerable because women are expected to be open to others and especially to men, who are assumed to need them. What is expected of a woman extends to the teaching of a feminist course, or a course focusing on women. These courses are viewed as soft, available, womanlike, as ideal environments in which all needs are met, that are taught by caring, goddesslike women. To close the door of such a course in the face of a man is to do an entirely different thing than to close the door of an advanced physics course to someone whose closest prerequisite is geography. To give as one's reason, as I did, that the man is unprepared, or even hostile, does not make much sense when the important fact is that the man is being denied access to a woman, and that this denial of access is considered unacceptable. After the man is refused, the course gets scrutinized more than another course might because with feminist courses, as with women, it is assumed that everyone has a right to see them, to expose them, to make them as fully available as possible.

Finally, in addition to being a lesbian and a woman teaching a course on women, I was vulnerable because I was a lecturer. It seems to me that

I was less respected, and more interfered with, than other women with higher status who were involved with this incident—the woman dean, the chair, other senior women faculty. No one can prove this one way or another, but there is a distinct possibility that none of the public questioning and challenging I received after saying no to the male student would have occurred were I a full professor. People with status, or those who have no experience with status injuries, might not think this true, however. To them, I was probably more vulnerable because I was a woman than because of my lack of institutional status, and indeed the two are related, compounding each other.

Add to these some other facts: that I was vulnerable because I was teaching a course emphasizing the personal aspects of research, often considered soft and female; because I drew primarily on my own experience to teach it (rather than on external expertise); because I do relatively unconventional work for a sociologist; and because I apparently do not look like a very well-protected person. Much as I try to look like a man for protection, I do not really succeed. To others, I often look as if I do not have a hard shell, or enough of a shell, a condition I think I live with more safely than others suppose. However, the students in my class were not likely to know this, or it was not what mattered. When they looked at me, they saw vulnerability and they saw that I was attacked—by the male student, the woman dean, other women faculty, other students in my class—and they did not want to be like me. They did not want to be as easily hurt, or to be as unprotected in the academic world or within themselves.

One can, of course, side with a vulnerable woman who is attacked— but if one is insecure oneself, and inexperienced, and if one feels very unprotected, the response can instead be aggression and withdrawal. Fear of their own vulnerability affected the students in my class very centrally, I think, because the system we were in did not value the unprotected. It was a milieu of many strategies for allying with those perceived to be powerful and for camouflaging one's own insecurities. When I spoke to the students in my class about my own vulnerability, and about the degree to which the negative responses to my saying no undermined me and caused me pain, it did not relieve the situation or help the students to feel close to me, as I would have hoped. Why side with this woman who speaks about her pain? Who wants such pain? they must have felt. Mine was an easy class to take a swipe at, with big effect. It was an easy class in which to capitalize on the students' potential for identifying with an aggressor. Nonetheless, some of the students felt the aggressor was me—I gave grades, I had brought all this on. Yet if I had all the power some of them thought I did, I would have given us a better experience.

During the quarter, several of the undergraduates in the class said they were glad I had said no to the male graduate student. They would not have wanted to engage him. The one graduate student who wholeheartedly supported me wrote in her final paper: "The newspaper is interested in X's story, not mine." One of the undergraduates wrote: "I am sorry that negative consequences resulted for Susan over denying permission to X because, perhaps for the first time, I felt my needs as a woman were being looked out for." The campus women's newspaper, published the last day of the quarter, carried an editorial in support of my decision, saying it was important for women students to have classes where the legitimacy of studying women was not questioned. One of the undergraduates in my class was a member of the paper's collective. The statements by these students in support of my decision were rare and they touched me.

Despite our difficulties, throughout the term the students in my class wrote emotionally moving, candid weekly papers about their research and writing. They spoke in the first person, expressed their feelings, and discussed troubles they had in acknowledging themselves in their work. I would read their papers and think, Everything is all right. Then I would go into the classroom the next week and the feelings expressed in the papers would seem bottled up, as if it was easier for many of the students to speak privately in writing than publicly in class discussion. I think the students must have learned something valuable to them in our course, and probably they were less upset by its failures than I was. But the failures and hurts were real, although often hidden.

When I think back on what I could have done differently, I think it might have helped if, early on and continually, I had talked at length with my class about our problem—my saying no to the male student and the responses, especially the responses within each of us. If we, as a class, could have talked about it—and it would have taken talking again and again at the expense of discussing the course assignments—maybe that would have helped. However, it seemed wrong to me at the time to let the trouble of the situation focus our attention; it seemed too vague and too big a trouble, and I was not feeling on good enough terms with my class to lead such a discussion. I did receive important support from the few people close to me during the quarter, and I am not sure what a lot more support would do. It has occurred to me, however, that a woman in a position like the one I was in needs a great deal of encouragement for her right to act on her own, and for her individual value, far more so than it would seem. It might also help for people, in general, to know how sensitive is the central unit of a class, how easily affected the teacher and students can be when the teacher is attacked.

I am left speaking of my experience afterward, seeking to share it in the hope that someone else will be able to deal with an event such as my saying no to this male student better than I did, or to experience it with less guilt, or less pain.[2] My class and I did not act together to form a deliberate response to our experience. We were together only in being undermined by it. We were divided, pitted one against another, and estranged often from one another.

At the start of the quarter, after the students had done their first week's readings and papers, they took turns going around the table, speaking of what they felt they had found in our course. This was to be an ideal class for them, the perfect class, useful for their futures and for each person in an intimate way. Perhaps it was useful in the end as a dramatization of some usually hidden pressures in a university, especially the pressures on women to ally with men. For me, it was a hard lesson about my own vulnerability as a teacher. My saying no to one man had many unsettling effects. It stimulated fears in other women and in myself, and caused others to question my judgment. I then confronted a situation in which respect for women's independence was not the norm, where women were easily turned against one another, and where the fragility of female relationships was easily undermined. To say no to a man is often a necessary act, and, as often, extremely difficult. Saying yes to women stands on the other side of that refusal. It seems to me important to say no to men, when needed, in order to protect the space of female intimacy. Only then can what is in the female space begin to be explored.

Seven

LESBIAN IN ACADEME

NOT LONG AGO, A GRADUATE student called to interview me for a master's thesis on experiences of lesbian and gay sociologists. She was interested in the effects of being gay on their academic lives. Was prejudice an issue? What happened in their universities and over the course of a career? I agreed to do the interview, but I told no one about it, for I felt I ought not to speak with her. Although I do have relevant experiences as a lesbian, I have always felt these experiences are not supposed to matter. Being a lesbian is, internally, a source of strength to me, but I feel it is a private choice I have made with full knowledge that this choice must often be hidden. Although I know discrimination exists in academic settings, and that I have experienced it, it feels to me as if it violates a code to turn around and point this out. It violates the code of accepting the conditions of my chosen status, and I fear something awful will happen to me as a result—the homophobia, or discrimination, that affects me will get worse.

Such a fear of making things worse by calling attention to them probably accompanies any stigmatized minority status or sense of personal vulnerability. With homosexuality and, in particular, lesbianism, the secrecy aspect of the status stands out more than in some other cases, for it is assumed that homosexuality can be hidden, that an individual can pass (as straight), and often should, thus disappearing as gay. One consequence of passing is that in becoming invisible to the outside world, one often becomes invisible to oneself. Lesbianism adds to the invisibility, since lesbians are women, and women and their choices are often viewed as unimportant and so they are not seen. When I seek to identify experiences I have had as a lesbian that have affected my academic career, I often feel I am pointing to something not there, or to a factor that does not matter much, or that should not be pointed to anyway because it is too private.

Initially, when I thought about speaking with the interviewer, I was apprehensive because of the nature of the subject, although I was interested to speak about it. We scheduled a time to conduct the interview on the phone long-distance. When the interviewer called and our discussion began, I immediately became afraid, much as people I have interviewed have become afraid. I feared what would happen to me as a result of this research. Specifically, I feared having it known in the outside world that I was a lesbian, odd as that may sound, and worse, having it known that I had recently acted like one.

My fear was particularly acute at that moment because the incident of my denying the hostile male graduate student permission to take my Feminist Methodology course had occurred the spring before, and it continued to have effects. Articles drawing from the story about it that ran in the campus right-wing newspaper were published, months later, in a national newsmagazine and in a local city paper, disparaging me for denying permission to the male student. During the following fall quarter, the campus ombudsperson called me into her office because two women graduate students who had been in my course—one of whom, I suspected, was a closet lesbian—needed to pursue the matter. They had spoken with the ombudsperson, not mentioning the incident of the male graduate student, saying only that they wished to complain about my approach to teaching. That winter, ten months after I had denied permission to that one man, my teaching contract was not renewed for an upcoming three-year term. The next spring, both of the courses I was teaching were affected when students in them were unusually homophobic in their responses to me. Hard to prove as related to any of this, but disturbingly coincidental, just when the male student's story hit the campus papers, both my car and my lover's car began to be repeatedly stolen and vandalized in front of our house. "Anyone hate you?" asked the police officer who came out to investigate. "Give any student an 'F' recently?"

When I spoke with the interviewer on the phone, all these events were on my mind. Thus, I was afraid perhaps far more than the situation of a master's thesis warranted. I was sure that people would know it was me in the thesis the interviewer would write, or in an article based on it, or they would hear about me through researchers' gossip networks. They would know I had said no to a man, and they would expect the same, or worse, from me. I would be seen as a person who is unsafe to hire, as a betrayer of the trust that holds up the system. No one in the whole country, I felt, would ever hire me again if they knew.

I may have had an exaggerated expectation of adverse consequences from a master's thesis, but I did not, I think, have an exaggerated fear. There are consequences of saying no to men. The instance of my saying no to the male student had already unleashed a set of them for me. This incident became controversial, in large part, I felt, because it raised the specter of my being a lesbian—a separatist, a man-hater, not a male-aligned woman, a woman who chooses women over men, who does not take care of men, a woman who risks being denied male privileges and who is, therefore, vulnerable. Even though I felt my lesbianism had affected what happened to me, it was difficult for me at the time of the controversy, and even after, to identify the consequences I experienced as related specifically to my being a lesbian. For example, during the more recent spring term, when I saw students in one of my classes avoid looking directly at me at times when I expected they would, or when they had trouble talking about the content of *The Mirror Dance*, my book on lesbians, I thought I was probably a bad teacher, or that I was feeling distant from the students, or maybe the students were right that there was not much provocative in my book to discuss. I did not think the students were afraid of me because I was a lesbian, or that this fear was related to the controversy of the year before when I had said no to the male graduate student.

The previous year, after I denied the male student permission to take my class, I had thought that the silences in class discussions, the fragmentation of morale, and the various oppositions to me from the students occurred because I was not doing well as a teacher, or as a person. I thought the students had really different values than mine, or that they simply did not like me. At the time, I did not think, "I am a lesbian. I have said no to a man publicly. They are scared of me, of being like me, and of losing the support of men." When I heard the conservative women faculty members at the meeting asking, "What do you mean by woman-centered?" and "Why didn't you take care of this man?" I felt hurt, and I was not sure why they were picking on me. I knew I was a lesbian and they were straight, and that this made a difference, but exactly what difference was hard to determine when the challenges were so indirect.

Now I told the interviewer about my fears concerning this still troublesome incident and what might yet happen to me, and she agreed to substitute another example when she wrote her thesis and article, rather than saying what I had actually done. I felt cowardly requesting her to hide my situation, and I hoped such a change would not harm the truth. We next discussed the many more usual circumstances when it is not clear to me whether my being a lesbian is affecting responses I receive. When I see women secretaries and administrative staff in university offices looking at me, for instance, I always wonder, Am I attractive to them, or frightening? Do they see me as a woman, or a lesbian—a mannish woman? What difference is it to them? What about the male administrators who pass judgment on my hirings and interview me, do they see a woman who is a lesbian and, therefore, threatening to them? Do they assume that because I am a lesbian, I will not do their bidding, and, therefore, who needs me? What about male students—is it only a facade when they defer to me, or seem to like me? Do they fear that because I am a lesbian, I will not like them? What about other women faculty, whether friendly on the surface, or formal and distant—does my lesbianism scare them? No one speaks of these things. The women students, who am I to them? "Are you afraid of me because I am a lesbian?" I asked one woman student who kept challenging me in class this past spring. "No," she swore up and down, she was not. Some of her best friends were lesbians. That just could not be.

When I did not get my teaching contract renewed, the obvious reason was that the university was having a budget crisis and lecturers were easy to eliminate. It seemed to have nothing to do with my being a lesbian, maybe it had something to do with my being a woman, certainly nothing to do with my having said no to the male student the year before. Usually when my contracts are not renewed, they say it is because of the nontraditional nature of my work. When I am not hired, that is also the reason given. I have found it is very hard to put a finger on anything important that has ever been denied me as a sociologist and say, "This is because I am a lesbian." There always seem to be other, better reasons. The lesbian part of the picture always disappears, as it does, for instance, when gay people say, "We are just like you. We have families. We raise children. We want to be loved." Yet we are different, or else why the consequences? Why the choice to be a lesbian in the first place?

When our cars were repeatedly stolen and vandalized, the police finally decided it might be a hate crime, but the hate crime squad never came out to get the facts. The threat hung there, unsolved. This type of crime, we were told, was usually impossible to pin down. If my hostile male graduate student had any link to our cars being attacked, I concluded, I was not going to find out. I was not of the mind to send the cops after him. Why stir up the antagonism? The police, were they to question him, would probably find nothing to link this shy, ivory-tower, third-year graduate student to car thieves.

So I said to the woman interviewer, feeling very tense just then about my prospects for another job, thinking about the cars, and wondering about the ways I sometimes think people look at me in hallways, "I might as well walk around in black leather and chains. I might as well rub it in. Maybe that would be better than being nice about it." She laughed. We both laughed. It was the highest, most intimate moment of the interview. I felt the interviewer, too, had had this thought. She was also a lesbian, as well as a good interviewer. It was a funny image— the two of us who had never met, talking on the phone, each imagining the other in black leather and chains walking around her relevant university wearing a sign saying, "lesbian (hates men, rejects being feminine, seeks to seduce other women)," or with a star symbol conveying the same meaning emblazoned on her forehead. We discussed how we each tried to hide it, but we always felt other people knew.

During the interview, I wished not to remember facts of my past. The interviewer tried repeatedly to get me to go back through the experiences of my career in a chronological way, beginning with graduate school, to trace the effects of lesbianism or discriminatory treatment related to it. I was reluctant to trace myself in that way. Instead, I felt mostly the jeopardy of my present. We did, however, identify some events of the past. There again, it felt to me like secrets I was not supposed to tell, for fear others would think I was betraying the system or acting improperly by speaking. My secrets, however, are probably not uncommon. On my first job, for example, as a visiting assistant professor, a senior male faculty member wrote me a note after my interview. It was on a pretty little card with a pressed, dried flower included in it. I figured he had some sort of fantasy, and that it was harmless. When I arrived to take the job at the start of the fall term, he picked me up at the airport and drove me around to look at houses. The damage was soon done. The first night, when he offered, I refused to stay with him at his house. Two days later, when I took an apartment that he drove me to see, I again refused his offer to spend the night with him, explaining that I was a lesbian. He quickly disappeared. Later in the semester at a faculty and graduate student party, I remember the rose-colored sweater I was wearing and how he kept looking at my breasts. Not long after that, the faculty of my department considered the continuation of my appointment. He strongly opposed it and his senior position helped to put an end to me at that university. Of course, other reasons were given—the nature of my work, for instance.

I am not saying that sleeping with male faculty members is a way to get ahead. I am saying I think it might have helped had I been wearing black leather and chains. At least, the betrayal element would then be missing. This man would have known who I was from the start. But then, again, men do not always accept what they see.

From that first job, I moved to a position at another university, again as a visiting assistant professor. I remember I did not attend a faculty party at the start of the year. The night of the party, I wondered whether I should have gone. Generally, I did not socialize with the members of my department in a way that suggested it mattered to me, and at that university such socializing might have mattered, since the faculty were unusually young; they were all my age or younger. But I was a lesbian. Moving to a new town, I had sought out other lesbians for my social life. When I finally went to a faculty party late in the fall, I came and left quickly. I still remember the dark interior of the male faculty member's house where the party was held. The living room was crowded and I was not interested in meeting people's wives. I had another party to go to that night, at a gay woman's house, and I had a lesbian lover who was waiting to go there with me. I walked through the straight faculty party quickly and did not engage anyone in conversation of more than a few syllables. I was glad not to have to take all that very seriously.

At that second university, there was, again, a senior male faculty member, although he was younger than the senior male at the first school. He came over to my house one night after a preliminary show of interest. I knew why he was coming and I planned to tell him I was a lesbian. I hoped we might be friends. That was my first experience with a man who takes it as a challenge when told that a woman is a lesbian. After I informed him, there was some wrestling on a bed that served as a couch in the living room, and finally he gave up.

Three of us had been hired that year as visiting assistant professors. One of us would be kept on. It was not me, and it was not the nicer of the two men. It was a man who had a dark brown beard, and who, when he got dressed up, wore a white linen suit, and whose wife had recently left him. There was nothing particularly wrong with him. He was more like the man who had come over to my house than like anyone else on the faculty.

The man who came over that night was one of the three male faculty members who formed the committee that decided on who to hire permanently for the organizational position. They made their decision before Christmas, although the appointment would not start until the next academic year. For some reason, they wished to make a decision quickly. I remember walking to my car one day not long after I was told that I would not be hired, thinking that if it took a dress to get a job, I would wear one to my next interview. I would ask people I knew if a dress would make a difference, and if so, I would do what I had not been willing to do before and get one. As it turned out, I did not wear a dress to either of the job interviews I went to that year, and I did not get either job. I never took seriously wearing a white linen suit like the bearded man who got the job in my department, but a vision of myself in a white suit, looking just like him, often occurred to me.

At one point, I visited each of the three men who formed the committee that made the hiring decision, and asked them why I did not get the job. I was told that the bearded man was more conventional. He was more the straight-line organizational type and could bring members of the nonuniversity community into the department's organizational program. I had brought nonuniversity people into my courses as guests, and I felt hurt that what they were saying was not true of me. I had probably already brought in more nonuniversity people than he had, but that was not the point.

These are blatant examples, two cases where a man I rejected sexually later rejected me in an institutional sense. Most cases are less clear. The clear ones, it seems to me, are less hurtful. At least they are less hurtful emotionally at the moment of their occurrence. In the long run, however, any rejection, or loss of a job, has consequences. In the second university, the job I did not get was one I very much wanted. I had developed attachments to people there and to that part of the country. I still think about how my life might have been different had I been able to stay. By this second time, too, I was beginning to feel that I should expect rejection when people got to know me, as they do when one is a visitor rather than a set of credentials on a curriculum vitae. Whether or not I was rejected because I was a lesbian, I felt I had been rejected because I was myself.

There are other less clear examples of experiences in which my being a lesbian has been tied to rejection, or to my being held at a distance by others. I have taught temporarily at a variety of universities, for instance, and I have noticed that my social circles are not those of the heterosexual women around me. They have husbands and I do not, and this often seems to be the problem. I sometimes feel hurt because the lesbian/straight divide limits the friends I can have at any place. The effect is not necessarily institutional disadvantage, since women do not have great advantages in universities. Mostly, I feel a loss. I notice the lesbian/straight divide and I never like it. It is another invisible presence, something supposedly not a matter of gay and straight, but of personal choice, and assumed not to be of much importance. Yet it is important to me, for I lose relationships with other women.

Another kind of example concerns my research, since I have done work on the subject of lesbians in *The Mirror Dance* and in articles about lesbian identity and about researching lesbians.[1] When I think about my work, I usually do not think it is marked by the fact that I have studied lesbians. However, it must be and, of course, this must make a difference. What if I had studied something else? Banks, for instance, or government, or men and women in high-technology industries? When I first did the research for *The Mirror Dance,* I felt I had a great advantage: here was a fascinating community of lesbians, and as a member of it, I had access as an insider. I did not think that a study of lesbians, because it is about a "marginal" group of women, would have marginalizing consequences for me within sociology. Yet even in feminist and women's studies, I would find the study of lesbians would set me apart, carrying with it the same discomforts that lesbianism does: a discomfort with sex between women, a fear of being called man hating, and a fear of losing ties with men and of losing privileges from men.

I would discover that there is a deep-seated fear, which can lead to hostility, both in women's studies circles and elsewhere, as if lesbians would take over the institution if granted more than minimal courses to teach and minimal faculty positions. When known to be an academic couple, lesbians are often closely scrutinized, more so than heterosexual couples in the same university. I have found such scrutiny to be intimidating, especially when used as a device of institutional control. It has seemed to me a shocking invasion of privacy. But then the boundaries of women, whether as individuals or as a couple, are often not respected. Unfortunately, I think, it still pays to be invisible, whether for financial reasons or to defend against the hostility and homophobia of others entering into one's private life. Self-protectively, I have tried to be quiet and to keep to myself in the institutions where I have worked, but I have not been able to be invisible.

If studying lesbians, and studying them as I do—visibly, like a woman, speaking in the colloquial, dealing with the personal—has disadvantaged me, however, I have tended to overlook that disadvantage. What I study, and how I study it, has seemed to me so much my choice, and my virtue, that I have a blind spot when it comes to thinking that others might devalue my work because of its subject, or because of my own life. But they do. After one hiring meeting, in particular, which occurred a few years after *The Mirror Dance* came out, I was told that the faculty, all men but one, did not find my work interesting or exciting. No wonder, I thought.

If I have been marginalized—disregarded, devalued, pushed aside—because I have studied lesbians, I have never felt I could do much about it, which may be one reason I have ignored it. I have also felt that judgments about my work that reflect a bias against lesbians are not judgments about me—that they do not really affect me personally, or cause me to think less well of myself. However, that is probably not true.

Responses to my work are responses to its style and content—and to me—which sometimes confuses me, and often obscures the lesbian issue for me. Yet I do think that my experimenting with narrative form is related to my perspective as a lesbian. *The Mirror Dance*, written in an unusual multiple-person stream of consciousness style—from the points of view of the seventy-eight women I interviewed—reads like gossip, like overhearing women in a small town talking about themselves and each other: "There was a lot of gossip, said Emily. It was not ill intentioned. It was Hollywood-type gossip, infatuation—'Last night she was seen with her.' She made hopeless attempts to control it sometimes."[2] There is a lesbian feel to this gossip, joined with a sense that *The Mirror Dance* breaks barriers of convention by inventing its own style of expression, as do many lesbians, and as I did in attempting faithfully to depict this lesbian community.

My subsequent study, *Social Science and the Self,* which argued that the social scientific observer should be acknowledged more fully in our studies, dealt, too, with lesbianism, but in a more indirect way. In large parts of *Social Science and the Self,* to illustrate my thesis, I spoke about my personal experiences related to my work, and I spoke about being a lesbian. This study was unusual in that it combined my self-reflections with discussions of self and knowledge by women artists—Georgia O'Keeffe and Pueblo Indian potters. The book concluded with discussions by eight feminist scholars whom I interviewed about self-expression in their work. Four of these eight scholars were lesbians. Except for one, however, I did not identify them as lesbian in the book, in part because they did not mention it when I interviewed them, and in part because I thought identifying them would cause readers to discount what they said. I feared readers might view their comments as the peculiar views of lesbians, rather than as more broadly relevant. I do not know if I would closet my choice of subjects again, but that I did so bears noting because it illustrates how easily lesbianism becomes invisible. It seems not to matter, or it seems to be something that should not be singled out for fear of adverse consequences.

The issue of closeting lesbianism aside, *Social Science and the Self* raised questions about narrative form: how is this study to be categorized? How does valuing self-expression and originality change a sociological work? How does speaking from a woman's view change social science? Although I did not explicitly discuss the issue of a lesbian approach to knowledge in *Social Science and the Self,* I think that being a lesbian and seeking women's perspectives—especially nonconforming ones—go together for me. To a significant extent, both *The Mirror Dance* and *Social Science and the Self* are lesbian expressions. They break away from male academic forms and seek to use an inner female voice in ways that challenge conventional expectations. *The Mirror Dance* presented a collective lesbian voice. In *Social Science and the Self,* I articulated my own individual voice more, and I sought out individual statements from others. In both studies, I was concerned with the difficulties of women's efforts to create their own forms of expression.[3]

Recently, I have been asked by people who know my work and its concern with lesbianism, "Given the current rage for lesbian and gay studies, why don't you have a regular job by now?" I was startled, at first, to be asked this question. It caused me to think about why I have not been swept up in this wave of popularity. Although I am a lesbian, I am not a particularly trendy or entrepreneurial one. I think that the current vogue for gayness in academia, including the interest in "queer theory," will further other women who play the male academic game far more so than I do, and those who already have security, or a high status, at a university. It is deceptive, I think, to see those few token lesbians who are rewarded for studying lesbians, and then to assume that everyone will be rewarded, or that I will be.

As a writer and scholar, I am marked by who I am. Although I wish it were otherwise, I may never become a conventional success in terms of salary, position, and popularity. In part, this is because, for me, being a lesbian is part of a desire not to fit a mold. My lesbianism, which is central to my work in general, has different value premises than those aimed at proving I can do as others do. Queer theory, like much that becomes popular in academic circles, is male theory, which may account for its appeal.[4] I wish to express a female sensibility. Further, it seems to me that any trend in scholarship, whether female or male, brings with it its own kind of standardization. I may always be slightly too different from what is standard to be fully embraced in the academic world, even as a representative of a minority. My lesbianism, in some way, stands for my difference. I do not mean by this to understate the costs to me of that difference. I have sought to follow my own values in my work, but I have never wanted to be penalized for doing so.

Finally, I wish to speak of homophobia. It runs through all my experiences like an invisible thread. It seems not to determine something major, like whether or not I receive a job, but rather to consist of small slights toward which I try to turn the other cheek. Yet the small slights have a way of building. Last spring, for instance, I heard, by word of mouth, a piece of anonymous gossip about a woman graduate student I knew and liked. It was introduced to me as something too horrible for the student herself to speak of. The item was this: a senior male faculty member on the dissertation committee of the woman student—who may, or may not, have been a lesbian—had suggested that the student seek my advice for some part of her study because it was about lesbians, and I was a lesbian. The awful part, according to the gossip, was the way the faculty member referred to me when he made his suggestion. He spoke with his hand held up to his face, looking off to the side, as if he were speaking of something dirty, and in a snide tone. "You know," he said of me, "she's an out lesbian," with the emphasis on "out." When I heard this story, I was not horrified but, rather, I felt let down. So what? I wondered. What is wrong with being known as a lesbian? The student, however, was so hurt and frightened by the remark that she never came to ask me for advice.

I usually think it is not the gestures like this man's, in which the scorn is on the surface, but those in which the scorn is covered up that are more serious in their consequence. The covered-up affronts are more difficult to identify and thus to deal with. I tend to think I am more hurt by the student in a classroom who sits across from me in silent distrust because she wishes not to be homophobic, but still is, than I am by the man in the background who disdainfully tells a graduate student to look me up, and also, I suspect, votes negatively on my hiring. However, the two are related. The student keeps her distance because the man is there. The man speaks his mind because no one stops him. I may not be hurt when told of the man's scorn, but I am hurt by the graduate student when, in not seeking my advice, she seems not to value me. Homophobia has a hidden nature because it is a fear. Acts that stimulate that fear are interrelated. They are also, I think, disabling. I have found the repeated job rejections I have experienced to be disabling, not only externally, but internally, in terms of my self-confidence and ability to do my work. However, I know that those who attempt to conform, to be invisible, also are disabled by not being able to be themselves in their work.

When I think about hurts of the academic system, I do not usually think I have been hurt because I am a lesbian. I think of things I can see more easily, and of explanations that have nothing to do with my choosing women. My main hurt in academia is lack of a regular job—a full-time, full-status position. I also think I have been hurt because of the ways people have spoken to me over the years about my not having such a job. They make comments such as: "I wish I could have all that time off." "If you just were willing to move." "You are happier this way." "You would not be so productive if you were full-time employed." "You don't do mainstream work, what do you expect?" meaning, of course, "you deserve what you get." I feel hurt by these words, to the point of tears, every time I hear them. Over time, however, I have learned to speak back to the words and eventually to focus on the insensitivity of the speaker: "This person does not realize, she does not know. I do deserve. I would be more productive. I am not happier. I have reasons for not moving, and for not taking just any job." Yet the hurt continues.

I have learned to think of my hurt in the academic world as very much related to the nature of my work—to my unconventional choices about what my work is, and where I do it. I have also learned to see this hurt as related to a larger economic circumstance that has existed since the time I completed my degree. I did my graduate work at a time of plenty. The academic world subsequently became more constricted, and it came to have less room for people like me. Such an economic explanation seems, at times, very clear to me. I see it with pain, but I see it.

What I almost never see is that my choice to be a lesbian is significant in all this. I can see that being a lesbian is an element in the whole bundle that is me, but it is hard for me to feel that this lesbian element is more important, say, than my refusal to keep moving for a job, or my penchant for doing things my own way. However, I now think I must take into account how I felt in the interview with the master's student, how great my fear was, how strong my denial, how shocked even I was by my own constant dismissal of the facts of my past and present. By the end of the interview, I was sweaty and tired and I wanted to stop early. "These are things I do not like to think about," I kept telling the interviewer. "These are things I do not want to know," and yet I know them.

In the past, I have viewed parts of my lesbian experience as incidents not to be spoken of in the same breath as I speak of my academic career.[5] I have feared I would be making the situation worse for myself by speaking of events that are too petty or too private. I feared that just as I dismiss the importance of these events, others would too. Yet my being a lesbian is not a private, or separate, part of my life. It is not separate for me, nor for those who respond to me. It is not unimportant for any of us. As a lesbian, I choose women over men, I align myself with women, and I often deny men access to me. To the extent that I do so, I am alternately vulnerable, threatening, and disposable in a system where male-based choices and alliances are the important ones. My experience is not that of every lesbian, but there may be elements of it that others may share, such as the sense of having a stigma that is accepted, and a pain that is not felt, or of having a wish that black leather would solve the problem, or simply wishing that the system had other rules.

PART THREE

Feminist Teaching

Eight

A FEMINIST CLASS

I HAVE TAUGHT A COURSE called Women and Organizations for the past eight years, seven times at one institution and once each at two others. Students, most of them women, take this course because they wish to be successful in a man's world and not to be disadvantaged because they are women. I teach the course for a different reason, because I like women and am interested in women's worlds. There is a basic set of topics in my course: women's development, boundaries, and styles of communication; women's experiences in organizations; women's work; and female separatism. But equally important are implicit processes that occur during the term, reflecting the students' needs for their own growth, their resistances and fears, and my own.

Because this seminar has provided many of my main ideas for understanding women's social patterns, I wish to give a sense of the key learnings by describing the flow of ideas and experience over a quarter's time. I wish also to convey a sense of the dynamics of a feminist course, where a teacher is often in a struggle with students over the development of awareness. In the following three chapters, I invite the reader to take the course vicariously by becoming involved with the materials and the classroom experience.

The first substantive week of the course is titled on the syllabus "Women's Development, Women's Boundaries, and Girls in Groups." My purpose is to start with a familiar topic—the growth and development of the individual—to suggest that women, from early on, learn different experiences of self and different ways of relating to others than men do. More broadly, my suggestion is that gender socialization is not only initial, but repetitive throughout life, which is why it is so very effective. If one does not learn properly how to be a girl as a child, for example, one learns this later as a teenager or an adult. We read Nancy Chodorow on the many unconscious ways that female gender identity is established in the first years of life.[1] Especially relevant for my purposes is her discussion of how female children have different personal boundary experiences than male children. The idea that a person has a boundary, which is treated differently if she is female, seems to me important because it leads to grasping how women might develop a different sense of self than men. Later, this idea of a personal boundary will be useful for understanding behaviors of adult women—for example, when women on the job need to say "no" in big ways to seemingly small requests because they do not feel a sense of clear boundary between themselves and others.

Chodorow explains that the female ego boundary is more "permeable" than the male ego boundary because a female mother separates less clearly from a daughter than from a son. The boy, for his part, separates more from a mother than a girl does in order to achieve gender identity, since being male means "not being female." The point, I think, can be taken further. Throughout their lifetimes, both girls and women experience themselves as more open because they are more frequently invaded by others—both female and male, both strangers and intimates. Female boundaries are more often invaded because women are viewed as accessible and manipulable, whereas men, because they are more respected, are treated as more separate and as more inviolable.

The idea that a female sense of self is less separate and less protected than a male sense of self may be viewed in positive terms. Carol Gilligan suggests that a woman develops a more relational, connected, less isolated sense of self than a man does, and that this requires relevant types of interpretations. I find especially interesting her discussion of how women experience danger when their relationships are severed, while men more often experience danger in intimacy and security in isolation. I use Gilligan's book on psychological theory in the first week to provide gendered descriptions that are very clear and that lead to organizational extensions—to seeing how female social forms might emerge from characteristics ascribed to women. Because there is no body of literature on women's social forms, I must often use readings that emerge from the study of one thing—of individuals and of women's moral development, in this case—to suggest broader organizational patterns. When Gilligan, for instance, says that women are more oriented toward relationships than men, and have a self delineated through activities of responsiveness to others, or of care, there are organizational implications. Gilligan suggests some of these with her images of web and hierarchy, noting that the male's more separate positioned self may be more comfortable in hierarchical relationships, while the woman's more socially embedded self may find extension in more weblike relationships.[2]

Although Gilligan's study draws from a white middle-class population, similar themes can be found in other groups as well. In a study of eight- to thirteen-year-old African American children on the streets of Philadelphia, Marjorie Harness Goodwin focuses on the relationship between language and social organization in children's same-sex task groups. The girls use more inclusive language among themselves, more "we" and "us," words that do not differentiate speaker and hearer. The girls' speech implies symmetrical relationships among group members. The boys, by contrast, use more commanding styles of speech that reflect and perpetuate hierarchy. Important for the girls are issues of alliance formation and of ostracism—of whether one is in or out of the group. For the boys, what counts is whether they are up or down in the structure of positions in their group. When the boys have a dispute, they change positions in their group, preserving the structure of the group. When the girls have a dispute, their dispute often lasts longer, internal alliances form and reform, and members are more likely to be excluded or to leave the group. The girls' groups are thus less stable and more short-lived. Because the girls' groups are interactionally different, looking at them requires seeing them in terms that are fitting, avoiding a common tendency to interpret female groups in the same way one would male groups.[3]

Goodwin's lower-class, African American children show similar patterns to those found in Gilligan's and Chodorow's studies of middle-class white children and adults. In both cases, interpersonal boundaries are less strictly defined among girls and women than among boys and men, with a quest for equality being a more important feature of the female social relationships. Similar gender-segregated patterns also appear in other studies of children.[4] Later, we will find these patterns again when we read about women and men in corporate settings. My point is not that all gendered patterns are the same, but that some similar styles of social organization can be found, with important variations, in strikingly different places.[5]

I like Goodwin's study of African American street children very much, both because of its setting and because of its organizational lessons. The students respect this study but are more stirred by Gilligan and her suggestion that women have definable characteristics. The students criticize psychoanalytic thinking when they read Chodorow. They criticize gender definitions, and the very idea of gender, when they read Gilligan. In response to Gilligan, many of the students, sometimes a majority, react hotly and angrily that women are not the way she portrays them, or not like that anymore. They claim they themselves are not like women but like men, or that they are a mix of characteristics. The male students often say, at this point, they feel they are like women. The students generally do not like what they see as the untrue stereotypes presented by Gilligan, and I sit there looking at these twenty or more stereotypes sitting around the room—noticing how they dress and how they speak, how they hold their bodies, the makeup the women wear, noticing my own female silence—and feel suddenly unpopular in my viewpoint. It only occurs to me later to ask those who protest, "Why this denial of the difference that gender makes?"

At this point in the course, I give the students their first research assignment. I ask each to interview four women of different ages and socioeconomic backgrounds about their experiences of participation in women's organizations. This assignment immediately raises the question, what is a women's organization? I tell the students that, to me, it is an organization in which women set the tone, and that it need not be a formal organization—it could be a friendship network or a family. I ask them to define it as they like and to pay special attention to the words the women they interview use to describe their experiences and to the feelings conveyed by these words.

The initial gender characteristics suggested in our readings are soon found again, at the student's own hands, in the words of women they know—their grandmothers, mothers, sisters, and friends—whom they have interviewed for this assignment. The students speak with women from different class and racial backgrounds about experiences in both work and nonwork organizations, providing a useful variety of groups for us to consider in class discussion. The types of organizations sampled include: hospital emergency rooms, church groups, businesses, women's companies, women's professional associations, sororities, sports teams, branch banks, dorms, women's committees, schools, women's centers, YWCAs, Hadassahs, Latvian women's groups, DAR groups, African American sororities, Asian women's groups, Chicana women's groups, public service and government agencies, fundraising organizations, volunteer networks, rape education projects, book clubs, investment clubs, SPCAs, 4-Hs, Girl Scouts, women's self-help groups, daycare centers, accounts payable departments, consulting firms, religious groups, and feminist collectives.[6] Similarities in the ways the women interviewed describe their experiences surprise the students. It now gets a little harder to dispute that there may be a reality to the stereotypes we have read about, even if that reality is discomforting.

In their interviews, the students find words such as these describing women's organizations: "cooperative, warm, comfortable, democratic, close-knit, fluid, friendly." These are "groups in which you can share personal things. They are better organized than coed groups. They attempt to include people; they weed people out. They are detail-oriented, open, trusting environments. They are places where you can get away from your husband. Their members communicate in incomplete sentences. They operate by a consensus process, which means you go around and around in the group hearing what people are thinking, but you wish someone would just come in and make a decision. Women's groups are nitpicky, bitchy, indirect. They are nonhierarchical, polite, almost formal; they share responsibility. They are family-like, educational, philanthropic, caring. People in them value equality; people talk about how they feel. There is attention to process and a lot of gossip. The groups are cliquish, backstabbing, forced, unnatural, time consuming. They are a wonderful opportunity, a brave new world. They run at too high an emotional level, are unpredictable, are a colorful range. The women in them are each others' sisters and mothers. Their members love each other and are bitchier with each other than in any other organization."[7]

Each year, I listen closely to the words the students find when they do this assignment, looking for nuances I had not seen or heard about before and for expressions I like. Last year, for example, when one student reported, "Work cannot be done in these groups until the dust has settled and everyone is happy with each other," I felt "how true" and I liked the warmth in the expression. Similarly, I liked the phrase, "they give awards," which, to me, pointed to the need I think women often feel to recognize and affirm each individual in a group. Although it may seem contrary to the idea that women do not care about individuals, but rather value groupness, I think that women are very aware of the need for affirming the individual, in part because such affirmation has so often been denied us.

The research assignment I give for the next week also has the effect of encouraging the students to believe there is a reality to the gender stereotypes they initially rejected. I ask them to look at patterns of communication among women to see what happens to these patterns when a man, or men, enters a previously all-women's group. The students observe women in settings familiar to them—informal conversation groups, secretarial offices, meetings, work groups, parties, among friends in their dorms. They find that women stop relating to one another when a man enters their group. They disperse or stop talking to each other, and defer to, and focus on, the man or men. The women alter their body language to lean away from a male presence, at the same time as they attend to the male. Their voices get louder when a man enters; their words change; the topic of their conversation changes to what the man wishes to discuss. When the man leaves, a previously all-women's group often breaks up, its moment of existence gone, although sometimes the group simply picks up where it left off. If a man even passes by a women's group, while the women are talking among themselves, and if one of the women notices him, the tone of the whole group changes. The woman who notices the man stiffens and gets watchful and her demeanor affects others in the group.

The results of this assignment suggest to me, each year, that women's groups are highly sensitive social units with boundaries that are easily invaded. The consequence of male entrance into a women's group is that the style of social relating characteristic of the women's group disappears. For the women's group, male presence means change toward a male way of being. Seeing such change before their eyes, in their own social settings, and participated in by themselves, the students are horrified and believe a little more in the presence of gender.

Our readings during this third week focus on effects of gender on group dynamics. Again, many of the students do not at first believe what they read. Even after conducting their research, they wish to conclude that perhaps their findings are not more generally true. On the syllabus, this week is titled "Women, Communication, and Invisibility." We begin with a classic social-psychological study by Elizabeth Aries that compares interactional patterns in female, male, and mixed-gender groups, and that points out that mixed groups advantage men more than they do women.[8] Mixed-gender groups expand the range of options for male styles of relating—they allow men to be more personal in style—and they give men an audience. By contrast, women in mixed groups become more restricted. They become divided from other women and oriented toward men. They speak less often, and in more limited ways, than when among only women. Finally, both women and men report preferring to be in groups with women.

When we read about these gender biases in group interactions, I think of the more general point that when people speak of advantages of gender integration—of coeducation, for instance—they note that women are advantaged by it because they gain access to male resources.

It is not often noted that if women are advantaged by integration, men are advantaged more. In part, this latter point is overlooked because we are used to seeing men as the more valuable resource, and we are not used to seeing how women's interactions with men restrict women.

The effect of gender on interaction appears in studies of male interruptions of women's speech, which report that men interrupt women far more frequently than the reverse. Male interruptions disturb not only a sentence a woman is speaking, but also penetrate into the woman's inner self. Male interruptions demonstrate power, and assumed superiority, while women's interruptions more often show identification with another; women interrupt to continue another's thought, or to express mutuality. Our article on interruptions, "Small Insults," views interruptions as micropolitical acts that both reflect and perpetuate a larger situation of gendered hierarchy.[9] We also read a study that offers a cultural, rather than political, approach, arguing that women and men come from different subcultures, and thus learn different ways of using and understanding words, which accounts for difficulties between them.[10] The students in my course are usually far more comfortable with a "cultural misunderstanding" view of female-male troubles than with a political view. They would rather view gender difficulties as having their source in women and men being different, than as having their source in men's greater power over women. I think this is because an analysis of power suggests more of a rift between the two genders and points to problems that are harder to rectify. I prefer a political view.

Overview studies of women's and men's communication patterns contain both types of views. A central observation of many of these studies is that men's styles of speech appear strong, while women's styles seem weak. For example, a woman says, "Oh dear, I've pricked my little finger," while a man says, "Oh shit, I've cut my hand," referring to the same degree of injury, and the man's injury and dignity both appear greater.[11] When I come across this example in our readings, I am aware that I wish to speak like a man. Still, I am surprised when the students respond similarly, when, in reading about women's speech, they see it as less effective, or less good, than men's speech and wish to change their own habits so they will sound more like men. The students now become self-conscious about their female speech habits—their asking questions rather than making statements, seeming uncertain and tentative, and using softeners in language and a style of indirectness. They notice especially how they are self-effacing in their speech and wish to change that.

Yet the students quickly move from rejecting their women's speech habits to seeing how their women's speech has its own value. It is not simply weak language, but conveys a different meaning. They begin to think it may be good to acknowledge uncertainty, or to show respect to another by asking a question rather than assuming compliance. Perhaps women speak more truthfully by making limited statements. Perhaps it is good not to be self-important. Why turn oneself into a man? Why use men's speech? The conflict between using the gestures of men and the less-assuming styles of women is not settled here, however. Men's speech seems clearly to be more effective when among men. But at what cost to the women who use it? And what happens when among other women? Male speech is often felt as offensive when women use it with each other. The women students in my class, for instance, do not like it if I speak too much like a man with them. They also will sometimes become anxious if I speak too much like a woman.

Our readings about gender and communication are peppered with observations I find fascinating—for example, that men answer questions not addressed to them, and that women are observed more, and are more conscious of their visibility. Women smile more—the woman's smile is the "servant's shuffle," says one author. When women adapt their behaviors to men's characteristics, they suppress themselves nonverbally and inwardly. Women wait more.[12] I have found that the insights in these studies are also fascinating to the women students, who realize, from their own experiences, the importance of the gendered intricacies of social interaction. They have been hurt by words and seemingly minor gestures, and they have learned how to be careful in using words. They demonstrate their socialization as women by having, often, a special flair for deciphering micro-interpersonal material. The women students, I think, often have skills in this regard that the men students do not have, or have not developed as well. I have noticed that the kinds of papers I assign, which are self-reflective and observational, favor the abilities of women students. The women "do better" on my assignments, although I do not penalize the men. In most classes in a university, the approaches that men students have learned are favored—approaches of rationality, detachment, and glossing over details in order to make larger statements. Women students can be as rational and grandiose as men, but I think there are other things women can do well, that are usually not required. I did not plan my research and writing assignments to favor the skills of women students, but I am pleased that they have.

So often, the subtleties of women's experiences are invisible to the untrained eye. I try, in my course, to train the students' eyes to see gender, and to see it where they might not have before, and where they still resist seeing it. To close our section on communication, we read an article by Patricia Williams, an African American woman, on invisibility. Williams speaks of how people do not see her, both because they overlook her and because they see through her—they assume they see her when they do not: "What was hardest was not just that white people saw me, but that they looked through me, that they treated me as though I were transparent."[13] Williams' statement could, I think, be applied to female experiences in many settings. Women often are not seen, or are seen in ways felt as untrue and humiliating.

The initial weeks of the quarter seem to me to contain all the central ideas of my course. By the start of the fourth week, because the students now have this foundation, I expect them to be at my level of understanding and to share my biases about how to interpret social interactions in a gendered way. When they do not, I become frustrated and impatient with them. During weeks three and four, I repeatedly feel the students are stuck in first grade. I feel they are incredibly slow to learn, and that they do not want to learn what I am teaching. I drive home after classes feeling that I hate teaching and that the students hate me. They make long faces in class sessions. They leave long silences between comments. I feel I am pulling teeth to get discussions moving. At this point, I would guess, the students feel I am trying to take them where they do not want to go, or that I wish to make them see what they are not prepared for.

Of course, students vary individually and much occurs beneath the surface that I am unaware of. A sense of opening up to new ideas may contribute to a silence in class discussions as much as may a closing down. There are moments of elation and breakthrough in many class sessions when individuals announce that something they have read, or heard, is exactly how they feel, and that they are glad to know they are not alone. This past year, one graduate student said she had felt inadequate, for many years, in discussions with men and had felt she was stupid compared to them. She had cried when she found explanations in our readings that did not blame her, but instead tied her feelings to gender differences.

About this time in the quarter, I have also noticed that the students start to get irritable with each other when they feel that others in the class do not think, and feel, as they do. In my own case, I begin to feel that my way of thinking is shared, at best, by one other woman in the room. As I watch her, she seems to me to be a loner, someone who speaks with tears in her eyes and who feels she is not heard by anyone else. For the past few years, this student has been a heterosexual woman with straight blond hair, who looks to me as if she could be in a sorority. She looks nothing like me, yet I feel for her as if she were me. If I tell her I agree with her, however, and that she is not alone in the room, she still feels alone. I begin to grasp that what matters to her most is the response from other students. This is far more important than agreement with me. I think that the students' importance for one another is a major influence in the course all term, although I do not wish, by saying this, to understate my role as the teacher. Affecting us all is the fact that, even when men are present, our class is, by and large, a women's class. It has the dynamics of a women's organization. Individuals in the class often feel invisible to one another and boundaryless. Their needs for acceptance and approval from each other are great. Affect, especially feelings that are never spoken of, are extremely important to what happens in the class. Finally, this is a group that is afraid of itself and of its own internal ties, in short, homophobic. None of this is easy to discuss.

WOMEN IN FORMAL ORGANIZATIONS

At this point in the course, the beginning of the fourth week, I am determined to break down the students' resistances, to challenge and shake them up, to make them feel absolutely miserable if I have to—anything to cut into the silences in class discussions that I repeatedly experience as too long. Our next topic, titled on the syllabus "Women in Corporate America and in Bureaucracies," deals with women's experiences in formal work organizations—corporations, universities, hospitals, governments, small businesses, professions. These organizations are usually viewed in male terms, as hierarchies with positions, ranks, procedures, and goals, and as competing with one another for survival.

In formal organizations, women have traditionally occupied interstitial and subordinate positions, and their activities have been spoken of in nonorganizational, or informal, terms. For example, women have occupied secretarial "pools," not secretarial departments. Women have, in large numbers, provided support and administrative "services" to the more formal divisions of large organizations. Individually, women are often found as assistants, in shadow and helping roles, and in decorative and prize roles. A token executive woman, for example, decorates the ranks of upper management and is a prize for a company because she is at that rank. Whatever women's rank, their major power in organizations is said to lie in their use of gossip and personal skills, and in their social networks. When women form social units, whether within large organizations or outside them, we are usually reluctant to give their unit a name with the word "organization" in it. Instead, women's organizations are called by softer names. They are networks, families, communities, societies, sisterhoods, groups, ladies' auxiliaries, branches, clubs, klatches, circles.

For the students in my course, our "Women in Corporate America" week is, I think, supposed to be about how women can become successful in formal male-style roles in male-style organizations. However, I have noticed as we start this week that many of the students are, by now, also feeling a strong need to celebrate women's ways. For some students, this need to celebrate starts the first week of the course as soon as female gender characteristics are identified. The students speak joyfully of the positive functions of how women speak and act. In the first year I taught the course, the students' statements of celebration took me by surprise. Why put so much energy into celebrating? I felt. I ask them only to see what is women's. However, I have learned to respect the students' celebratory responses. Although not written into my syllabus as part of the progression of ideas in the course, these responses actually are part of that progression because ideas about women are heavily tied to emotions and often viewed in very negative ways. A sense of celebration is required for the students to take in facts about women because these facts are normally just the opposite of celebrated. The realities I want the students to see are realities they want to escape. These are discredited, repudiated, stigmatized realities, unwanted truths, rejected facts, just as women so often are unwanted and rejected. "It's too hard to live with," the students say of much that I want them to see. "It's too painful to know about." When they celebrate, the students turn their pain into joy. They convert their feelings of inferiority to a newfound strength.

This year, because I did not feel satisfied with the way my "Women in Corporate America" week seemed repeatedly to be a letdown for the students, and because I felt their disappointment must be a result of how I had been teaching the subject, rather than of the situation of women in corporations and bureaucracies, I decided to put an emphasis on one theme. We would focus on experiences of complicity in one's own subordination as a woman. I gave the students a quote from Kathy Ferguson's *The Feminist Case Against Bureaucracy:* "The distortion of powerlessness affects women's deepest psychic structures and cannot be dismissed as artificial externalities confining the real person. We would not object so strenuously to oppression if it did not in part accomplish that which it is intended to do, to elicit the complicity of the oppressed in their oppression and to produce subjects appropriately readied for subordination."[14]

I asked the students to write about experiences of their own in which they felt they had been complicitous in their subordination as women. What was the organizational setting? What happened? How did they feel? My wish was to suggest that although it is desirable to become aware of how women are denied opportunity and reward in large organizations, it is, in some ways, more useful, and more difficult, to see how one complies—the hidden bonds, one's own acceptance of an inferior status, the pain felt upon internalizing the terms of female oppression, and the lack of choice a woman usually has to do differently—

for oppression, or subordination, is part of the definition of a woman. As with other interpretations I offer the students, I like such a dire picture. It conforms to my sense of what my own experience has been. The students, however, feel differently, for they have been schooled to believe they have freedom. They think they can be whoever they want to be, and that most of the obstacles facing women can be overcome, at least in their individual cases.

Ferguson describes characteristics of women as traits of subordinates. Impression management, pleasing others, being open and available, being attentive to detail, being supportive—all these help one to get along when dealing with others who have a superior status, or who have a great deal of control over one's life. Female traits, says Ferguson, have little to do with being biologically female and a great deal to do with being politically powerless and with "learning to play the role of the subordinate in social relations." We also read about the need for radical feminist alternatives to bureaucratic systems, and about the harassment of women, especially the experiences made public in the Anita Hill case. Harassment raises similar issues to complicity because women repeatedly accept harassment and stay quiet about it, feeling they have no other choice. We read about how the situation of women in the workplace is not getting better as much as is usually claimed, that statistics often understate the disadvantages women still experience.[15]

There is a great deal of popular "advice literature" written for women that offers tips on how to succeed in the corporate world. Because that literature is colorful and provocative, I have the students read some of it. I especially like Betty Lehan Harragan's classic *Games Mother Never Taught You* on corporate gamesmanship for women. Harragan describes the metaphors and rules of male sports teams and of the military and encourages women to learn these rules in order to succeed. She tells women to use feminine wiles, but to play hardball like the men, to reject their early female socialization, which makes them unfit for the male world, and to adapt and fit in with male socialization. The objective of the game of corporate politics, she says, is money and power. The rules are ridiculous, but rigidly adhered to. It's a childish and, heretofore, strictly a boys' game. Yet if women learn the rules, they can get to be dealer, and then change the rules to dealer's choice.[16] I ask the students whether a woman who climbs to the top in an organization in the same way a man does will still have a choice. Who will she be by that time? Will she even want to change the rules? I want the students to see that there are inner consequences to external behaviors.

Rosabeth Moss Kanter's *Men and Women of the Corporation* is our basic academic text on corporate organizations. Although written more than a decade ago, Kanter describes a structure of opportunity and reward that persists to the present day in large organizations, despite flexible or progressive management approaches and the appearance of change. At upper levels in corporations, Kanter notes, women become increasingly visible because as minorities, or tokens, they stand out. At the same time, professional and managerial women are expected to be increasingly invisible, to blend in with men at upper levels and to serve the same organizational ends as men do. Women at the higher levels often feel pressure to repudiate what is female, both in themselves and in other women. Women at lower levels, by contrast, are expected to act like traditional women and to provide "pockets of the personal within the bureaucratic." It is around secretaries, says Kanter, that people at higher levels can "stop to remember the personal things about themselves and each other (appearance, dress, daily mood), could trade the small compliments and acknowledgments that differentiated them from the mass of others and from their formal role."[17]

Much that Kanter says about secretaries could, I think, be said of women at any rank in an organization when they act like women or are taken for women. Secretaries, she says, have a contingent status—they "derived their formal rank and level of reward not from the skills they utilized and the tasks they performed but from the formal rank of their bosses." Similarly, higher-level women are often seen as achieving recognition not in their own right, but because of relationships with high-ranking men. The case of Georgia O'Keeffe and Alfred Stieglitz comes to mind, for it is often said that she never would have become so famous had it not been for him. When Kanter says that secretaries "were doled out as rewards rather than in response to job needs," I think of how, at universities, affirmative action appointments of women faculty are often given out as prizes, or rewards. They are won in competitions between departments. The secretarial job, says Kanter, is "a job with low routinization in terms of time planning, characterized instead by a constant flow of orders." Women faculty, similarly, are often besieged. They are asked to do more than men and to be responsive in all directions rather than in control. Like secretaries, women faculty are often given symbolic rewards rather than material rewards for their work; they are paid with compliments and appreciation rather than with money.

Kanter's purpose in *Men and Women of the Corporation* is not to show likenesses between secretarial and managerial women, however. Nor is it to show truths about women, or gender, but to show how organizational structure determines individual behavior. Given the same structure, women and men will behave in the same way, she says. I ask the students to question this assertion and to see how Kanter's study does illumine the situation of women.

As we read her discussions of corporate women, I find that the students in my class separate themselves especially from Kanter's description of the secretaries. Kanter's secretaries are people with whom they do not identify, and whom they do not ever expect to be like. They think that by becoming doctors or lawyers, they will not become secretaries. Therefore, I must take the secretaries chapter and go over the details of it, pointing out how this chapter is not just about an occupation now replaced by computers and administrative personnel. It is about people like them and me.

More generally, in our discussions of women in corporations and bureaucracies, I find that many of the students do not want to accept that women are still disadvantaged. The older reentry students in the class, who have more workworld experiences, know about the difficulties, however, and they help me by describing these to the others. The more radical feminist students often speak fluently about the need for change. Yet although the students frequently have, and gain, words for seeing the faults of a system that discriminates by gender, and that puts women in impossible positions (damned if you act like a woman, and damned if you do not), most of the students are far from grasping the costs of behaving in ways that challenge such a system. For they are here at this elite university to enable themselves to do just the opposite, to do what the advice books wish—to succeed, to get ahead, to learn the rules and to use them—and they see themselves as already advantaged. They feel they come from relatively privileged backgrounds and that their education will further privilege them.

In other words, I think the students tend to see their class advantage, and their potential class mobility, as canceling out their gender disadvantage, or their caste immobility. Gender, like race, is a caste in the sense that it marks an uncrossable line between two separate systems of opportunity—one for men, one for women, the two unequal. When I ask the students to identify with secretaries, or to reflect on experiences of complicity in their own subordination as women, that is hard for them to do. They find isolated instances—when they once worked as a maid, or had a specific humiliating experience on a job—but they usually do not find a life full of such experiences.

Yet a life full is what I want them to see. Often, at this point, I feel I am alone in the room in identifying fully with this statement in one of our readings: "Imagine thinking yourself lucky to get any job, no matter how servile or poorly paid, any partner, no matter how brutal or dull, any roof over your head, no matter how costly the psychic mortgage payment. Imagine believing that's what you deserve. Imagine feeling guilty if you fail to feel grateful."[18] Similarly, I am far more likely than the students to associate my whole life with Kanter's description of corporate secretaries. When we discuss the complicity assignment, I have no difficulty identifying with experiences of subordination. Because the students have trouble doing so, I try to describe certain of my experiences to help them to see theirs. I sit there and, in an unsteady voice, tell them about my life. It is the hardest statement I make all term.

I tell the students about how my work, which means my writing, is very important to me, and about how I have accepted a second-class status for it. I speak about my periods of unemployment, my working as a secretary, my not climbing an academic ladder, my many unpublished manuscripts, my wish not to compete in the standard way. I describe how I have taken myself out of the running, in a sense, by doing work there is no comparison for, and by not continuing to move around the country for an academic job. I talk about how my work is valued by some people, but it is not viewed as worthy by those who determine who gets widely published or who gets hired for long-term jobs, and how I have not insisted they view it as worthy. I have turned away when rejected for jobs and continued on my own. I have not built an empire. I have not been particularly aggressive.

As I speak of this, I feel I am telling the students I am a failure, and I feel ashamed. My whole life seems to me, at that moment, to be a product of bad choices, which only with a flash of clever thinking can I credit to my gender—to my being a woman and having values other than the standard male ones, and to my being treated differently as a result. To step to one's own tune is, I think, different for a woman—a woman seems less successful, her difference looks less valuable. But I do not believe this applies to me. I tell the students that usually I think it is my nature to be good for nothing, or relatively worthless, that I feel I fail because I am myself, not because I am a woman. When I speak in this way, giving specifics of my complicity—of how I am part of what happens to me—I feel very alone in the classroom. I feel that the students do not want to be like me and that most of them do not grasp the commonness, and unavoidability, of my experience. It is a terrible feeling—to sense that others look at you and find you so wanting, or your predicament so frightening, that they feel they must, and can, do better.

Of course, I do not know how the students really feel. Perhaps they see me simply as a curiosity, or as the product of one woman's choices. Perhaps they do identify with me. But my point is that, for the moment, I see my own predicament as if through their eyes, and I feel the horror and pain and defeat of it. We each, perhaps, have our occasions to feel such pain, to feel caught in a trap with no way out and for which we feel responsible. In my own case, the trap is clearly particularly female, full of feelings of unworthiness. I think that false consciousness is often the best defense against being a woman. When I tell myself, "It is not my gender, it is me" that causes me trouble, and when I feel that I could have made other better choices, that is easier—by which I mean, less painful—than to feel that I have no better choices because I am a woman.

At intervals during the quarter, as I have mentioned, the students speak of not wanting to become aware of the situation of women because such awareness feels too painful. When they say this, I often do not understand what is painful for them. By the end of our "Women in Corporate America" week, after speaking of my own subordination and sense of failure, I begin to feel that something similar may be involved for the students. For them, a pain similar to mine may be felt when they realize that women do not have equality with men, or not as much equality as they had thought, that women face a glass ceiling in corporate worlds, or are not taken as seriously as men, and probably will not be taken as seriously in their lifetimes. These are prospects that highlight constraints. I am asking the students to be aware that female gender brings with it unwanted constraints that shape our lives in ways totally out of keeping with our ideas of who we are, and of what our opportunities should be.

The week we look at women in corporations and in bureaucracies is a letdown for the students because this was the week we were supposed to learn about how to succeed, or at least about how the corporate world is bad (patriarchal) and we are good (we are fighting women with better values). Instead, I have chosen to use this week to dramatize the problem of female gender by locating it not institutionally "out there," where it may have legal and political solutions—where harassment may be redressed, for example, or a woman may be reinstated in a job if discriminated against because of gender—but by locating it "in here," in each of us, where the costs are felt. The central question we are left with is, What do you do when a system denies your worth?

WOMEN'S WORK

Our tone becomes more positive the next week, for we study "Women's Work." This is something the students can feel proud of. Women may be limited and may not be rewarded well, but the nature and variety of women's work shines through as having great meaning. We read, first, about the "interaction work" women do—the work of making conversations succeed, providing the connective tissue in interpersonal relations, acknowledging others and asking them questions—work that women do for other women and for men, but that men usually do not do in return. In discussing conversations as interaction work, Pamela Fishman presents a sociological idea I find extremely useful for understanding gender, an idea also suggested in some of our other readings: that female characteristics are not the result of biological heredity, nor of a cultural nature experienced passively, but are, rather, accomplishments. A woman works at being a woman. She learns how to "perform" a female act, often self-consciously and so deeply it seems to be natural. Says Fishman, "the activities involved in displaying femaleness are usually defined as part of what being a woman is, so the idea that it is work is obscured. The work is not seen as what women do, but as part of what they are."[19]

Women's language is one form of expressing women's work. Ursula Le Guin speaks of "the mother tongue," the language of housework and daily life in which one thing rushes into another and power and success are not meaningful words. The mother tongue is colloquial, banal, "repetitive, the same over and over, like the work called women's work; earthbound, housebound. . . . It is language not as mere communication but as relation, relationship. It connects. It goes two ways, many ways. . . . Its power is not in dividing but in binding, not in distancing but in uniting."[20]

Along with language, we read about what Arlie Hochschild has called the "emotion work" women do—the work not simply of displaying emotion, such as might occur on the surface in personal relations, but the work on the self behind an emotional display that makes an emotional display convincing. When a woman puts on a smile, acts sympathetically, or, more generally, "plays the woman," she often does deep acting and emotion work. Hochschild studied airline flight attendants and the emotion work they do, especially the work of "enhancing the status and well-being of others." She writes of how women flight attendants work on their emotions to produce the smiles and friendliness of airline service. Although the job description is the same for both genders, women flight attendants do different emotion work than men, both because they receive more abuse—they receive more rude and surly treatment, angry tirades, and blame—and because they have less protection against abuse, having lower status and less of a "status shield" than do men. The women attendants are expected to defer to others and to provide the traditional female services of "loving wife and mother" and "glamorous career woman." Male flight attendants, on the other hand, have more of an "authority shield" protecting them against abuse. A passenger, says Hochschild, may not move her luggage when asked repeatedly by a woman, but will immediately do so when asked by a man.[21]

As we read about the women flight attendants, I encourage the students to see Hochschild's discussion as not only about flight attendants, or about women in stereotypical female service occupations, but about all of us. Some of the students see my point, but many find it hard to identify with the flight attendants. As with Kanter's discussion of secretaries, I sense a wish on the students' parts to be different from these women. They wish to escape traditional definitions of female gender and not to be subservient, which gets in the way of their identifying with other women across status lines.

The economic organization of women's work contributes to the gender distinctions we see. We read next about the difference between "time discipline"—an approach of standardization, unit organization, and wage labor characteristic of industrialism—and "task orientation"—a preindustrial, or more primitive, approach to the organization of work that involves doing many things at once, or "what it takes" to get a job done.[22] In modern economies, time discipline is associated with men and men's work. A task orientation is more often associated with women and women's work, such as housework and raising children. Sometimes, a task orientation is labeled as superior, such as when men do it (Kanter describes the organization of men at the top as familistic and nonmodern), or when women praise women's work. Le Guin, for example, elevates women's work, referring to "the art of making order where people live. Housekeeping is an art, so is cooking," she says.[23] Yet even when a female orientation is praised, it is hard for me to escape feeling that women's skills are not really valued. In a larger system where advance, and advantage, are measured by conformity to a standardized norm and by time efficiency, women's ways, especially when attached to women, are not, in an economic sense, an advantage.

On the other hand, in a different system, within the bounds of a women's world, for instance, there can be a different kind of economy, one with different goods and services and with its own richness. Marjorie DeVault suggests that difference in noting the nonpaid nature of women's work, and the violation of the character of that work that occurs when a dollar value is assigned it, when an attempt is made to translate into the terms of wage labor the worth of women's "caring work." Women, she says in a study of feeding families, "certainly recognize that feeding a family requires time, effort, and skill. But it is different somehow from paid work." A woman she interviewed tells her, " 'I think love has a lot to do with it.' "[24]

Women's leadership is also a form of women's work, as we see in a book titled *Feminine Leadership, or How to Succeed in Business without Being One of the Boys*. Although I hate the word "feminine" in this book's title and the way that the author views women as incomplete without men, I use Marilyn Loden's advice book because it gives legitimacy to a sense that the students have been feeling increasingly—that women have valuable, even superior, ways of doing things that should be sought after by organizations. For example, says Loden, women often encourage others, rather than trying to control them. Women have a more cooperative management style and teach basic positive values that bring out the best in people.[25] I find that the students like this advice book, for it talks about leadership (and they want to be leaders, not secretaries), and it makes them feel they can be valued as women in a male world without disrupting that world or changing themselves into men. It makes them feel they can succeed after all. Some of the students become irritated with me at this point, because having assigned a reading they liked, I then say there is something wrong with it.

For their research project due at the end of the week, the students examine different types of women's work that interest them—for example, women preparing meals in a kitchen, women administrators working in an office, women on duty in a hospital emergency room, mothers and daughters talking with one another, women cleaning other women's houses, women taking care of other women's children and their own, women managers doing more work to complete a job than men would do because the women see more work as required. As an alternative, the students can study relationships between women, focusing on feelings at deeper emotional levels that are often not spoken of and that are difficult to describe.[26]

To supplement their basic readings and research, the students select additional specialized readings. In one, DeVault discusses how the work women do in planning meals for a family is often invisible, like much of women's work, because it is embedded in other activities. Hochschild, similarly, speaks of how work like housecleaning is not seen: when the work is done well, it is not noticed. We have several readings about sex work—prostitution, massage, and erotic dancing—that show how women face similar dilemmas in sex work as in other occupations. A massage worker, for instance, discusses the problem of losing a sense of herself because her work is other-oriented and requires denial of self. An erotic dancer discusses how her work provides her with a sense of power and self-esteem, yet it is still based on her subordination to men. Women's work often has that kind of double meaning—it is, at once, a show of strength and of deference, or subordinance. An article on transsexualism discusses the extensive work that goes into "passing" as a woman that is often taken for granted, arguing that gender—a cultural fact—is more fundamental than the biological fact of sex. Much that women do is cultural, yet because it is looked at as natural and biological, it is often underappreciated as work.[27]

One means of countering the devaluation of women's work is through women's workplace networks. A study of Chicana cannery workers by Patricia Zavella describes the informal self-help ties that enable cannery women both to learn skills on the job and to help each other emotionally. However, although the cannery women's networks serve the women, they also serve the cannery company. Says Zavella, "Ironically, women's solidarity sometimes encourages women to bear the negative aspects of their jobs. Women's criticism of work conditions are blunted, for they see work friendships as a way to create a 'family' at work and thus the whole situation seems better."[28] When we read about the cannery women's networks, I think of faculty women's networks at universities. These informal networks enable faculty women to help each other and to join in feminist efforts. Yet what Zavella says of the cannery women would also apply—the faculty women's networks bolster the university by making its environment feel more tolerable, at the same time as they support women within it. Even those more independent women's networks considered radical or feminist are, in part, I think, similarly conservative.

With completion of the women's work section, we come to the end of the first half of the course. The next week, we will read about women in the Army, after that about female separatism, feminist processes, and lesbians. I will soon touch on many fears. But, for now, our basic work is done. The students have learned to see women's subordinate status in organizations and to look at how social interactions are affected by gender. I have learned to be sensitive to the students' feelings about what they are studying. When first planning this course, I approached each topic in an intellectual fashion. In teaching it, I have had to realize the highly emotional nature of the subject matter. The students have strong feelings about each topic we discuss, and so do I, and there is often a great difference between our views.

It is frequently said that feminist teaching is preaching to the already convinced. I have not found that to be so. As with any good teaching, feminist teaching seeks to jog and change the mind.[29] In a feminist course, the students are often greatly resistant to learning about gender and the situation of women, indeed far more resistant than they are to learning principles of chemistry. A feminist course, in addition, often seems to have no content, and the teacher to have no expertise, when quite the opposite is true. The content is so vast as to be hard to isolate and the expertise of the teacher lies in combining, at least in my case, a dogmatic stubbornness about the importance of seeing gender with a high sensitivity to the emotional needs of the students. Most courses do not require as much emotional sensitivity, but in a feminist course, both the teacher and the students assume it is extremely important.

The students expect the teacher to be careful of their feelings, not to do anything they do not like, and to be an absolutely wonderful person who has triumphed over the difficulties facing women. I have found this a more than challenging task. I have found it is often lonely to be a teacher in a feminist classroom. It requires a great deal of invisible women's work in class sessions in order both to push the students and to care about their fears, for they often feel very strongly that what they are being taught will be the death of them. While I am teaching this course, I try to increase my understanding of my subject, to improve my sense of how to relate to the students' emotions, and to increase my ability to deal with the problem that, given what I am doing, the students will often look at me with suspicion. They will feel that I am not adequately taking care of them, that I am not a good enough mother.

Because such criticism is hurtful and can be undermining, teaching a course like this requires a continuing belief in one's purposes. I have had to sustain such belief during many weeks when the students feel their old moorings failing and, at the same time, grasp for new insights that will help them in the future.

One of the most impressive things for me has been to see how much the students come to my course—as they do to feminist courses generally—wanting a valuable experience, not a throwaway class, and how pleased they can be with themselves, in the end, to find that they now believe much that is the opposite of what they believed before. They truly do wish to learn, although they often object in the process. At this point in the course, the greatest challenge, separatism, is yet to come. But if we were to stop right now, I think that the students would have begun a fundamental process of change in their views.

Nine

SEPARATISM

My CENTRAL GOAL IN Women and Organizations is to enable the students to recognize the importance of female separatism. I also want them to understand the problems of women's groups. For, if separate women's organizations are important, then it is desirable to grasp the difficulties these groups face, especially the internal difficulties that often threaten the groups' survival. Women's organizations are treated differently by the external world. They receive fewer material resources than men's and mixed organizations, and their boundaries are invaded more carelessly, with greater destructive effect. But the biggest problem for women's organizations is that women themselves devalue what is women's. Women withdraw from women's organizations, fearing contamination by being with other women, or loss of advantage by not being with men. They feel that women's groups are less good than similar male or mixed groups, or that they are unnecessary, or for someone else and not them. Often, women are members of women's groups but do not recognize their membership. "I have never participated in a women's organization," women say, when they have been raised by a single mother, or an extended female family, and are dependent on women's friendships.

Women bring different expectations to women's organizations than to male or mixed groups, and they often have such high expectations of women's groups, and, at the same time, take them so for granted, that the groups perish under both pressure and neglect. Usually, women see women's organizations as failures because they are not like men's groups, rather than interpreting them on their own terms. Separate women's organizations are a major source of power for women—of pride in their own lives and effectiveness in the larger world. Yet when women make gains because of the political functions of their separate organizations, we often abandon the organizations, thinking them no longer useful. Unfortunately, when we lose our organizations, we subsequently lose the basis for sustaining our gains.

When I first put together the syllabus for my course on women and organizations, the value of female separatism seemed to me the main lesson to be learned in the later weeks. By female separatism, I mean women organizing apart from men. I mean organizations composed of women, and run by and for women, to which men are denied access, or, when included, are required to conform to women's terms. The need for separate women's organizations has always seemed to me to follow from what we learn earlier in the course about the subordinate status of women and the permeability of women's individual and group boundaries. Yet, in the later weeks, I find that embracing separatism requires more than logic. I find that the students have deep prior emotional investments in gender integration. They feel separatism to be an assault on their way of life and their expectations for the future. Similarly, I have a deep investment in separatism. When the students reject separatism, as they often do at first—or, if not separatism, lesbianism (and if lesbian is a frightening word, it is mostly because it means separatism)—I feel they are rejecting me.

At the start of the second half of the term, I am faced with a group of women students who are, for the most part, heterosexual. They are more worried about how to take care of men, and how not to exclude men from their lives, than they are about how to open up the range of choices available to them. They see women's worlds as less good than men's worlds and do not want to give up access to male privileges by leaving men behind. I am a lesbian and I depend on women's worlds. I cannot reject them even if I dislike aspects of them, and even though I am often afraid of being among "just women." By the end of the quarter, I want the students to feel as I do. I want them to see their ties with women as so important to them that they are willing to overcome their fears of losing the support of men.

Ideas about separatism are not new in the second half of the course. When I asked the students, in their first research project, to look at characteristics of women's organizations, I wanted them to have images of women's groups as an initial frame of reference, rather than have men's groups come first. When I had them look at what happens to women's groups when men enter, I wanted them to gain a lesson that would be useful later for understanding why separatism is important. The students initially are so oriented to male-world success that they fail to grasp fully my intent in these early research exercises, but the important thing for me is that they do them. In the first two class sessions of the quarter, I make clear to the students deciding about whether to enroll in the course that we will be a class in which women will set the tone. The men present are here to learn about women. This is not a course to take if they are hostile to women. I ask the men to take their lead from how the women in the class speak and act, and to try to follow and blend in. They should not attempt to provide a male viewpoint, or "the" male viewpoint, but to speak for themselves. I ask the women to avoid taking care of the men, or focusing on them. I say that if they turn to the men in the class and say, "How about a male point of view?" I will stop them. This is to be a class centered on women.

The need to work at being women-centered, and at not becoming male dominated, is discussed further during the second week of the course when I divide the students into subgroups. These are groups of four to five members each that will meet every other week outside of class to enable more intimate discussions than are possible in the larger class of twenty to twenty-five. I have noticed that the size of a group is often an important issue for women, who tend to break groups down into ever smaller units to increase intimacy. When I give the students their first subgroup assignment, I tell them that if they have a man in their group to treat him like a woman, which means, "Treat him as an equal. Bring him up to your level. Act as you would if you were a group of all women." The students, of course, will find this hard to do, but it is, I think, an important thing to attempt.

MIXED COMPANY: THE ARMY

We begin the separatism section by reading about women in the United States Army, that large hierarchical, standardized organization that is considered the measure of men. Helen Rogan's *Mixed Company: Women in the Modern Army* is the best book I know of for seeing gendered organizational patterns in a branch of the military. Rogan traces the history of the Women's Army Corps from its inception in 1942 to its ritual dissolution in 1979 asking, What happens to women in a male system, first with, and then without, their own separate women-run organization? For their assignment, the students go through *Mixed Company* thinking about the question, "What got lost when the Women's Army Corps was dissolved?" I ask them to note both specific passages in the book and implicit suggestions, such as feeling tones, and to report these in a paper, identifying, in the end, how they felt about what got lost. Did it make them sad? for instance. They are also to note, in the end, whether they thought the dissolution of the WAC was a step forward or backward for women, explaining why. This assignment plunges us directly into dealing with the question of separatism versus integration. If the students think the dissolution of the WAC was a step backward for women, they are arguing in favor of separatism. If they think the destruction of the WAC was a step forward, they are arguing for integration.

At its peak, the WAC numbered 100,000 women. When the Corps was dissolved and women were then integrated individually into the male Army, they became divided from each other. They faced an environment of harassment and withdrew as individuals, adapting strategies of merging and blending in with men in order to make themselves less conspicuous as targets. There was reason, Rogan says, for male hostility against the women: "Women soldiers deprive men of their masculinity by showing that soldiering is not so terribly hard and by usurping the profession." After the WAC was gone, policies negatively affecting women could not be effectively countered. With the WAC, the women had the power of numbers and of organization; now each woman had the power of one. In their papers, the students mention many losses after the demise of the WAC: loss of "a chain of women protecting, encouraging, and looking out for other women in a world of men," loss of an ability to produce young women leaders, loss of real power, of a WAC esprit, of a sense of closeness and solidarity among women. They mention loss of lesbian inner cliques of power, of special ways of training women, of higher standards for women. Without the WAC, they note, women lost pride and a chain of command that could be used against sexual harassment.[1]

The students' conclusions about whether loss of the WAC was a step forward or backward for women work out differently each year. I was surprised the first time when a majority of the students favored separatism. Last year, I was surprised when a majority favored integration. Even when only a few of the students favor integration, I feel that their arguments for it are irrational. The evidence about losses cited in their papers clearly shows a step backward (the losses are so great), and the students' feelings about these losses are always negative—the losses sadden and anger them. Yet they often argue that integrating women individually into the Army is better than women having a separate organization furthering their interests within the Army. In part, I think, the students argue for integration because events that have occurred historically seem inevitable. In part, the students have a personal investment in integration—they have chosen a coeducational college. I think they also have a prior prejudice in favor of integration that asserts itself despite the evidence in the Army case. When I mention the possibility of such a prejudice to the students, some think it likely. They can see how there might be a bias toward gender integration in our culture. In previous generations and other cultures, separate gender arrangements have seemed natural and desirable, but in our culture, gender integration seems the more desirable arrangement. Some of the students feel their favoring integration does not reflect a cultural prejudice, however, that it is simply a difference between their views and mine.

I often feel a tension in the classroom at this time in the course. One year, several students complained of feeling that suddenly, when we discussed *Mixed Company,* there was a correct way I wanted them to think and they felt that was unfair. Since then, I have sought ways to avoid causing a reaction against me on the students' parts when I seek to teach about the value of separatism. My main solution has been to encourage the students to grasp separatism in intellectual terms. Beginning with *Mixed Company,* I tell the students that I want them to understand the logic behind separatism, despite possible negative feelings they may have, so that they will have a choice. I want them to be able to choose separatism—at times, and if it is useful to them—and to support others who choose it even when they do not. At this point, most would not choose separatism and would criticize others for doing so. The *Mixed Company* assignment provides an opening that enables me to encourage the students to question their prior assumptions about the desirability of integration.

SEPARATISM AS STRATEGY

The topic "Separatism as Strategy" is so emotionally sensitive that its placement in the course has varied. I used to schedule this topic in the next to last week. I felt it belonged at the very end of the course as a culmination, or answer, to all of the problems of "women and organizations" raised previously. Two years ago, I decided to move it up two weeks earlier because I felt there was too much tension in the air beginning with the *Mixed Company* assignment. The students felt pressure from me to believe in separatism, but our readings presenting rationales for it were still weeks away. Moving the separatism readings and discussion two weeks earlier has helped to relieve this tension. In the later weeks, the students now focus on other issues and have time to reconsider separatism. But curiously, although the tension surrounding separatism has been relieved, the students' dissatisfaction simply moves on to the next topic. (I discuss this in chapter 10, "Desires for an Ideal Community of Women.") It seems to me that no matter what I do, feelings of student frustration linger over the last weeks of the course.

I often think that the students feel frustrated at this point because I have failed them—because I do not have a positive enough outlook, or offer them "individual success" solutions, or conduct my classes well enough. I do not usually think that their frustrations reflect the larger world in which solutions to the problems of women are sought, or the fact that no sooner have the students immersed themselves in my course than they must think about leaving it and returning to situations in which others they know do not share the views I have been encouraging.

Our key reading on separatism is Estelle Freedman's "Separatism as Strategy: Female Institution Building and American Feminism, 1870–1930." Freedman poses the question, "What happened to American feminism after the suffrage victory in 1920?" She finds that the achievements of feminism at the turn of the century came through "building separate female institutions." After 1920, when a new generation of women opted for assimilation, feminism and women's gains declined. "As soon as male politicians realized there was no strong female voting block or political organization, they refused to appoint or elect powerful women," Freedman says. "When women tried to assimilate into male-dominated institutions, without securing feminist social, economic, and political bases, they lost the momentum and the networks which had made the suffrage movement possible."

Freedman argues that a lesson of the past is that it is important to create female interest groups and support systems and to continue separatism. "Otherwise, token women may be coopted into either traditionally deferential roles, or they will assimilate through identification with the powers that be." It is also important, she writes, not to be "self-hating of that which is female as we enter a world dominated by men."[2]

In each of the years I have taught my course, I have asked Estelle Freedman to come as a guest to my first separatism session. She teaches at the university where I have taught the course most frequently, and when I first read her article, I felt she sounded so sane and rational about separatism, while I felt so emotional about it, that I wanted her to come to my class to help me explain separatism to the students. I feared they would reject the rationale for it if they heard about it only from me. When she comes as my guest, Freedman addresses the concerns and fears of the students. She amazes me by making separatism acceptable to them. In addition to discussing her article, she asks the students to name their fears—fear of being lesbian, of excluding men, and of losing the advantages of gender integration. She points out that these fears cause the students to reject separatism perhaps unfairly, and she discusses the value separate women's organizations have had in her own professional life.

For their papers this week, the students write about a situation in their own lives in which the issue of female separatism arises for them, identifying insights from the readings that help them to understand this situation better. Marilyn Frye's discussion of "separatism and power" also helps them understand their fears. Separatism, says Frye, is "denial of access," that is, women denying men access to women. There are many kinds of "feminist separations," she says, ranging from lesbian separatist communities, to women leaving a home or marriage, to more ordinary withdrawals from interactions with men. In Frye's view, both women and men rightly fear separatism because "when women separate, they are insubordinate." Separatism is an assumption of power— "the slave who decides to exclude the master from her hut is declaring herself not a slave." Separatism, says Frye, generates in women fear of punishment and reprisal, and in men a fear of loss of the goods and services they receive from women, a fear that is often buried beneath men's expressions of hostility. "When those who control access have made you totally accessible," Frye says to women, "your first act of taking control must be denying access, or must have denial of access as one of its aspects."[3]

Frye speaks as a lesbian and a philosopher (separatism, she says, is "undeniably connected with lesbianism"). At first, I thought the students would reject her essay because of its outrageous tone. However, they do not. It clarifies issues for them. The Frye essay was given to me one year by a graduate student and was not on my initial reading list for the course. Had I known about it, I probably would not have included such a blatant lesbian reading, assuming it would make separatism too hard for the students to accept. It has been important for me to see that avoiding confrontation with the students' fears of separatism is not the best way to deal with this subject. Both Frye and Freedman suggest to the students that there are grounds for their fears of separatism. This acknowledgment helps relieve their fears.

We read several other discussions of separatism. Regina Morantz-Sanchez' historical study of women physicians in American medicine describes how separate women's organizations have served women in medicine in different ways than mixed-gender organizations. Women's medical colleges and hospitals provided training receptive to the needs of women; an atmosphere in which women set the direction; female role models; and distinguished programs in such fields as preventive medicine and gynecology. Although laboring under a "stigma of inferiority" and having fewer material resources than male institutions, these women's organizations met longstanding needs. When the women's colleges and hospitals closed their doors at the end of the nineteenth century, women entered integrated institutions and had to deal with problems of male dominance and an ethos of professionalism that stressed aggressiveness, scientific objectivity, impersonality, individual advancement, and "cure over care," rather than the more traditional women's values of devotion to family, compassion, use of feeling and intuition, and collaboration in caregiving. For women, Morantz-Sanchez says, coeducation would "ultimately prove disappointing."[4]

I find Morantz-Sanchez' study useful for indicating that separate women's organizations are not just fringe groups, like failing bookstores, but part of mainstream institutions, like medicine. At this point in the course, I want the students to see women's organizations as not outside their expectations for their own professional lives and to feel they may need such organizations in order to advance some of their values, such as the "sympathy" in science. I want them to feel they have a stake in making sure that women's organizations survive, or in creating new women's organizations.

Paula Giddings' book on Delta Sigma Theta and the Black sorority movement attests further to the value of separate women's organizations. Giddings speaks of the history of African American sororities and of how they have represented a lifetime commitment for many Black women. African American sororities have had large and coherent memberships (Delta Sigma Theta had a membership of 125,000 at the time of Giddings' writing) and they have been a source of community service, leadership, pride, and solidarity for Black women. Says Giddings, "It struck me that Black women may be among their freest, their happiest, and, in some ways, their most fulfilled when they are together in their organizations."[5]

Bernice Johnson Reagon, in an article "Coalition Politics," also discusses experiences of African American women and the value of women's organizations. These groups can be like being in your own "barred little room" with people just like you, she says, or they can be like going out of that room in order to be in a broader coalition. By comparison with the small room, the broader coalition is often an uncomfortable experience. Although its members may all be women, they will be different kinds of women who may not feel they have much in common. Says Reagon, "Wherever women gather together it is not necessarily nurturing. It is coalition building. And if you feel the strain, you may be doing some good work."[6] Similarly, Alma Garcia, in a discussion of Chicana feminists, suggests an image of women feeling uncomfortable—conflicted, alienated, and alone—when among other women different from them in important respects—class or race, for instance—and thus needing more specialized separatisms.[7] A Chicana feminist group allows a Chicana to feel more identified with other women than she would in a white women's feminist group, for example. Among other Chicanas, she feels closer to home. Echoes of this sentiment are found in discussions of other specialized separatisms. In Esther Chow's study of Asian American women, in studies of lesbian communities, and in studies of other women's groups, a repeated theme is that women feel more at home in small groups of others like them.[8]

Our readings on specialized separatisms suggest to me the nature of a large-scale women's organization, such as a women's movement. It is a coalition, or confederation. It is separatist in the sense of drawing a more than usually selective boundary between itself and an outer male world, but also in the sense that, within itself, it is composed of many different female separatisms. It is made up of ever smaller units in which women can relate increasingly closely with other women with whom they feel an affinity. Although the outside world's way of viewing a women's organization is often to call it "factionalized" (to view it as a failure to be coherent or whole), more properly, it may be seen as a mosaic of tiny separatisms. These groups touch occasionally at their borders, or in spirit, or through a vague knowledge of one another. But that is all.

My point is that all organizations need not look like the United States Army. They need not have a chain of command, a structure that contains all the members, or even procedures for working out disagreements. The image of a women's organization is different. It is less defined by standardization (by the imposition of a uniform style of behavior, or of a worn uniform) than by affinity—by congregations that form because of likeness, or attraction, or to close gaps between members. It is less defined by "power over" than by "conformity with," less defined by conflict than by avoidance of conflict. It is also often short-lived. A women's organization will dissolve and reform rather than survive for power's sake and become like a men's organization.

FEMINIST AND WOMEN'S PROCESSES

To enable further discussion of the nature of women's groups, I have titled our next week "Feminist Processes and Alternative Organizational Forms." Our main reading is an essay on feminist process, self-published in 1974 by a four-member women's collective.[9] It is notable to me that I need to turn to 1974 to get the kind of statement I find useful at this point. Some of our other readings in the course are also older, and for a similar reason. Recent studies of women's organizations tend to be less proudly self-assertive, less critical of men, and less down-to-earth about women's experiences than those written in the 1970s. The more recent works are more theoretical and assimilationist, and they focus on different issues—success, professionalism, equal treatment, stages of growth, multiple identities, divisions between women, and how women's ways are similar to men's, or, if different, not threatening. The more recent writings are less about creating alternatives and making change than about women taking their rightful place as part of a mainstream. They are often written by academic feminists, whose commitments are different—more careerist, and more constrained—than those of the previous political feminists.

The authors of the essay "Feminist Process" describe dynamics of their collective group, such as use of "mosaic logic" and anecdotal speaking. The women in their group tell stories about their experiences, using multiple images, and seeking insight through processes of mutual identification. They avoid speaking in a debating manner that uses linear logic, techniques of persuasion, and other speech forms that establish hierarchy. Instead, they work to relate to each other as equals, which requires overcoming expectations that a woman who is more verbal, or older, or who acts like a "good woman" is superior to others. Although women may start with a good deal of equality, even among women, it seems to take determined effort to keep interactions from becoming "hierarchical and competitive." The dynamics of this feminist group are similar to many noted during our first weeks of the course as characteristics of women's groups more generally. Deborah Tannen discusses one such feature, "women as cooperative overlappers," noting how women often finish each other's sentences, and seem to interrupt each other, when they are actually deliberately overlapping to maintain connection or rapport.[10]

Joyce Rothschild-Whitt speaks further of equality and of how collectivist organizations should not be judged by the same standards as those used to assess bureaucratic organizations. They should be assessed "not as failures to achieve bureaucratic standards they do not share, but as efforts to realize wholly different values." She notes that collective groups often seek ideals of consensus, community, and equality, and the integration of intellectual and manual labor and of the emotional and the intellectual. They seek relationships that are defined by individual whole persons, rather than by roles and a segmentation of tasks.[11] Women's groups are, I think, natural collectives in that female socialization makes many collective ways first nature for women. I ask the students how women's organizations are nonetheless different from other collective groups, such as mixed-gender collectives or Japanese-style, or participative, management groups, which also have egalitarian goals.

I always have problems answering this question about the difference of women's groups, but the students, by now, have learned to see gender. They say that it changes an organization when women are members because women bring with them female gender socialization from the outside world—habits of deference and invisiblity, different styles of speech, different feelings of comfort. Their socialization affects how women act and are perceived by others. Simply imposing a collective group structure on individuals does not obliterate effects of gender differences. I ask the students about the difference of women's groups because when I have described women's group characteristics to organizational theorists, they often say, "Oh, that's just like a modern management group," or they say it is like any other egalitarian group. I want the students not to let such responses make women's group characteristics disappear for them, as they often have for me. To bolster their sense of gender difference, we read about how women create "centrarchies"—structures of "circles with central coordinators but no hierarchical leaders."[12]

Women's groups often encounter problems of conflict between hierarchy and equality. In "Women Working with Women in the University," Carol Ascher describes a women's studies program in the 1970s that had egalitarian goals for students, faculty, and staff and, at the same time, operated within a university and was therefore heavily affected by hierarchy. Female faculty striving for advancement in the university often held themselves apart from, and above, others in the program. Ascher found this disturbing because of her egalitarian feminist goals and because, in her position as program administrator, she was often exposed to the hurts that resulted. The university hierarchy, she says, contributed to "perpetual obfuscations of honesty, underground alliances and convoluted agendas among women who, overtly, were trying to work together in an egalitarian feminist manner." Under the stress, "some days were particularly bad, my neck and shoulders became rigid concrete bricks." Ascher speaks of male behavior patterns among the women in the program, such as career climbing, as "conscious but unexamined," while female patterns are often unconscious. "A women's studies program is a collection of mothers and sisters," she says. "It is a composite of intimacies, rivalries, rebellions." Yet these and other strong feelings were often "diffused and disguised," and lesbianism was the "soft spot" that everyone was afraid to discuss.[13]

I like Ascher's description of the women's studies program and find it very real. The students in my class, however, are not as glad as I am to stumble across this glimpse of reality. They want women's organizations not to be conflicted and disappointing of their ideals, and they do not want to have to deal with lesbianism. Yet the Ascher reading illustrates how women's organizations are never strictly egalitarian, or strictly women's forms, but are always infiltrated by hierarchical, and often bureaucratic, forms of social organization. The result is a hybrid that is sometimes difficult to tolerate because of how it fails women's ideals.

When we speak about feminist processes in this section of the course, I am aware that I see feminist strategies as having much in common with traditional women's ways. In large part, these strategies are a deliberate valuing, rather than a devaluing, of women's socialization. Similarly, feminist organizations are, in many ways, like traditional women's organizations. Both a feminist organization (a feminist collective, or a women's studies program) and a traditional women's organization (a female extended family, or a charity, or church group) will have many similar characteristics. For instance, there will often be a bias toward equality among members, a valuing of the personal dimension of members' lives, indirect styles of expression, and strong conflict avoidance tendencies. There will, of course, be differences. The feminist organization will be more self-conscious about having a goal of changing a male system of oppression, rather than being a ladies' auxiliary to it. The traditional women's organization will take more pride in standing behind its men and in engaging in customary female activities, such as caretaking, deferring, and supporting. But the traditional women's organization also has strategies of undermining male systems. Consider the traditional women's habit of manipulating men for women's purposes, of working around a husband or father, for example, and of keeping men (husbands, bosses) out of separate women's spheres—the kitchen, the nursery, women's social circles, and work groups. A recent literature on cultures of resistance in organizations such as department stores, restaurants, and families discusses women's ingenuity, self-direction, and the maintenance of special women's worlds even in subordinate statuses.[14]

Differences between feminist and traditional women's organizations are not unimportant, I think, but they are mainly differences in emphasis. For the feminist organization, the values of system change and of individual liberation (or reversing habits of subordinance) are usually more important in the life of the organization, and more prominent in the self-concept of members, than these values are in a traditional women's organization. The difference in what its members value causes a feminist organization to overestimate its nonauxiliary function, just as members of a traditional women's organization will overstate their organization's male support role. In my readings about women's organizations, I have been surprised by the many similarities in women's interactional styles that appear across different cultures and in different types of organizations. In studies of Nazi women's organizations, of women of the Ku Klux Klan, of Mary Kay Cosmetics and other women's businesses; studies of nuns, women's church groups, women's schools, extended female families, different racial and ethnic women's groups, and of feminist movement groups, the most striking thing to me is how similar the patterns are. In all these groups, in ways that seem to me significant, women seek to avoid conflict with each other. They seek a oneness, or sense of solidarity, with one another and equality in their relationships. Their disappointments with each other are often great and their expectations high. Women's groups tend to be life sustaining for their members, although often they are spoken of disparagingly. In these groups, women seek to assert female styles of social relating despite conflicts with male styles. In many of the groups, women seek fervently to protect their different way.[15]

I think that the similarities in the dynamics of women's organizations are due to women's subordinate status—to the fact that women's gender characteristics are the characteristics of people who have learned to defer in order to survive. The similarities are also due to the fact that women's particular type of subordination has historically been linked to certain kinds of work, such as childcare and the care of men. Both the subordinate status and the link to caring work give female characteristics much of their definition, even when that definition is embroidered very differently in different settings.[16]

REACHING FOR SEPARATISM

During these later weeks of the course, as we focus on the functions and problems of separate women's organizations, I feel that the students are reaching. They are often seeking to take an intellectual position to which they were previously opposed. The strain of reaching for separatism, and the complications that separatism raises for the students, are reflected in their papers, which often speak of a past in which separatism was unacceptable to them:[17]

> I never expected to be for separatism. (Peggy)

> For most of my life, I have rejected coalitions and separatism as negative things. (Maureen)

> In the past, I would never have identified with a separatist female organization. In fact, the reason that I never considered myself a "feminist" is that I did not consider myself a separatist. (Ann)

> I had an integrationist bias, but after reading, I have converted into a separatist. However, I realize the issue is more complex than I had anticipated. Thus, although I now favor separatism, I still harbor mixed feelings about it. (Kelly)

Although I want the students to accept separatism, I am always surprised when they do. For if they are reaching for separatism, I am reaching for a sense that my encouraging them to value it is legitimate. In another feminist course, the teacher might have, as a goal, that the students accept, and identify with, the term "feminism." In my course, the term "separatism" carries that weight. These are, I think, conversion terms. They are tools in the process of effecting a change from old to new values. In my case, the change sought is a valuing of alliances with women.

It matters a great deal to me to accomplish the shift to separatism. I sometimes wonder whether my emphasis on separatism is my lesbianism passing. Two weeks later in the course, we discuss a lesbian community, but I do not then demand that the students become lesbians, or that they open themselves to a lesbian choice. I seem, instead, to use separatism to get as far as I can toward having them value relationships with other women.

Often in these weeks of the course, I stay awake at night thinking about my experiences with separate women's organizations. I want to tell the students about these experiences, in part to indicate that feeling conflicted about participating in a women's group does not mean one has to reject such a group, and, in part, because when I see the students wrestling with separatism, I know I have also done so. In class, I speak to them first of my experience at a women's college, painfully thinking back to my first year. In my first two weeks at the college, I tell the students, I decided to transfer out. Then I stayed for two years because people said transferring right away would not look good on my transcript. I wanted to leave because that Seven Sisters' women's college felt like a summer camp to me. It felt artificial—not like part of the real (male) big-city world. Most of the faculty at the college were male and I felt they talked down to the students. In classes, the students knitted, were quiet and polite, mostly listened to the teacher, and did not challenge the teacher or one another. The classes felt deadly to me.

As importantly, I think, I left that college because I was afraid of lesbians. I did not know the word "lesbian" at the time, nor did I know what a homosexual was.[18] I only knew that when I saw certain women socializing with one another—women who were members of sports teams, for example—I felt excluded, sick in my stomach, and frightened. When I saw certain student leaders, I felt similarly. I wanted to get away from them. I then transferred to a large coeducational university in a big city, where I found the air of challenge in the classroom that I sought. The students, mostly men, spoke out in classes. I was glad for the change. I felt safer. The courses I took at the big-city university were far easier than my courses at the women's college. Later, I concluded that my college education really occurred during my first two years at the women's college, when I stayed up late many nights reading in the library and felt alone and out of place.

A second type of experience I mention to my class occurred when I first became a lesbian. I was, by then, a graduate student. I had been sexually involved with women for several years while married to a gay man, but now I was moving out of the marriage and seeking a comparable relationship with a woman. I started to attend meetings of a lesbian group in order to meet other lesbians. The group met every two weeks for mutual support and discussion. It was large for its type, numbering thirty-five to forty women a session, with members drawn from the university and the surrounding community. I was uncomfortable in this group, which was my first lesbian group. I felt that the women present sat around getting nowhere in their discussions, only supporting each others' prejudices and saying "far out." They avoided conflict, avoided talking politics and intellectually challenging one another, were cliquish and quiet, and seemed to want just to bask in each others' presence.

In each meeting I attended, probably because I felt frightened, I challenged the "nothing happening" nature of the group. In one meeting, a handful of undergraduate students from a psychology class came and asked to study our group. The undergraduates were both women and men. When the larger group was about to refuse to let them stay, I said, "You kick them out, you kick me out too." Then I walked out with the students and waited in the hallway outside the meeting room door until someone came to get me. When the larger group wanted to have a guest come to speak with us, I asked, "Why do we need a guest?" I wanted us to discuss ourselves. I proposed that we go around in a circle and each tell why we were there. We went around the circle and I marveled at my nerve. I still had a wedding ring on my left hand. I wanted the group to talk about politics and do something radical, and I kept bringing that up.

After a while, the group's attendance started dropping. From a high of forty, soon only half a dozen women came. The meeting where they kicked out the undergraduates seemed the last straw. In the next meeting, the few women who showed up played guitars and sang moody songs and lay around on the floor with the lights turned low. Everyone present ignored me. They did not even look in my direction. "We are going to be happy in spite of you," I felt I was being told.

I managed to destroy the whole group, I told my class seventeen years later. The students laughed. They felt I could not have had so much power as to destroy a group of forty women. Yet I felt I had. Women's groups are fragile, it seems to me. They do not absorb disturbing events in the same way male, or bureaucratic, groups do. Instead, they splinter and disappear, ostracizing a disturbing member, and blending back into the environment. I was reminded of the students' research in the third week of the course when they looked at women's groups and what happens when a man enters—the women's group often disbands.

The year after I joined my first lesbian group, I joined a smaller lesbian group building a women's coffeehouse. At an initial meeting, disturbed again by the passive nature of a women's group, I requested that we conduct our meetings in a more organized fashion, with an agenda, and starting on time. Someone called me a male chauvinist, got up, and walked out, and one-third of the group went with her. I decided I would, in the future, remain quiet in lesbian groups. The next year when I moved to the Midwest and joined the lesbian community portrayed in *The Mirror Dance,* I was careful not to challenge anyone, or any way of doing things. I had, by then, learned to be more respectful of lesbian groups. I also did not want to be ostracized from the group.

With these examples, I try to convey to the students in my class that participation in women's groups is often difficult. One is likely to have conflicting feelings toward women's groups, even to flee them. However, by now, I think the students have a different priority than understanding the troubles of women's organizations. They have read about separatism, they are familiar with women's styles of social relating. They wish now to experience what is good about women's groups.

STUDENTS ON SEPARATISM

Because the students have put much work into accepting separatism, I wish, in closing, to give a sense of their efforts in their own words. Their writing lets me know how hard it is for them to accept the principles of separatism. When I ask them, in their papers, to discuss their feelings, they say:[19]

> RACHEL: I feel as if I am working toward embracing separatism, but right now I feel guilty that I may not be able to do so.

> CATHY: I find separatism a confusing issue. I believe that it is something positive for women, but I also do not want to separate from everything in this world that is "male."

> YOKO: Although I can better understand the merits of separatism, I must admit that I still feel somewhat uncomfortable with it. I wonder how groups will ever come together if they re-

main so separate. Or perhaps I am afraid that if I participate more fully in such groups, I may never want to rejoin the "rest of society." (A thought that is extremely unsettling for me—I don't know why!)

The students use their papers to work toward accepting separatism, using insights from the readings to help them. I find their comments moving—both because they show a strong sense of problem solving and because they show an effort to embrace something initially felt as frightening and repugnant. As the students seek to embrace separatism, they seek to embrace themselves:

> MARIE: Although intellectually I see the value of separatism, I first reacted strongly with fear and aversion. Insights from the readings and discussion helped me understand and reduce this fear. In Frye's article, she explains why people react so strongly to a woman who owns her own power, who doesn't "subordinate." Another insight that is meaningful to me concerns the fear of lesbianism. I grew up devaluing relationships with women and, quite frankly, avoiding them. As I face this truth, I find a load of pain and loss. And I embrace that part of me that hungers to be accepted, nurtured, cared for, loved by a woman/in woman's ways. And this hunger scares me. Does it make me a lesbian?

> MARTA: The hardest topic I have had to wrestle with in this class is the issue of separatism. Before this class, I was not sure what separatism was. I thought it was a lot of men-hating women living in their own fantasy world away from reality. However, as I read, I realized that separatism was not so simple. It is about a movement within a bigger social capsule. It is about claiming your own strength and power. It is about defining yourself. After doing the readings, I discovered that I had been wrong. Separatism was good. However, I only thought of it as "good to an extent," and I did not think of it as a personal choice for me because of the race issue and the need

for Chicana-Chicano unity. Then I did my research paper on Chicana separatism. After I wrote my paper, I realized that I wanted to become involved in a separatist Chicana group.

LESLIE: Frye's article helped me see that separatism doesn't necessarily mean joining an all women's organization, that actions I'd always attributed to my "independence," and my desire to take care of myself, were also separatist actions. Reagon's assertion that not enough women recognize that the definition of "woman" is very broad—and that this causes many women to reject feminism because they are made to feel they are not woman-identified enough—spoke to me. I have felt rejected by, and resented by, other women for not always being the "nurturing" type at all times.

After reading the articles, I ached so badly to have close women friends, and I realized how much I've isolated myself from women because I felt I didn't qualify as a woman. I think women have carved for themselves a very limiting definition of what is "feminine" and this makes it difficult. I've had a relatively easy time finding men with similar interests and qualities as me, but these relationships leave me unsatisfied. I feel they've stunted my reflective side and made me feel isolated, as if I can't relate to other people. I told a male friend recently that I felt lonely because I felt like I didn't have any peers. I think I meant women when I told him that.

ROSE: Separatism was not a word I had seen or used prior to the past few weeks but it now has a considerable significance for me. When I entered the workforce, I believed I had no choice but to try to integrate by emulating the males. There were no other women in my area of engineering. But behind me in school were more and more women earning proper credentials. When they entered the workplace the effect was almost immediate. As a lone woman, I could be treated as a man, but with several women in the group, the men began to adjust their behavior. Office arrangements started to equalize. The term "girls" began to be exchanged for "women." Because of witnessing this, I am encouraged, but I am also concerned that we will slip back into a deep valley.

ARNIE: I have always believed that separatism is at the heart of all the world's problems. This year I have been forced to take another look at separatism as a result of this class. One thing I really got out of the readings was the concept that there are a lot of different ideologies and ideas that the term separatism encompasses. This makes the idea slightly easier for me to deal with.

JULIA: I no longer see the choice between integration and separatism as simple. If the valuation of women is furthered through an organizational form, I say the form is a good one.

Separatism is the one topic in my course that most reveals to me the process of education. With time, intellectual nourishment, and a strategy that allows them to deal with their emotions, the students come to view the world and themselves differently. The degree to which they change their views to accept separatism sometimes frightens me. But the openness with which they seek a change and accomplish it, and the satisfaction they often express over their change of views seem positive to me. It is as if adopting new views is the reason they have come to college. I think that teachers are often discouraged from changing the minds of students on controversial social issues because it is considered brainwashing, or political, to do so. It takes nerve to suppose one has a right to bring students around to one's own way of thinking. But such nerve is needed or things fall to the nerveless, to those who will act less on principle than in order to conform. It is when the students deal with separatism that I most feel their needs of other women and their distinctly female desires for strength and for freedom from subordination. The students initially fear that separatism will make them into man-hating women, but, in the end, it makes them more in touch with the female in themselves.

Ten

DESIRES FOR AN IDEAL COMMUNITY
OF WOMEN

THE EIGHTH WEEK OF Women and Organizations is titled on the sylla-bus "Circles within Circles: Dilemmas of Belonging in a Women's Group." Here I begin to pale, for I know what is coming. We are going to read my book about a lesbian community. From experiences of past years, I know that the students approach this book with high expecta-tions that, within its pages, they will find an ideal women's community. If women are good, then lesbians, they now expect, must be exception-ally good in their relationships with one another.

An important part of the students' experience in reading *The Mirror Dance: Identity in a Women's Community* will be coming to terms with the fact that a lesbian community is primarily real.[1] It is not a social expression of ideal female sensitivity and responsiveness, but rather an expression of many of the women's ways we have been reading about all along in the course, with the added dimension that its members are les-bians. These are women who are willing to be intimate and erotic with other women, and who are more acknowledging of the depth of their emotional needs for other women than straight women often are.

The lesbians in my book formed an informal self-help community in a midwestern town. The book presents a collective portrait of their community through the voices of its more than sixty members. *The Mirror Dance* is written in an unusual way, I tell the students. Reading it is like being taken into the community. The book focuses on conflicts between merger and separation, between an individual's feeling part of a group and feeling apart from it.

HOMOPHOBIA IN THE CLASSROOM

I am often impressed with the work the students do when they read *The Mirror Dance*. In the first few years I taught the course, I was moved when students who had initially been biased against lesbians would come to a different conclusion after reading the book and writing a paper about it, and they would be proud of having changed their views. The assignment I give on *The Mirror Dance* asks the students to trace their feelings as they read the book and to write about these feelings in a paper. In the end, they draw conclusions about the import, to them, of their own responses. What insights do they gain by considering their feelings?

The first two times I gave this assignment, I asked the students to add to the end of their papers a paragraph identifying characteristics of the lesbian community described in *The Mirror Dance* that were those of a women's organization. To my shock, each year, several of the students said, "I just cannot see this lesbian community as a women's organization. It is the opposite of what I think a women's group is." To these students, it seemed, lesbians were not women. After receiving such responses in the second year, I decided to delete the extra paragraph from my assignment. I was not ready to take on the problem of rejection of lesbianism that the students' views pointed to.

In their papers about *The Mirror Dance,* the students reveal a range of emotional responses:[2]

> I could really identify with the women in *The Mirror Dance* who were searching for their own identity within the group. (Yoko)

I saw many parallels to my own experience. (Rose)

I found myself very emotionally involved. . . . I felt confused and frustrated. I also felt fascinated by the complex workings of the interactions of the women. (Julia)

I was disappointed by the community examined in *The Mirror Dance* because it was far less noble and infused with political meaning than I thought it should be. (Kim)

As I progressed through the book, my feelings switched from surprise to acceptance, because all of a sudden the community didn't seem that weird. . . . The chapter on children really hit home with me. (Peggy)

I was sad because so many of the women felt they could not tell their parents. (Arlene)

In general, I feel the students appreciate *The Mirror Dance* and its multivoiced style, and they use it to come to valuable recognitions about lesbians and about themselves. The problems that arise concern how they judge the social reality described in the book. In class, when the students discuss their feelings in response to the study, I mostly listen, for I have found that the students feel very differently when reading *The Mirror Dance* than I did when writing it. The main difference is that they view the community depicted in the book as a group that does not live up to their ideals. To say they feel disappointed puts their response mildly. They feel disheartened, painfully let down, disturbed, confused, and angry. Not all feel this way, but most do. They do not like the way members of this lesbian community gossip about one another, or exclude male children from a Thanksgiving dinner, or conform to group dress norms that stress androgynous clothes, or how they deal with their personal relationship difficulties. They do not like how the women speak of themselves in terms of other women—that Mary is Jo's lover and Amy's former lover, for example.

The students report feeling most positively about the community after reading the chapters in the last section of the book that deal with the outside world, and with how members experience difficulties at work and among their families that cause them to keep their lesbianism a secret. The students like being drawn into the lesbian world described in the book. However, most say they would not want to be part of a community like this one. For these students, the community is "them," and the students have specific troubles with what "they" do.

It always seems curious to me that when the students read *The Mirror Dance,* they take as true many of the negative statements about the community that are made by the women in the pages of my book. They assume the community is what its members say it is, without seeing beyond the surface nature of the complaints to the more underlying social reality. In a way, despite their protests, the students in my classes become extensions of the voices of the women in the book. For instance, a student will say, "Marge says the group felt suffocating to her. That's how I felt." Or, "Leslie says the community was only interested in emotional trauma. I wouldn't be able to stand that." However, I have noticed that the students are selective in which complaints they identify with. Certain criticisms made by the women of the community are seized upon more than others, which suggests to me that something more is occurring than simply personal identification.

After I have listened to the students' responses and read their papers, I come to the next class session seeking to explain a few of the community dynamics I think some of them do not understand. I want to explain how a social group may not be exactly what its members think it is. Especially, because it is highly criticized by the students, I want to explain how gossip (talking about others and being talked about) is not necessarily bad, but, in this community, helpful and desirable. Individuals need to talk about each other in lesbian communities in order to learn about how to be a lesbian, or how to get along with each other, or to solve their problems. There are no lesbian television shows or large numbers of books, magazines, and public images, or grandmothers and mothers passing down instructions. Most self-knowledge must be created in face-to-face interactions and through word of mouth. When I offer such an explanation to the students, I think I am doing so because they lack skills for analyzing interactions in a lesbian setting. I do not think, although I often feel, that there is an emotional dimension to the students' apparent failure of sociological understanding.

To reject a group because it gossips too much seems to me a bit strange. In part, this may be a rejection of what women traditionally do. It may represent a wish not to be associated with women's more familial and down-to-earth ways. By extension, I think, given the subject of our reading, it may also reflect a wish not to be caught in a web of lesbianism—a web of women being intimate with one another. In brief, I think I have overlooked the extent to which the students' discomforts with the community in *The Mirror Dance* are products of homophobia—of fears of being among lesbians, and of being a lesbian. Thus one distances oneself. A student says, "It's okay for them, but not for me," and points to specific behaviors she feels are intolerable, in order to keep intact a sense of herself as heterosexual, or as a woman apart from a lesbian community.

When I discuss *The Mirror Dance* with the students, I try to be careful of their emotional responses to the book so they will not feel intimidated by the fact that I wrote it, or by the fact that I am a lesbian. When I think about their feelings after they first discuss them, I consider what the students do not understand. In other words, I deal with their criticisms in intellectual terms. Thus, I do a parallel distancing to that done by the students. I do this to protect myself, for the community in *The Mirror Dance* was once my community. I was friends and lovers with women in it. When I lived there, I felt it was a very good community. It was not too constraining or too gossipy for me. When the students criticize this community, they criticize something I am very much identified with.

I think that, in part, the students judge the lesbian community in *The Mirror Dance* harshly because they are largely unaware of the degree to which heterosexual culture is so taken for granted as to make anything lesbian seem tainted and wrong. Yet I, too, have this problem. Why else would I shrink from confronting it in the students? I may see the lesbian community in my study as good and as acceptable, but I certainly view the lesbian in myself as less than acceptable. Or why would I feel I cannot tell the students they are hurting me with their views, that they are not granting to lesbians—and, by implication, to me—the same quality of respect, and equality of judgment, they grant to themselves? I have taught my course on women and organizations for eight years, but I have never once talked about the way lesbianism is rejected in it and viewed, by most of the students, as undesirable. I urge the students to identify with separatism when we study it, but I do not make a similar request that they embrace lesbianism. Yet if I can ask the students to question their integrationist values, surely I can ask them to question their heterosexual values.

I have only recently come to feel that I ought to discuss with the students the issue of homophobia in our classroom. Sometimes, such as this past year, the homophobia is more evident to me. This year followed that in which I denied permission to the hostile male graduate student to take one of my courses. I felt that the students in my classroom now, who knew about that episode, were more afraid than usual. They avoided talking about the lesbian content of *The Mirror Dance*, and one graduate student attacked the book's style "on literary grounds," with a vehemence I could not understand other than as an attempt to separate herself from its lesbian subject matter. Usually, however, the homophobia is more masked and more invisible.

Sometimes, I think, it is visible only to me. The first year I taught the course, for instance, I was afraid to have the students read an article titled "Beyond 'Subjectivity': The Use of the Self in Social Science," which I had written about the process of researching and writing *The Mirror Dance*.[3] It discussed my personal experiences in the community and, in particular, my having sexual desires toward some of the women I interviewed. The article had already been published in a sociological journal, but I kept it out of my course reader because I feared that if the students were to read it, they would fear me in the classroom. I thought that if I subsequently put a hand on a student's shoulder, she would feel I was trying to seduce her and that everyone in the class would look at me and see a child molester. Finally, approaching the week when we were to read *The Mirror Dance,* I reconsidered my decision. I wanted the students to have my story of how I did my study. I also wanted not to be driven by fear. Fortunately, the students liked the article. It seemed not to frighten them so much as to make them feel more appreciative of my study and of me. I think it helped relieve their fears because it spoke of sexual matters explicitly and in a way that was personal to me.

But my point is not the students' fears, but my own degree of fear. Homophobia has affected my Women and Organizations class not only because the students fear lesbianism, but because I do. Occasionally the homophobia in my classroom is evident to me, such as when I feel the students in a class withholding themselves when we discuss *The Mirror Dance,* or when I am aware of withholding myself, as in not giving out my article. However, most of the time, the fear of lesbianism—of being intimate with other women, and of choosing women over men—is present in the classroom but underground. I would like to speak more about homophobia in my classes, but I am not sure, at present, how to do so.

DESIRES FOR AN IDEAL CLASS

By the time we have finished *The Mirror Dance,* the students are edgy. We are near the end of the term and something has not happened yet. There remains, I think, a nagging question, What about that ideal women's community? I have found that, before I know it, this question can become, what's wrong with this class? Although I have moved separatism two weeks earlier, divided the class into subgroups for greater intimacy, and offered *The Mirror Dance* as a way to come to terms with the disappointment a community of women can arouse, the students still are unresolved on this issue. In the later weeks of the course, some of the students now find our class the women's group that is not ideal enough. They look around the classroom and at me and say that when they speak, they do not get a connected enough response from other students. They say they feel alone. What good is this class as a women's organization if such a sense of isolation exists for them?

Hearing their complaints, I feel at fault. Why could I not have done better? I think. If I ask the students what I can do to relieve the difficulty, they tell me to change the place where I sit, or to direct the conversation so that it relates them better to one another and leaves them feeling less alone. However, since I feel that the underlying problems are such that I cannot fix them in this way, I refuse to change the place where I sit, or to direct the conversation differently. Instead, I try to explain to the students the source of the problem by discussing dynamics of women's groups. I hope that if the students understand our situation better, they will not judge the class, and me, so harshly.

The main explanatory variable I point out to them is that, it seems to me, there is a strong desire for union among women. In our class, we feel we should all be as one, that no individual should feel isolated from others. Yet the way I teach tends to frustrate that desire. In my classes, I often isolate individuals. I ask each student to speak from her experience—about her own inner thoughts and feelings—and to have that always be the focus. This is different from an other-orientation, which women often feel more comfortable with, and it is different from challenging others' thoughts, as is common in most university classes.

My goal is the very different one of having the students articulate their own individual experiences in response to our readings and research assignments. This results in a classroom where what happens, most often, is that one person speaks and everyone else listens attentively. Then another person speaks. We develop a whole that sounds more like a mosaic, in the sense referred to in our "Feminist Process" reading, than it sounds like a traditional classroom discussion, or even like the normal exchange in a women's group. The exchange in a women's group will usually not be as directed by one individual—in this case, by me as the teacher—nor will it have as great an internal psychological focus. Rather, the priority will be the creation of a surface feeling of agreement among the women present. Yet I seek to individualize women precisely because we are usually merged. I feel more comfortable with such individualizing, and more threatened by a surface sense of merger, than perhaps others do.

I feel good listening to all the different individual experiences that are discussed by the students in the kinds of classes I create. I therefore probably overlook the discomfort my method of teaching may cause others. For me, in hearing about everyone's experiences, and offering my own, the air seems full of so much evidence for learning that I do not stop to think that this type of class process will be foreign to many of the students. Their classes have been about challenge and counter-challenge and about dealing with disembodied ideas. Their desire, in a women's world, is for a high connection between speakers, an explicit bridge between experiences, a oneness among women who elsewhere are divided from one another. My approach produces a oneness, with its focus on women's experiences, but it is not the type of oneness the students expect.

I think there is a similarity between the way I run classes and the way I structured *The Mirror Dance*. In both cases, I wished to present multiple voices reflecting on different aspects of a common reality—a lesbian community, or women's experiences in organizations. In both cases, I offered these voices without much authorial intervention—without much explicit narrative commentary in the case of *The Mirror Dance*, and without much traditional teacherly authority in the classes. In both, I have avoided summarizing, or linking, statements made by individuals, but instead want the experiences presented to speak to one another. I say this because when I am criticized for how I teach, I often feel I have failed to do as I should, rather than seeing that I am doing something different. When I look at my study and see that I created this kind of process before, I can then view my approach to teaching less critically and see that it has its own integrity.[4]

If I have drawn one conclusion about "women and organizations" from teaching my course over the years, it is that the key to understanding women's groups is to think about the desire for oneness. I think this desire is central to how women feel about women's groups, to why the groups exist and fall apart, and to the problems the groups have. Oneness is what women most wish for, and fear, in their relationships with other women. It is why lesbianism is both sought and feared. Often, because much conspires to divide women from one another, women feel a great hunger for connection with each other. They bring that hunger to feminist classes.

When I try to tell the students in my class about my thoughts on desires for oneness, however, I never think it makes much difference. We are near the end of the quarter and all I seem to have done is to raise their desires for an ideal community of women only to frustrate those desires. This past year, because the students' frustrations were more near the surface than usual, I asked the students to go around the room in one of our last class sessions and to say what an ideal women's organization would provide for them. What would they like in their ideal women's group?

I can find no notes of what they said that day. Perhaps I just listened. I remember that the students answered seriously: "My ideal women's group would accept me." "It should be nonsexual." "Maybe it's a lot to ask. . . . " "I know I'm supposed to be realistic about this." "It would understand me." "I don't want false support, but. . . . " "It wouldn't be a big group." Their voices cracked and were tearful and hesitant and the room was very quiet. I had been asking the students, with the previous *Mirror Dance* assignment, to come to terms with the reality of women's groups, rather than having expectations the groups could not live up to. The students were, therefore, reluctant to admit to having idealistic desires, so they prefaced many of their remarks—"I still have these wishes." "I know, maybe it's unrealistic." "I don't know what to do about it, but this is how I feel." We went around the circle and the class ended in silence. "If I want something, I go out and make it happen," one of the students said toward the end. "I don't know if I'll ever find it," said another.

Although I do not know if that tearful discussion meant much to the students, it meant a great deal to me. I liked hearing them speak of their ideals. The students may have felt so far from having their ideals met that the discussion mainly saddened them. They may have been thinking of tests they had to take and other classes they had to go to. But they did stay around longer than usual after the class was over, planning their next subgroup meetings.

LOOKING BACK

The readings for the final week of the course fall under the title "Transformative Visions." These readings suggest to me the importance of acknowledging the "I"—the idiosyncratic and the individual—in women's experiences, and also the importance of processes of identification across boundaries between women. If women's experiences are to transform other ways of being, says Evelyn Fox Keller in her book on women and science, their difference must be seen. Further, we want our awareness of women's experiences to change our sense not only of what is true, but also of how truth is to be revealed. Keller discusses the life of geneticist Barbara McClintock, who approaches scientific understanding with "a feeling for the organism" and an attitude of "listening to what the material has to tell you." Only when McClintock feels "at one" with the corn plants she is studying can she truly understand them, Keller says, suggesting that "questions asked about objects with which one feels kinship are likely to differ from questions asked about objects one sees as unalterably alien."[5]

Dealing with self-knowledge in an essay, "On Keeping a Notebook," Joan Didion advises her readers and herself to remember the personal basis for our observations. "Our notebooks give us away," she suggests, "for however dutifully we record what we see around us, the common denominator of all we see is always, transparently, shamelessly, the implacable 'I.' " Nancy Mairs, in an essay about her experience in a psychiatric hospital, speaks of what her female gender has to do with her ending up "behind bars," and of how, on getting out of the hospital, "I did not get well. I got functional, which is another condition altogether." Similarly, I think, women often can be extremely functional, our strength hiding our feelings of discontent and despair. Patricia Hill Collins, in *Black Feminist Thought*, discusses African American women's experiences and how, in looking at different women's experiences, one must "pivot the center," focusing on each experience as a totality, or as the main frame of reference, rather than imposing a frame of reference from outside. I have tried to encourage the students to do such pivoting in looking at their own and others' experiences in the course. To illustrate the process, I also assign a reading about the Pueblo Indian potter Maria Martinez and the representation of self in clay, as well as several other discussions by women about developing vocabularies relevant to their experiences, especially in art. I want to suggest to the students that there are many forms for expressing female individuality and that they ought to continue to write about themselves after the course is over.[6]

The students' final research papers are due at the next to last class. The students have been working on these papers for a month, independently of me, pursuing a topic of interest to them. They have chosen topics such as female leadership, what if female ways of doing things were valued in organizations, subtle gender dynamics in organizations, glass ceilings, role models and mentors, mothering in organizations, women viewing themselves as men, managing family and career, women comparing themselves with other women, dynamics of minority women's organizations, dynamics of women's collectives, women's professionalism, superior-subordinate relationships among women, women's boundaries and invisibility in organizations, why women deny gender and oppression, sexual harassment, entrepreneurial women, and self-reflection on one's own gender history. The students write personally about their feelings in relation to their findings. They put a great deal of work into their research and feel that their final papers are extremely rewarding and the climax of their individual work in the course.

For the very last class session, the students write a course summary paper in which they review their experiences during the entire quarter—experiences in class discussions, in subgroup meetings, in doing research and papers, and in doing readings. I ask them to identify insights and key learnings that were especially important to them, and to describe their learning process over time. Often I do not know how much this course has meant to the students until I read their summary papers at the end. The students say, for instance:[7]

CHARLENE: My viewpoint has changed dramatically.

JULIA: I look back and feel proud for all the reading and writing I did.

KELLY: Initially, I was hostile to your teaching methods. However, since I knew you had something to offer, I tried to keep an open mind. This has been a struggle for me. Upon reflection, I am glad that I sat and listened. Instead of trying to fill my head with facts that I will probably forget, this class has changed my mental processes.

RACHEL: I think I have reacted to and learned from the structure of the class as well as from the content of it.

YOKO: Throughout this course, I realized how much I have adopted "masculine" ways of looking at and interacting with the world. In a desire to do well in school and please others, I think I lost the little girl and consequently the woman that is inside me. Discovering that I had shoved my "femaleness" aside was a very difficult thing to admit. Although I am looking forward to getting back in touch with the woman inside me, it is not easy and I know that doing so may upset the status quo of my current life. I feel like a baby bird that was just pushed out of the nest by the mother bird in order to learn how to fly. I haven't flown before, but I know that I will learn how before I hit the ground.

The students often speak emotionally:

MARIE: When I began feeling the pain and reality of these wounds that I had been hiding for so long, I wanted to just barrel in head first. I wanted to scream and cry in our class discussions. I remember the power of some of the emotions I was having but knew that I must be careful—these types of feelings frighten people and I knew that I didn't need, couldn't take, more alienation and rejection. Eventually, I began to feel more comfortable. I very much appreciated the structure of the class. I felt secure in the details of the class—how the chairs were set up, what order business was taken care of.

I now feel a bit like a woman warrior. I am proud to be a woman. It's funny because during my undergraduate years, I was very ashamed of being female and pretty much denied all female traits that I had. I feel like this class gently ventured with me to my insides, where I found parts of me that I can now reclaim, embrace, and rejoice in. It empowers me and gives me pride in myself. It's accepting, loving, and valuing me. If I'm to live, this is necessary for me, instead of trying to kill myself, part by part. I look at it now as a life or death situation—that's how serious it's been for me.

ROSE: I have grown immensely. Compelled as I am to assign numbers, I would say this is 25% due to my "single-mom" existence, 25% due to applying myself to hard work and study in my engineering master's program, and 50% to WS-235. This course has caused a permanent change in my thought patterns. I will catch myself at the start of self-doubt and analyze a situation as a combination of being both an engineer and a woman. While I still profess a desire to achieve financial and personal success, I no longer feel like adding the phrase, "like a man." I want the same opportunities certainly, but I like being a woman. Accepting this, I can now say, gulp, that I am a feminist.

ANGELICA: Before the class, I had never considered starting my own business. I assumed that I would simply enter corporate America and deal with the "old boy" network. But out of this class, I got the idea of starting my own law firm. Maybe it will not happen, maybe it will. I don't know, but I feel this class has given me other options for life that I would never have turned to.

BETH: I have started to rely on women more, and seek only women to share my time with. When we focused on women's work, I felt like calling my mother and telling her how much her commitment means to me. She has done invisible work in our house for twenty years, and I didn't realize it until we began our discussion. I have learned to open up doors inside my mind, doors that I didn't even know were there.

STEVEN: Well, I was one of only two men in a class filled and dominated by women and women's issues. This alone should be enough to figure out that I have learned a great deal.

Because the students' course summary papers tell me what the students value about their learning, they put a buffer between me and the official university course evaluations that I will read later. The official evaluations, written on computer forms, give numerical rankings to features of a course and to the teacher. They are statements I would do away with if I could. The evaluation forms are known to be biased against women teachers and feminist classes and to provide an opportunity for students to strike out at vulnerable teachers. Although I have done very well on these forms, I dislike them, and I always find the experience of reading them to be painful. I have never gained information from them that has helped me to improve my teaching. For that, I need to elicit in-person qualitative responses from the students, which I do, to some extent, with the course summary papers.

The students' discussion of their papers in the last class provides a sense of closure for the course. To me, the last session of the quarter is always important. I warn the students, for weeks beforehand, that they should not miss it. However, the significance of the course does not lie in any one final outcome. All along, there have been important moments. In my view, the most significant learning lies in the deeper, and often unselfconscious, emotions and insights that the students take with them, and that I take with me. This course is not easy to summarize. When I think back on it, the best I can ever do is to remember a few vivid events from my experiences in the classroom that have the feel of vignettes.

The first year I taught the course, for example, it was not until the next to last class session that one student told the class, quickly and softly, her words slurring together, "I am a lesbian." Two years later, another student would not tell the class that she had been Miss America the year before. She was afraid that if the other students knew, they would think she was an empty-headed blond and not take seriously anything she said. She was, in fact, a feminist and highly critical of the beauty pageant system.

An African American man sat quietly in class one year, not speaking much even when I encouraged him to speak. At the end of the quarter, he wrote in his final paper, "I feel I have been in another culture by listening to the women in the class. Had I spoken, I would not have had this experience." A member of the men's football team took the class one spring. Growing up, he was closer to his mother and sister than to his father, who had been a Nazi. In his papers, he spoke as if, on the inside, he felt like a woman.

A few times, women in the subgroups, which met in student homes or cafes, worked it out so they could meet without the man in their group. One year, one of the men blended in with the women in the larger class to an unusual degree. He bent his head down among the women around him and spoke with similar feelings and confusions as they had. He was a business student working toward an MBA and he had been a feminist for a long time. He said he felt more at home in our class than in his other classes. Another year, one woman decided to challenge everything I said.

Members of the women's swim team sat together at one end of the table one year. The other students complained that they passed notes and talked among themselves. Another year, three members of different women's sports teams did not sit together, but often when they spoke at the start of the term, I felt an increase in homophobia in the air. At the start of the first class session one quarter, a woman student introduced herself by saying, "I am a black feminist butch dyke and I hate men." Everyone liked her.

One year, one member of the class was a sixty-year-old undergraduate completing her BA. When other students in the class were having trouble calling themselves feminists, she said, "I have seen all these words change. Now it's 'feminist.' I think it will change again. One day I just decided to take the plunge and I started calling myself a feminist."

One year, a businesswoman returning to school thirty years after graduating took the course. She commuted down from her job in the city, was always on time, did the readings voraciously, spoke in class often, and appreciated me. Another older reentry student was present that year, a woman completing her master's degree in engineering. She also did all the work and even more, spoke her mind in class, and appreciated the opportunity of the class. Although undergraduates will often complain about the amount of work in a course, especially a course with a heavy load like this one, no one complained that year. Class discussions were unusually thoughtful and had a strong sense of, "Yes, this is true in the real world," which was provided by the two reentry women. The attitude of the students toward me was a valuing one. The class had a warmer feeling than it did any other year.

The first year I taught the course, an Austrian woman sat in as a guest in one of our sessions. She told the class about a two-thousand member traditional women's business organization she was studying in Switzerland and spoke of many of the same characteristics the students in the class had found when they interviewed their grandmothers and friends at the start of the quarter. These characteristics included consensus decisionmaking, personalized relationships, gossip, flex time, and a decentralized, leaderless organizational structure. Consensus decisionmaking takes longer, she told the students, but implementation time is then shorter. The students, that day, seemed shocked and relieved to hear her, as was I. We had all, I think, been uncertain about whether there was truth to the characteristics we had found. One year, I had two graduate student auditors from Denmark. They took in all the material of the course looking for parallels with their country. One of them said repeatedly, "In our country, the women and men look more similar in how they dress, but it is the same. It's very bad there. The system is not equal."

One year, an engineering student cried inexplicably in a class session near the end of the quarter. We were discussing separatism and she said she felt she already had too many burdens. Now she was being asked to add another—to find time to become a member of a women's group. I told her she need not join a women's group, but that did not solve her problem. By now, she had a strong desire to be part of a women's group. She fell off her bike on her way to our last class. I kept feeling I had caused her to fall by upsetting her with my course.

After the course was over one year, I received a letter from an undergraduate who had sat in class with her head down glowering into her notebook very often, making it known to me that she approved of neither what I was teaching nor how I was teaching it. "I've had time these past few days to think," she wrote. "In the class, I rejected again and again what you said. Perhaps that is because you wanted so much for us to believe it and you were so sure we eventually would. I didn't want to be predictable, but I'm afraid I am. And now when I say what you said, people think I'm as crazy as I thought you were."[8]

Each year when Estelle Freedman has been my guest, I have introduced her as a professor of history and an expert on the subject of separatism, whom I know as a colleague. I never tell the class that she is my lesbian lover and has been for over twelve years. I have been afraid the students will look at us and see sexual images and then discount the importance of separatism. I fear, too, that they will view my having Estelle as a guest as morally wrong because she is my partner (nepotism), or that they will view my having her help me with separatism as a weakness on my part. Yet, is it better to learn about separatism from an acquaintance of your teacher, or to learn about it from a lesbian couple at your university? The latter has implications for why separatism is important, and who it is important to—who will fight to keep it as an option for themselves and other women.

It was not until my third year of teaching the course that I began asking the students to write all their papers in the first person. Their papers then became more interesting for me to read. It was as if the students were sitting at their computers typing out their ends of personal conversations with me.

One year when the course was still cross-listed with the business school, ninety students turned out at the first class session for a seminar that would be limited to twenty-five. The turnouts were big for a couple of years afterward until we dropped the business school listing. Since then, I have had to learn not to measure my success by numbers.

The composition of the class has made a difference to how it has gone each year. I think I do best or, at least, I like best having people of mixed backgrounds, ages, and levels, both undergraduate and graduate students, and students from different professional programs in the university—engineering, business, education. I do fine with men present even if I think it would be better for the women students if the class were only women. The course has been easier for me to teach, and more rewarding, when I have had more older returning students in it, and when a small but significant number of the students are committed feminists. The students do work I cannot do myself by affecting each other and indicating their importance to one another, even when they are afraid to let others know who they are. Their behaviors indicate, I think, the extreme importance women's groups have for their members.

This is not a course I will always teach. It has, therefore, seemed desirable to me to record some of the ideas and experiences of it. This course has been central to the development of my thinking about women. Perhaps one's first feminist, or women's studies, course is often like this one has been for me. It requires that a teacher figure out her basic views, such as, "How do I feel, and think, about women? How can I bring others along with me?" From these two questions have emerged both the substance and process of my Women and Organizations course.

I did not initially view my own teaching as an instance of feminist teaching, but I have come to feel it is.[9] I think that feminist teaching is often hard for those who do it because a great deal is expected of us—by both others and ourselves—and because we often feel we fail to meet those expectations. Especially, I think, feminist courses are hard to teach because of the involvement of the teacher. She gives a great deal and often feels, "This is not about them—the students, or other women. This is me." When students reject the feminist teacher's lessons or viewpoints, they are not rejecting a distant subject or an intellectual conclusion, but something more sensitive, the teacher's way of being. Feminist classes are based on a shared stake in a movement for women's freedom, or in the fact of being a woman. Beyond that, there are many differences among their members. The classes require that a teacher remain open to her students in a way that parallels the openness she asks of them. It is, I think, a shared vulnerability to other women that gives feminist classes their excitement and their distinct character.

Finally, students expect feminist classes to fulfill ideals they have that are often frustrated elsewhere. The classes contain many of the conflicts between women's ways and a university structure that are a recurrent focus in my course. Although feminist classes cannot fully escape the male structure of a university that houses them, they often make their own kind of room within it. How much room, and what values that room encourages, depend on how much both a teacher and her students are willing to be present, in mutually helpful ways, during that brief period—in my case, ten weeks—when a miracle is expected to occur. I am always amazed at the big changes that can occur for students in so short a time. "This course has changed my life." "I will never see things the same again." "I will raise my sons differently." "I will quit my job." "I will join a women's law firm." "When I go back to my country, I will work for women," the students say, and I wonder about the truth of it, thinking all this must have been in the works anyway, and doubting that their ideals will be carried through. I tend to believe that nothing major can happen in a short period, but I forget how important ideas of gender are, and how students will work to produce learning that far exceeds the goals of any teacher.

Notes

NOTES

These notes are intended both to provide a context for my work and to be read as a bibliographic essay.

INTRODUCTION

1. Recent and important works on feminist approaches to knowledge include: Patricia Hill Collins, "Learning from the Outsider Within: The Sociological Significance of Black Feminist Thought," *Social Problems* 33:6 (1986): 14–32; Marjorie L. DeVault, "Talking and Listening from Women's Standpoint: Feminist Strategies for Interviewing and Analysis," *Social Problems* 37:1 (1990): 96–116; Jane Duran, *Toward a Feminist Epistemology* (Savage, Md.: Rowman and Littlefield, 1991); Ann Garry and Marilyn Pearsall, eds., *Women, Knowledge, and Reality: Explorations in Feminist Philosophy* (London: Unwin Hyman, 1992); Stanlie M. James and Abena P. A. Busia, eds., *Theorizing Black Feminisms: The Visionary Pragmatism of Black Women* (New York: Routledge, 1993); Sandra Harding, *The Science Question in Feminism* (Ithaca, N.Y.: Cornell University Press, 1986); Donna Haraway, *Simians, Cyborgs, and Women: The Reinvention of Nature* (New York: Routledge, 1991); Evelyn Fox Keller, *Reflections on Gender and Science* (New Haven: Yale University Press, 1985); Frances E. Mascia-Lees, Patricia Sharpe, and Colleen Ballerino Cohen, "The Postmodernist Turn in Anthropology: Cautions from a Feminist Perspective," *Signs* 15:1 (1989): 7–33; Shulamit Reinharz, *Feminist Meth-*

ods in Social Research (New York: Oxford University Press, 1992); Judith Stacey, "Can There Be a Feminist Ethnography?" *Women's Studies International Forum* 11:1 (1988): 67–79; and Liz Stanley and Sue Wise, *Breaking Out Again: Feminist Ontology and Epistemology* (New York: Routledge, 1993).

See also Jean Jackson, "On Trying to be an Amazon," in Tony Larry Whitehead and Mary Ellen Conaway, eds., *Self, Sex, and Gender in Cross-Cultural Fieldwork* (Urbana: University of Illinois Press, 1986), pp. 263–74; Camilla Stivers, "Reflections on the Role of Personal Narrative in Social Science," *Signs* 18:2 (1993): 408–25; and for discussions of writing and voice, Carolyn Heilbrun, *Writing a Woman's Life* (New York: Norton, 1988); Ursula Le Guin, "Bryn Mawr Commencement Address," in *Dancing at the Edge of the World: Thoughts on Words, Women, Places* (New York: Grove Press, 1989), pp. 147–60; and Nancy Mairs, *Voice Lessons: On Becoming a (Woman) Writer* (Boston: Beacon, 1994).

Within the literature on feminist method, there has long been a concern that women's experiences be viewed as real, important, and valid, as well as a more recent concern that women's (and lesbian and gay) experiences be viewed as interpreted, culturally created, or socially constructed. Recent debate has been prompted by Joan W. Scott's "The Evidence of Experience," *Critical Inquiry* 17 (1991): 773–79, which argues against a view of experience as natural and fundamental, in line with a general postmodernist relativism. Responses to Scott defending the importance of a concept of experience in the study of women include: Kathleen Canning, "Feminist History after the Linguistic Turn: Historicizing Discourse and Experience," *Signs* 19:2 (1994): 368–404; Laura Lee Downs, "If Woman Is Just an Empty Category, Then Why Am I Afraid to Walk Alone at Night?: Identity Politics Meets the Postmodern Subject," *Comparative Studies in Society and History* 35:2 (1993): 414–37; and Jane Roland Martin, "Methodological Essentialism, False Difference, and Other Dangerous Traps," *Signs* 19:3 (1994): 630–57. See also Celia Kitzinger, "Experiential Authority and Heterosexuality," in Gabriele Griffin, ed., *Changing Our Lives: Doing Women's Studies* (London and Boulder, Colo.: Pluto, 1994), pp. 135–44; and Chandra Talpade Mohanty, "Feminist Encounters: Locating the Politics of Experience," in Michèle Barrett and Anne Phillips, eds., *Destablizing Theory: Contemporary Feminist Debates* (Stanford: Stanford University Press, 1992), pp. 74–92. My view is that experiences are always interpreted, but that there are realities our interpretations may attempt to grasp. I think that not all those who speak a language of experience do so naively.

The idea of standpoint theories, or of views of reality as reflecting an individual's position, or social context, has become important among feminist and lesbian and gay scholars. Standpoint theories imply that each viewer has a partial, yet valuable, perspective. Influential recent statements include: Patricia Hill Collins, *Black Feminist Thought: Knowledge, Consciousness, and the Politics of Empowerment* (New York: Routledge, 1991); Sandra Harding, *Whose Science? Whose Knowledge? Thinking from Women's Lives* (Ithaca, N.Y.: Cornell University Press, 1991); Donna Haraway, "Situated Knowledges: The Science Question in Feminism and the Privilege of Partial Perspective," *Feminist Studies* 14:3 (1988): 575–99; Nancy Hartsock, "The Feminist Standpoint: Developing the Ground for a Specifically Feminist Historical Materialism," in Sandra Harding and Merrill B. Hintikka, eds., *Discovering Reality: Feminist Perspectives on Epistemology, Metaphysics, and Philosophy of Science* (Dordrecht, The Netherlands: Reidel, 1983); and Dorothy Smith, "Women's Perspectives as a Radical Critique of Sociology," *Sociological Inquiry* 44:1 (1974): 7–13 and *The Everyday World as Problematic: A Feminist Sociology* (Boston: Northeastern University Press, 1987).

2. Feminist theoretical views of gender congenial to my own are often sociological, or social-psychological. Important recent works include: Sandra Lipsitz Bem, *The Lenses of Gender: Transforming the Debate on Sexual Inequality* (New Haven: Yale University Press, 1993); Nancy J. Chodorow, *Feminism and Psychoanalytic Theory* (New Haven: Yale University Press, 1989) and "Gender as a Personal and Cultural Construction," *Signs* 20:3 (1995): 516–44; Paula England, ed., *Theory on Gender/Feminism on Theory* (New York: Aldine de Gruyter, 1993); Carol Gilligan, *In a Different Voice: Psychological Theory and Women's Development* (Cambridge: Harvard University Press, 1982); Suzanne J. Kessler and Wendy McKenna, *Gender: An Ethnomethodological Approach* (Chicago: University of Chicago Press, 1985); Judith Lorber, *Paradoxes of Gender* (New Haven: Yale University Press, 1995); Laurel Richardson and Verta Taylor, eds., *Feminist Frontiers III* (New York: McGraw-Hill, 1993); and Candace West and Don H. Zimmerman, "Doing Gender," *Gender and Society* 1:2 (1987): 125–51.

Postmodernist theories tend to make gender disappear in their efforts to subvert our ideas of gender categories. These theories try to escape essentialism, binary (or oppositional) thinking, and ideas of identity and experience. I have differences with much of postmodernist thinking. As a realist, I feel discomforted when these theories have as their goal the destruction of all existing categories of knowledge and ways of knowing other than their own, and when the theories are presented as if they were the only way to structure a contemporary, or progressive, vision. Yet postmodernism has encouraged much imaginative work. Important recent discussions of postmodernist-feminist views include: Seyla Benhabib, Judith Butler, Drucilla Cornell, and Nancy Fraser, *Feminist Contentions: A Philosophical Exchange* (New York: Routledge, 1995); Judith Butler, *Gender Trouble: Feminism and the Subversion of Identity* (New York: Routledge, 1990); Judith Butler and Joan W. Scott, eds., *Feminists Theorize the Political* (New York: Routledge, 1992); Diana Fuss, *Essentially Speaking: Feminism, Nature and Difference* (New York: Routledge, 1989); Linda J. Nicholson, ed., *Feminism/Postmodernism* (New York: Routledge, 1990), see especially Susan Bordo, "Feminism, Postmodernism, and Gender-Scepticism," pp. 133–56; Linda Nicholson, "Interpreting Gender," *Signs* 20:1 (1994): 79–105; and Joan W. Scott, "Deconstructing Equality-versus-Difference: Or, the Uses of Poststructuralist Theory for Feminism," *Feminist Studies* 14:1 (1988): 33–50. See also Linda Alcoff, "Cultural Feminism versus Post-Structuralism: The Identity Crisis in Feminist Theory," *Signs* 13:3 (1988): 405–36; Diane Elam, "Questions of Women," in *Feminism and Deconstruction* (New York: Routledge, 1994), pp. 27–66; and Mary Poovey, "Feminism and Deconstruction," *Feminist Studies* 14:1 (1988): 51–65.

For overviews of theoretical differences within feminism, see Diane Elam and Robyn Wiegman, eds., *Feminism Beside Itself* (New York: Routledge, 1995); Ann C. Herrmann and Abigail J. Stewart, eds., *Theorizing Feminism: Parallel Trends in the Humanities and the Social Sciences* (Boulder, Colo.: Westview, 1994); and Marianne Hirsch and Evelyn Fox Keller, eds. *Conflicts in Feminism* (New York: Routledge, 1990).

3. Among lesbian and gay scholars, it has increasingly become de rigueur to view one's work as a part of queer theory, or queer studies, using an outlook that draws heavily on postmodernist thinking. The new queer views challenge traditional "identity categories" of sexual orientation, such as lesbian and gay, substituting "queer," which represents an impulse to displace experience-based and essentialist concepts. A mixture of old allegiances and new ambitions, lesbian, gay, and queer scholarship has had a growth spurt since 1990. Special issues of scholarly journals providing overviews of this emerging field include: *Critical Sociology* 20:3 (1994), "Critical Studies of Lesbian, Gay, and Bisexual Issues"; *Differences* 3:2 (1991), "Queer Theory: Lesbian and Gay Sexualities," a special issue edited by Teresa de Lauretis; *GLQ: A Journal of Lesbian and Gay Studies* 1:1 (1993), an opening issue edited by Carolyn Dinshaw and David M.

Halperin that aims towards "the fractious, the disruptive, the irritable, the impatient, the unapologetic, the bitchy, the camp, the *queer*" (p. iv); *Journal of the History of Sexuality* 4:2 (1993) and 4:3 (1994), "Lesbian and Gay Histories," a double-volume special issue; *Radical History Review* 62 (1995), "Queer," a special issue edited by Jeffrey Escoffier, Regina Kunzel, and Molly McGarry; *Radical Teacher* 45 (1994), "Lesbian/Gay/Queer Studies," a special issue edited by Henry Abelove, Richard Ohmann, and Claire B. Potter; and *Sociological Theory* 12:3 (1994), "Queer Theory/ Sociology," a partial special issue edited by Steven Seidman.

Collections of scholarly essays providing overviews include: Henry Abelove, Michele Aina Barale, and David M. Halperin, eds., *The Lesbian and Gay Studies Reader* (New York: Routledge, 1993); Emilie L. Bergmann and Paul Julian Smith, eds., *¿Entiendes? Queer Readings, Hispanic Writings* (Durham, N.C.: Duke University Press, 1995); Corey K. Creekmur and Alexander Doty, eds., *Out in Culture: Gay, Lesbian, and Queer Essays on Popular Culture* (Durham, N.C.: Duke University Press, 1995); Monica Dorenkamp and Richard Henke, eds., *Negotiating Lesbian and Gay Subjects* (New York: Routledge, 1995); Diana Fuss, ed., *Inside/Out: Lesbian Theories, Gay Theories* (New York: Routledge, 1991); Ken Plummer, ed., *Modern Homosexualities: Fragments of Lesbian and Gay Experience* (New York: Routledge, 1992); R. Jeffrey Ringer, ed., *Queer Words, Queer Images: Communication and the Construction of Homosexuality* (New York: New York University Press, 1994); and Michael Warner, ed., *Fear of a Queer Planet: Queer Politics and Social Theory* (Minneapolis: University of Minnesota Press, 1993), see especially, Steven Seidman, "Identity Politics in a 'Postmodern' Gay Culture: Some Historical and Conceptual Notes," pp. 82–104.

For a discussion of discomfort with the phenomenon of the queer anthology, and of lesbian ambivalence about the term "queer," see Penelope J. Englebrecht, "Strange Company: Uncovering the Queer Anthology," *NWSA Journal* 7:1 (1995): 72–89. A statement of discomfort with the place of women in the new queer nation appears in Maria Maggenti, "Women as Queer Nationals," *Outlook* 11 (1991): 20–23. See also the view of queer in Lisa Duggan, "Making It Perfectly Queer," *Socialist Review* 22:1 (1992): 11–31; and see the views in *Differences* 6:2–3 (1994), "More Gender Trouble: Feminism Meets Queer Theory," a special issue edited by Naomi Schor and Elizabeth Weed.

Although my work can be subsumed under the "queer studies" heading, I am more comfortable viewing it as lesbian and feminist work, or as primarily women's scholarship. It seems to me that women's realities often become invisible under the queer heading. Recent issues of feminist scholarly journals devoted exclusively to lesbian scholarship address issues of how lesbian identity is defined. In a recent special issue of the *NWSA Journal* 7:1 (1995), "Sexual Orientation," Bonnie Zimmerman sets a queer tone in the introduction: "Where once we might have been able to say confidently that we knew what sexuality was, who among us now can use the word without immediately moving to a deconstructive stance?" (p. 1). Earlier special lesbian issues of feminist journals were not queer-identified, but were attentive to presenting diversity in views of lesbian experiences: *Signs* 18:4 (1993), "Theorizing Lesbian Experience," presented its selections as "revisionist" lesbian scholarship that included both postmodern theories and empirical research (pp. 757–59), in a special issue edited by Toni A. H. McNaron, Gloria Anzaldúa, Lourdes Arguelles, and Elizabeth Lapovsky Kennedy; *Feminist Studies* 18:3 (1992), "The Lesbian Issue," aimed to affirm "the multiplicity of lesbian identities" and to acknowledge the "instability of representation and meaning" in lesbian experiences (p. 463).

The first special issue of *Signs* 9:4 (1984), "The Lesbian Issue," acknowledged complexity in theoretical views and differences among lesbians, but emphasized a commitment to presenting scholarship normally not accessible because of prejudice against the subject (pp. 553–56), in a special issue edited by Estelle Freedman, Barbara Charlesworth Gelpi, Susan L. Johnson, and Kathleen M. Weston. A recent, and more traditional, sociological collection is *Gender and Society* 8:3 (1994), "Sexual Identities/Sexual Communities," a special issue edited by Beth E. Schneider.

Other important recent edited collections of lesbian scholarship include: Jeffner Allen, ed., *Lesbian Philosophies and Cultures* (Albany: State University of New York Press, 1990); Claudia Card, ed., *Adventures in Lesbian Philosophy* (Bloomington: Indiana University Press, 1994); Laura Doan, ed., *The Lesbian Postmodern* (New York: Columbia University Press, 1994); Karla Jay, ed., *Lesbian Erotics* (New York: New York University Press, 1995); Karla Jay and Joanne Glasgow, eds., *Lesbian Texts and Contexts: Radical Revisions* (New York: New York University Press, 1990); and Sally Munt, ed., *New Lesbian Criticism: Literary and Cultural Readings* (New York: Columbia University Press, 1992). Collections emphasizing class and race differences include: Catherine E. McKinley and L. Joyce DeLaney, eds., *Afrekete: An Anthology of Black Lesbian Writing* (New York: Anchor/Doubleday, 1995); Valerie Mason-John, ed., *Talking Black: Lesbians of African and Asian Descent Speak Out* (New York and London: Cassell, 1995); Julia Penelope, ed., *Out of the Class Closet: Lesbi-*

ans Speak (Freedom, Calif.: The Crossing Press, 1994); Juanita Ramos, ed., *Compañeras: Latina Lesbians (An Anthology)* (New York: Routledge, 1994); and Carla Trujillo, ed., *Chicana Lesbians: The Girls Our Mothers Warned Us About* (Berkeley, Calif.: Third Woman Press, 1991).

Significant recent booklength studies of lesbian subjects include: Terry Castle, *The Apparitional Lesbian: Female Homosexuality and Modern Culture* (New York: Columbia University Press, 1993); Elizabeth Lapovsky Kennedy and Madeline D. Davis, *Boots of Leather, Slippers of Gold: The History of a Lesbian Community* (New York: Routledge, 1993); Lillian Faderman, *Odd Girls and Twilight Lovers: A History of Lesbian Life in Twentieth-Century America* (New York: Columbia University Press, 1991); Lynda Hart, *Fatal Women: Lesbian Sexuality and the Mark of Aggression* (Princeton: Princeton University Press, 1994); Annamarie Jagose, *Lesbian Utopics* (New York: Routledge, 1994); Ellen Lewin, *Lesbian Mothers: Accounts of Gender in American Culture* (Ithaca, N.Y.: Cornell University Press, 1993); Esther Newton, *Cherry Grove, Fire Island: Sixty Years in America's First Gay and Lesbian Town* (Boston: Beacon, 1993); Judith Roof, *A Lure of Knowledge: Lesbian Sexuality and Theory* (New York: Columbia University Press, 1991); Esther D. Rothblum and Kathleen A. Brehony, *Boston Marriages: Romantic but Asexual Relationships among Contemporary Lesbians* (Amherst: University of Massachusetts Press, 1993); and Teresa de Lauretis, *The Practice of Love: Lesbian Sexuality and Perverse Desire* (Bloomington: Indiana University Press, 1994).

Influential individually authored essay collections include: Dorothy Allison, *Skin: Talking About Sex, Class and Literature* (Ithaca, N.Y.: Firebrand, 1994); Claudia Card, *Lesbian Choices* (New York: Columbia University Press, 1994); Marilyn Frye, *Willful Virgin: Essays in Feminism, 1976–1992* (Freedom, Calif.: The Crossing Press, 1992) and *The Politics of Reality* (Freedom, Calif.: The Crossing Press, 1983); Sheila Jeffreys, *The Lesbian Heresy: A Feminist Perspective on the Lesbian Sexual Revolution* (Melbourne, Australia: Spinifex, 1993); and Joyce Trebilcott, *Dyke Ideas: Process, Politics, Daily Life* (New York: State University of New York Press, 1994). Additional references to lesbian scholarship can be found in the notes to chapters 1, 2, and 7.

1. GENDER ROLES AMONG WOMEN

1. Gender ambivalence and confusion, gender play, and desires to transcend or change one's gender have been the subject of much recent writing. Significant recent works include: Anne Bolin, *In Search of Eve:*

Transsexual Rites of Passage (South Hadley, Mass.: Bergin and Garvey, 1988); Holly Devor, *Gender Blending: Confronting the Limits of Duality* (Bloomington: Indiana University Press, 1989); Julia Epstein and Kristina Straub, eds., *Body Guards: The Cultural Politics of Gender Ambiguity* (New York: Routledge, 1991); Michel Foucault, *Herculine Barbin: Being the Recently Discovered Memoirs of a Nineteenth-Century Hermaphrodite* (New York: Pantheon, 1980); Marjorie Garber, *Vested Interests: Cross-Dressing and Cultural Anxiety* (New York: Routledge, 1991); and Esther Newton, *Mother Camp: Female Impersonators in America* (Chicago: University of Chicago Press, 1979). See also Judith Butler: *Gender Trouble: Feminism and the Subversion of Identity* (New York: Routledge, 1990); *Bodies That Matter: On the Discursive Limits of "Sex"* (New York: Routledge, 1993); and "Imitation and Gender Insubordination," in Diana Fuss, ed., *Inside/Out: Lesbian Theories, Gay Theories* (New York: Routledge, 1991), pp. 13–32. Butler's postmodernist "performativity" and gender-problematizing views have been highly influential recently among lesbian scholars; these views challenge ideas about both the existence of gender categories and the locatability of the individual.

In the gender-change literature, a recent significant popular account is Kate Bornstein, *Gender Outlaw: On Men, Women and the Rest of Us* (New York: Routledge, 1994), about an initially biological male who became a (female) lesbian. Jacqueline N. Zita examines this phenomenon from both a traditional lesbian-feminist perspective and a postmodernist, gender-fluidity view, in "Male Lesbians and the Postmodernist Body," in Claudia Card, ed., *Adventures in Lesbian Philosophy* (Bloomington: Indiana University Press, 1994), pp. 112–32. Says Zita, "If men can become lesbians, if women who sleep with men can still be lesbians, if anybody can visit lesbian positionality or transsex it with anybody else, then what would such a category really name? Postmodernism not only makes the 'male lesbian' possible; it may in addition make lesbianism, at least as we have known it, impossible. The theory seems a bit pitiful" (p. 129). Similarly, anthropologist Judith Shapiro takes a cross-gender phenomenon and sees in it a deeper structure of gender that is effectively conserved by the gender crossing (Shapiro, "Transsexualism: Reflections on the Persistence of Gender and the Immutability of Sex," in Epstein and Straub, *Body Guards,* pp. 248–79). The views of both Zita and Shapiro are congruent with my own in this essay.

In her foreword to *Tendencies,* Eve Sedgwick describes a gay parade in New York City in 1992, noting a gender incongruity posed by a gay man that is similar to the one I describe at the opening of this chapter upon viewing the marionette; see Sedgwick, *Tendencies* (Durham, N.C.: Duke University Press, 1993), p. xi. Sedgwick's introduction to *Epistemology of the Closet* (Berkeley and Los Angeles: University of California Press, 1990), pp. 1–66, provides a literary-deconstructionist overview of the emergence of lesbian and gay studies. Terry Castle discusses the masculinist bias of Sedgwick in *The Apparitional Lesbian: Female Homosexuality and Modern Culture* (New York: Columbia University Press, 1993), p. 13. The man I describe in this essay as so convincing as a woman later wrote a book about her experiences: Holly Woodlawn with Jeffrey Copeland, *A Low Life in High Heels: The Holly Woodlawn Story* (New York: St. Martin's, 1991). Carole-Ann Tyler discusses gay male camp as "phallic narcissism" in "Boys Will Be Girls: The Politics of Gay Drag," in Fuss, *Inside/Out*, pp. 33–70.

2. Lesbian scholars have recently been interested in femme and butch roles, examining both the outer display and the inner sense of self involved. This new literature is concerned with a recent revalidation of gender roles that once were rejected by many lesbians as too heterosexual. Significant recent studies and writings that combine personal reflections with a search for interpretations include: Judith Butler, "Imitation and Gender Insubordination" and portions of *Gender Trouble* and *Bodies That Matter;* Sue-Ellen Case, "Toward a Butch-Femme Aesthetic," *Discourse* 11:1 (1988–89): 55–71; Ann Cvetkovich, "Recasting Receptivity: Femme Sexualities," in Karla Jay, ed., *Lesbian Erotics* (New York: New York University Press, 1995), pp. 125–46; Lillian Faderman, "Butches, Femmes, and Kikis: Creating Lesbian Subcultures in the 1950s and the '60s," in *Odd Girls and Twilight Lovers: A History of Lesbian Life in Twentieth-Century America* (New York: Columbia University Press, 1991), pp. 159–86; Amber Hollibaugh and Cherríe Moraga, "What We're Rollin Around in Bed With: Sexual Silences in Feminism," in Ann Snitow, Christine Stansell, and Sharon Thompson, eds., *Powers of Desire: The Politics of Sexuality* (New York: Monthly Review Press, 1983); Elizabeth Lapovsky Kennedy and Madeline D. Davis, *Boots of Leather, Slippers of Gold: The History of a Lesbian Community* (New York: Routledge, 1993); Sheila Jeffreys, "Butch and Femme: Now and Then," in Lesbian History Group, *Not a Passing Phase: Reclaiming Lesbians in History, 1840–1985* (London: Women's Press, 1989), pp. 158–87; JoAnn Loulan with Sherry Thomas, *The Lesbian Erotic Dance: Butch, Femme, Androgyny and Other Rhythms* (San Francisco: Spinsters Ink, 1990).

See also Biddy Martin, "Sexual Practice and Changing Lesbian Identities," in Michèle Barrett and Anne Phillips, eds., *Destabilizing Theory:*

Contemporary Feminist Debates (Stanford: Stanford University Press, 1992), pp. 93–119; Joan Nestle, "Butch-Femme Relationships: Sexual Courage in the 1950s," in *A Restricted Country* (Ithaca, N.Y.: Firebrand, 1987), pp. 100–109; Joan Nestle, ed., *The Persistent Desire: A Femme-Butch Reader* (Boston: Alyson, 1992), see especially Gayle Rubin, "Of Catamites and Kings: Reflections on Butch, Gender, and Boundaries," pp. 466–83; Esther Newton, "The Myth of the Mannish Lesbian: Radclyffe Hall and the New Woman," *Signs* 9:4 (1984): 557–75, and "The 'Fun Gay Ladies' " and " 'Just One of the "Boys," ' " in *Cherry Grove, Fire Island: Sixty Years in America's First Gay and Lesbian Town* (Boston: Beacon, 1993), pp. 207–34; Minnie Bruce Pratt, *S/HE* (Ithaca, N.Y.: Firebrand, 1995); Karen Quimby, "*She Must Be Seeing Things* Differently: The Limits of Butch/Femme," in Jay, *Lesbian Erotics;* Judith Roof, "Polymorphous Diversity," in *A Lure of Knowledge: Lesbian Sexuality and Theory* (New York: Columbia University Press, 1991), pp. 237–54; and Lisa M. Walker, "How to Recognize a Lesbian: The Cultural Politics of Looking Like What You Are," *Signs* 18:4 (1993): 866–90.

Popular lesbian literature has also explored gender roles, for example: Lily Burana, Roxxie, and Linnea Due, *Dagger: On Butch Women* (San Francisco: Cleis Press, 1994); Pat Califia, "Genderbending: Playing with Roles and Reversals," in *Public Sex: The Culture of Radical Sex* (Pittsburgh, Pa.: Cleis Press, 1994), pp. 175–82; Leslie Feinberg, *Stone Butch Blues* (Ithaca, N.Y.: Firebrand, 1993); and Tracy Morgan, "Butch-Femme and the Politics of Identity," in Arlene Stein, ed., *Sisters, Sexperts, Queers: Beyond the Lesbian Nation* (New York: Plume, 1993), pp. 35–46.

Generally, lesbian scholarship has been concerned with issues of how to interpret lesbian experiences, especially in light of ideas of heterosexuality, of gender, and of differences among lesbians. Additional recent significant works include: Gloria Anzaldúa, *Borderlands/La Frontera: The New Mestiza* (San Francisco: Spinsters/Aunt Lute, 1987); Yvonne Yarbro-Bejarano, "De-constructing the Lesbian Body: Cherríe Moraga's *Loving in the War Years,*" in Carla Trujillo, ed., *Chicana Lesbians: The Girls Our Mothers Warned Us About* (Berkeley, Calif.: Third Woman Press, 1991), pp. 143–55; Cheshire Calhoun, "The Gender Closet: Lesbian Disappearance under the Sign 'Women,' " *Feminist Studies* 21:1 (1995): 7–34; Ekua Omosupe, "Black/Lesbian/Bulldagger," *Differences* 3:2 (1991): 101–11; Katie King, "Audre Lorde's Lacquered Layerings: The Lesbian Bar as a Site of Literary Production," in Sally Munt, ed., *New Lesbian Criticism: Literary and Cultural Readings* (New York: Columbia University Press, 1992), pp. 51–74; Biddy Martin, "Lesbian Identity and

Autobiographical Difference[s]," in Bella Brodzki and Celeste Schenck, eds., *Life/Lines: Theorizing Women's Autobiography* (Ithaca, N.Y.: Cornell University Press, 1988), pp. 77–103; Adrienne Rich, "Compulsory Heterosexuality and Lesbian Existence," *Signs* 5:4 (1980): 631–60; Arlene Stein, "Sisters and Queers: The Decentering of Lesbian Feminism," *Socialist Review* 22:1 (1992): 33–55; and Dana Y. Takagi, "Maiden Voyage: Excursion into Sexuality and Identity Politics in Asian America," *Amerasia Journal* 20:1 (1994): 1–17.

2. BECOMING A LESBIAN

1. In the scholarly literature on lesbianism, "coming out" processes have been of central interest. My use of "becoming" is somewhat different but is still a variation on the coming out theme. A sociological classic dealing with coming out, and with the relationship between secrecy and lesbian identity, is Barbara Ponse, *Identities in the Lesbian World: The Social Construction of Self* (Westport, Conn.: Greenwood Press, 1978). An important early collection of stories is Susan J. Wolfe and Julia Penelope Stanley, eds., *The Coming Out Stories* (Watertown, Mass.: Persephone Press, 1980); in a foreword to this volume, Adrienne Rich refers to coming out as "that first permission we give to ourselves to name our love for women as love, to say, *I am a lesbian*" (p. xiii). A more recent collection is Karen Barber and Sarah Holmes, eds., *Testimonies: Lesbian Coming-Out Stories* (Boston: Alyson, 1994).

Other significant recent accounts include: Terry Castle, "First Ed," in *The Apparitional Lesbian: Female Homosexuality and Modern Culture* (New York: Columbia University Press, 1993), pp. 21–27, a story of a first love; Julia Creet, "Anxieties of Identity: Coming Out, Coming Undone," in Monica Dorenkamp and Richard Henke, eds., *Negotiating Lesbian and Gay Subjects* (New York: Routledge, 1995), pp. 179–200; Paula C. Rust, " 'Coming Out' in the Age of Social Constructionism: Sexual Identity Formation among Lesbian and Bisexual Women," *Gender and Society* 7:1 (1993): 50–77; Valerie Jenness, "Coming Out: Lesbian Identities and the Categorization Problem," in Ken Plummer, ed., *Modern Homosexualities: Fragments of Lesbian and Gay Experience* (New York: Routledge, 1992), pp. 65–74; and Shane Phelan, "(Be)Coming Out: Lesbian Identity and Politics," *Signs* 18:4 (1993): 765–90, also in her *Getting Specific: Postmodern Lesbian Politics* (Minneapolis: University of Minnesota Press, 1994).

Lesbian accounts often emphasize choice as characteristic of processes of coming out, or becoming a lesbian. Men, on the other hand, have tended to emphasize their gayness, or homosexuality, as a given nature, viewing it as something one knows about oneself, or eventually discovers. Jacqueline N. Zita comments on a gender difference between "cause and choice," in "Gay and Lesbian Studies: Yet Another Unhappy Marriage," in Linda Garber, ed., *Tilting the Tower: Lesbians, Teaching, Queer Subjects* (New York: Routledge, 1994), p. 264; Claudia Card discusses becoming a lesbian as a process of "many choices," observing that the meaning of one's lesbianism may be discovered only after this choice has been made, in *Lesbian Choices* (New York: Columbia University Press, 1994), pp. 47–50. Marilyn Frye turns the question around to focus on heterosexuality as a female choice, in "A Lesbian's Perspective on Women's Studies," in *Willful Virgin: Feminist Essays, 1976–1992* (Freedom, Calif.: Crossing Press, 1992), pp. 51–58. Joyce Trebilcott speaks of "taking responsibility for our sexual identities," and describes coming out as a process in which a woman "creates" a new lesbian self, in *Dyke Ideas: Process, Politics, Daily Life* (New York: State University of New York Press, 1994), pp. 97–109.

Lesbian desire and sexuality have been explored in recent works. Most interesting to me are those studies that aim to distinguish what is unique to lesbian desire and sexuality, making it different from heterosexual, or gay male, experiences. The mothering basis of desire in lesbian relationships, which I touch on in this chapter, is further elaborated upon in theoretical terms in Teresa de Lauretis, "The Seductions of Lesbianism: Feminist Psychoanalytic Theory and the Maternal Imaginary," in *The Practice of Love: Lesbian Sexuality and Perverse Desire* (Bloomington: Indiana University Press, 1994), pp. 149–202. De Lauretis speaks of the maternal female body as central to lesbian subjectivity and desire (p. 171), and of lesbian desire as a sexual and sociosymbolic search for an absent mother, rather than a nostalgic search for a memory of a past mother-daughter unity. She speaks of the mother's absence as producing in the daughter "a desire that is absolutely unrealizable, and hence must consist in the desiring itself" (p. 200).

In "The Lure of the Mannish Lesbian: The Fantasy of Castration and the Signification of Desire" (also in *The Practice of Love*, pp. 203–53), de Lauretis takes this thinking a step further in speaking of a woman's desire for another's female body as refigured in a desire for masculinity, or for the "fetish of masculinity" (p. 243). When a woman desires the love of another woman, she seeks "not a faulty woman," but "a woman embodied and self-possessed as a woman, as I would want to be and can become only with her love" (p. 249). Although de Lauretis' language is very different from mine in this story of my relationship with Fran, it seems to me the basic experiences reflected upon are similar.

See also Judith Roof, " 'This Is Not for You': The Sexuality of Mothering," in *A Lure of Knowledge: Lesbian Sexuality and Theory* (New York: Columbia University Press, 1991), pp. 90–118, a work to which de Lauretis refers; and Sharon P. Holland, "To Touch the Mother's C(o)untry: Siting Audre Lorde's Erotics," in Karla Jay, ed., *Lesbian Erotics* (New York: New York University Press, 1995), pp. 212–26. Lorde's imagery of her mother's body in *Zami*—"Her large soft breasts beneath the buttoned flannel of her nightgown. Below, the rounded swell of her stomach, silent and inviting touch"—reminded me of my own description in this chapter of Fran in the morning (Audre Lorde, *Zami: A New Spelling of My Name* [Trumansburg, N.Y.: The Crossing Press, 1982], p. 33; also cited in Holland).

In her essay, "Lesbian 'Sex,' " Marilyn Frye suggests that " 'sex' is an inappropriate term for what lesbians do," since our ideas of sex are male and phallocentric (in *Willful Virgin*, pp. 109–19). Frye suggests, instead, the creation of a new vocabulary and way of thinking more fitting to lesbian and female experiences—"Let it be an open, generous, commodious concept encompassing all the acts and activities by which we generate with each other pleasures and thrills, tenderness and ecstasy" (p. 117). Marny Hall explores Frye's suggestions further, speaking of "erotic connections" between women that are more difficult to describe than "sexual rapport," and of "patterns of intimacy" yet to be noticed and acknowledged that form "a new female framework of intimacy" (p. 45), in " 'Why Limit Me to Ecstasy?' Toward a Positive Model of Genital Incidentalism among Friends and Other Lovers," in Esther D. Rothblum and Kathleen A. Brehony, eds., *Boston Marriages: Romantic but Asexual Relationships among Contemporary Lesbians* (Amherst: University of Massachusetts Press, 1993), pp. 43–62.

This chapter is taken from an autobiographical novel, "Jenny's World" (manuscript, 1985).

3. THE FAMILY SILVER

1. As I wrote this chapter, I thought of Joan Didion's essay, "On Going Home," in which she speaks of returning to a family house "filled with mementos quite without value" to her husband: "what could the Canton dessert plates mean to him?" she asks. Didion speaks of wishing to

give her daughter "a sense of her cousins and of rivers and of her great-grandmother's teacups," in *Slouching Towards Bethlehem* (New York: Delta, 1968), pp. 164 and 167–68.

In *Inalienable Possessions: The Paradox of Keeping-While-Giving* (Berkeley and Los Angeles: University of California Press, 1992), anthropologist Annette B. Weiner speaks of possessions imbued with the identities of their owners that are "not easy to give away," and that are given as part of "an effort to make memory persist" and to reproduce the kin group or family (pp. 6–13). Weiner quotes Steinbeck in *The Grapes of Wrath:* "When everything that could be sold was sold . . . still there were piles of possessions. . . . The women sat among the doomed things, turning them over and looking past them and back. . . . How can we live without our lives? How will we know it's us without our past?" (p. 1). Weiner, interested in women's wealth, especially "cloth wealth," re-examines classical anthropological exchange theories, which assume that giving is done for reciprocity, and suggests instead a "gender-based power constituted through keeping-while-giving" (p. 17).

Anthropologist Jane Schneider writes of a more egalitarian women's wealth than silver that is nonetheless similar, "embroidered whitewear" in nineteenth-century Italy, a wealth requiring much female labor that women brought to a family. Like family silver, the whitewear (embroidered sheets and bedcovers) was largely produced "for use within the home" and "was also potentially exchangeable for cash or food" and could be pawned (p. 344). Schneider refers to whitewear and other trousseau goods as "prestige goods," "valuables," "precious things." She seeks to distinguish a "pattern of creating value" by women's labor in embroidering cloth from the "make-work" it was sometimes claimed to be: "If the wealth thus created was inferior to more liquid forms such as gold, this is somewhat beside the point" (p. 350), in "Trousseau as Treasure: Some Contradictions of Late Nineteenth-Century Change in Sicily," in Eric B. Ross, ed., *Beyond the Myths of Culture: Essays in Cultural Materialism* (New York: Academic Press, 1980), pp. 323–56. See also Annette B. Weiner and Jane Schneider, eds., *Cloth and Human Experience* (Washington, D.C.: Smithsonian Institution Press, 1989).

Discussions of the history, production, and art of silver tableware can be found in Herbert Brunner, *Old Table Silver: A Handbook for Collectors and Amateurs,* translated by Janet Seligman (New York: Taplinger, 1967); Philippa Glanville and Jennifer Faulds Goldsborough, *Women Silversmiths, 1685–1845: Works from the Collection of the National Museum of Women in the Arts* (London: Thames and Hudson, and Washington, D.C.:

The National Museum of Women in the Arts, 1990); Jessie McNab, *Silver* (Washington, D.C.: The Smithsonian Institution's National Museum of Design, 1981); Dorothy T. and H. Ivan Rainwater, *American Silverplate* (West Chester, Pa.: Schiffer, 1988); Charles L. Venable, *Silver in America, 1840–1940: A Century of Splendor* (Dallas: Dallas Museum of Art, and New York: Harry N. Abrams, 1995); and Peri Wolfman and Charles Gold, *Forks, Knives, and Spoons* (New York: Clarkson Potter, 1994). Traditionally, men have made silverware and women have used it. Discussions of American Indian silvercraft emphasize themes of ornamentation, use, symbolic meanings, and the craft of production: for example, John Adair, *The Navajo and Pueblo Silversmiths* (Norman: University of Oklahoma Press, 1944), an anthropological classic; and Larry Frank, with the assistance of Millard J. Holbrook II, *Indian Silver Jewelry of the Southwest, 1868–1930* (West Chester, Pa.: Schiffer, 1990).

Margaret Visser comments on the class difference between buying the family silver and inheriting it, in *The Rituals of Dinner: The Origins, Evolution, Eccentricities, and Meaning of Table Manners* (New York: Penguin, 1991), p. 185. For a discussion of family stories, see Elizabeth Stone, *Black Sheep and Kissing Cousins: How Our Family Stories Shape Us* (New York: Penguin, 1988).

4. THE PASSING DOWN OF SORROW

1. In my reading, I have found female sorrow to be a recurrent theme despite cultural differences. Amy Tan, in *The Joy Luck Club* (New York: G. P. Putnam's, 1989), speaks of the passing down of sorrow across Chinese female generations: says one auntie, "I was raised the Chinese way: I was taught to desire nothing, to swallow other people's misery, to eat my own bitterness. And even though I taught my daughter the opposite, still she came out the same way! Maybe it is because she was born to me and she was born a girl. And I was born to my mother and I was born a girl. All of us are stairs, one step after another, going up and down, but all going the same way" (p. 9).

   Nancy Mairs writes of her mother, "What I didn't see, and maybe she didn't either, was that behind her anger lay the anxiety and frustration caused by her helplessness to protect me from my pain." Mairs speaks of a "reflexive maternal guilt" felt by her mother and by herself, a guilt that seems to say, "I'm sorry"—" 'I'm sorry I can't keep you perfectly full, perfectly dry, perfectly free from gas and fear, perfectly, perfectly happy.' Any mother knows that if she could do these things, her infant would die more surely than if she covered its face with a rose-printed pillow. Still, part of her desire is to prevent the replication of desire," in *Plaintext: Deciphering a Woman's Life* (New York: Harper and Row, 1986), pp. 74–75.

Marianna De Marco Torgovnick writes, "The line between [my] worries and my mother's is the line between the working class and the upper middle class. . . . Now, as I write . . . I recognize that although I've come far in physical and material distance, the emotional distance is harder to gauge," in *Crossing Ocean Parkway: Readings by an Italian American Daughter* (Chicago: University of Chicago Press, 1994), pp. 10–11.

Patricia J. Williams, writing about her mother encouraging her to go to law school, recalls: "My mother was asking me not to look to her as a role model. . . . She hid the lonely, black, defiled-female part of herself and pushed me forward as the projection of a competent self, a cool rather than despairing self, a masculine rather than a feminine self," in *The Alchemy of Race and Rights: Diary of a Law Professor* (Cambridge: Harvard University Press, 1991), pp. 216–17.

Sara Lawrence Lightfoot speaks of her mother being "determined that her children's experiences would not parallel hers." She "promised herself that her daughters would wear colors—bold, intense colors, colors that would show off their beautiful brown skin," rather than the dark colors she had been taught to wear by her mother, in *Balm in Gilead: Journey of a Healer* (Reading, Mass.: Addison-Wesley, 1989), pp. 309–10.

The narcissistic wounding of a female child by her mother is discussed in Teresa de Lauretis, *The Practice of Love: Lesbian Sexuality and Perverse Desire* (Bloomington: Indiana University Press, 1994); de Lauretis suggests that "In a culture perversely homophobic" and gendered (so that females are both less valuable and less desirable), the mother wounds the daughter with a sense of "lack of a loveable body" (pp. 242–43).

Other relevant personal accounts include: Nancy K. Miller, "Coda: Loehmann's, Or, Shopping with My Mother," in *Getting Personal: Feminist Occasions and Other Autobiographical Acts* (New York: Routledge, 1991), pp. 139–41; Kesaya E. Noda, "Growing Up Asian in America," in Asian Women United of California, ed., *Making Waves: An Anthology of Writings by and about Asian American Women* (Boston: Beacon, 1989); pp. 243–51; and Carolyn Kay Steedman, *Landscape for a Good Woman: A Story of Two Lives* (New Brunswick, N.J.: Rutgers University Press, 1987).

For theoretical views, see Nancy J. Chodorow, *The Reproduction of Mothering: Psychoanalysis and the Sociology of Gender* (Berkeley and Los Angeles: University of California Press, 1978) and "Family Structure and

Feminine Personality," in *Feminism and Psychoanalytic Theory* (New Haven: Yale University Press, 1989), pp. 45–65; Evelyn Nakano Glenn, Grace Chang, and Linda Rennie Forcey, eds., *Mothering: Ideology, Experience, and Agency* (New York: Routledge, 1994); and Adrienne Rich, "Motherhood and Daughterhood," in *Of Woman Born: Motherhood as Experience and Institution* (New York: Norton, 1986), pp. 218–55. A recent review of feminist literature on mothering that includes works of French psychoanalytic feminists is Ellen Ross, "New Thoughts on 'the Oldest Vocation': Mothers and Motherhood in Recent Feminist Scholarship," *Signs* 20:2 (1995): 397–413.

5. HURTS OF THE SYSTEM

1. Susan Krieger, *The Mirror Dance: Identity in a Women's Community* (Philadelphia: Temple University Press, 1983); Marjorie L. DeVault, "Women Write Sociology: Rhetorical Strategies," in Albert Hunter, ed., *The Rhetoric of Social Research* (New Brunswick, N.J.: Rutgers University Press, 1990), p. 109; and Verta Taylor, *Signs* 9:4 (1984): 722. My first book, *Hip Capitalism* (Beverly Hills, Calif.: Sage, 1979), also used multiple voices and had an innovative narrative form.

2. Shulamit Reinharz, *Feminist Methods in Social Research* (New York: Oxford University Press, 1992), p. 228.

3. Susan Krieger, *Social Science and the Self: Personal Essays on an Art Form* (New Brunswick, N.J.: Rutgers University Press, 1991); Laurel Richardson, *Contemporary Sociology* 21:3 (1992): 409; and Barrie Thorne, *Gender and Society* 8:1 (1994): 138.

4. Anne Statham, Laurel Richardson, and Judith A. Cook discuss women in a male world in *Gender and University Teaching: A Negotiated Difference* (Albany: State University of New York Press, 1991); see especially the discussions of authority management, gender differences in personalizing in the classroom, and student reactions to the gender of faculty, pp. 65–122. Patti Gumport, in "Fired Faculty: Reflections on Marginalization and Academic Identity," discusses the internalization of pain when faculty lose their jobs because they are "targeted as marginal and hence dispensable" during university budget crises (in Daniel McLaughlin and William G. Tierney, eds., *Naming Silenced Lives: Personal Narratives and Processes of Educational Change* [New York: Routledge, 1993], pp. 135–52).

   Other discussions of gender-related dilemmas of women faculty, especially in women's studies and sociology, include: Margo Culley and

Catherine Portuges, eds., *Gendered Subjects: The Dynamics of Feminist Teaching* (Boston: Routledge, 1985); Sara Munson Deats and Lagretta Tallent Lenker, eds., *Gender and Academe: Feminist Pedagogy and Politics* (Lanham, Md.: Rowman and Littlefield, 1994); Susan L. Gabriel and Isaiah Smithson, eds., *Gender in the Classroom: Power and Pedagogy* (Urbana: University of Illinois Press, 1990); Diana Hume George, " 'How Many of Us Can You Hold to Your Breast?': Mothering in the Academy," in Elaine Hedges and Shelley Fisher Fishkin, eds., *Listening to Silences: New Essays in Feminist Criticism* (New York: Oxford University Press, 1995), pp. 225–44; Anne Goetting and Sarah Fenstermaker, eds., *Individual Voices, Collective Visions: Fifty Years of Women in Sociology* (Philadelphia: Temple University Press, 1995); Gail B. Griffin, *Calling: Essays on Teaching in the Mother Tongue* (Pasadena, Calif.: Trilogy Books, 1992); bell hooks, *Teaching to Transgress: Education as the Practice of Freedom* (New York: Routledge, 1994); Louise Morley and Val Walsh, eds., *Feminist Academics: Creative Agents for Change* (Bristol, Pa.: Taylor and Francis, 1995); Jean Fox O'Barr, *Feminism in Action: Building Institutions and Community through Women's Studies* (Chapel Hill: University of North Carolina Press, 1994); Barbara Omolade, "Invisible to the Naked Eye: Black Women and the Academy," in *The Rising Song of African American Women* (New York: Routledge, 1994), pp. 103–51; and Kathryn P. Meadow Orlans and Ruth A. Wallace, *Gender and Academic Experience: Berkeley Women Sociologists* (Lincoln: University of Nebraska Press, 1994).

Michelle M. Tokarczyk and Elizabeth A. Fay, eds., *Working-Class Women in the Academy: Laborers in the Knowledge Factory* (Amherst: University of Massachusetts Press, 1993) conveys a sense of female alienation from mainstream university norms and circles of inclusion. See also Joy James and Ruth Farmer, eds., *Spirit, Space and Survival: African American Women in (White) Academe* (New York: Routledge, 1993). Student disappointments when women faculty identify with elitist norms are discussed in Himani Bannerji et al., *Unsettling Relations: The University as a Site of Feminist Struggle* (Boston: South End Press, 1992). Jessie Bernard discusses a difference between "the teacher role" and "the man-of-knowledge role" in her classic work, *Academic Women* (Cleveland, Ohio: Meridian, 1966), pp. 115–20, a distinction relevant to my interest in "women's work." I further discuss women's work in chapter 8.

5. From a letter of invitation to contribute to a volume on "Gender, Life Histories, and Human Agency: 'The Missing Feminist Revolution in Sociology' Revisited," May 1992.

1. Judy Small, "Evil Angels," *Snapshot.* © 1990 by Crafty Maid Music (Fairfield, Australia). All rights reserved. Used by permission.

2. A few other feminist teachers have written of similar experiences with male hostility. Patricia J. Williams speaks of an incident with a male student who was an ex-football player whom she asked to do his coursework more carefully. He then burst into tears in the office of an associate dean and soon coalesced "both the student body and the administration against me" (p. 96). Williams notes: "I thought long about how a situation in which I thought I was being plucky and self-protective had turned into such a nightmare. How did my self assertion become so powerful as to frighten, frustrate, or humiliate this man?" (pp. 96–97). Mentions of such experiences and their inner psychological toll are rare in written accounts by women faculty, as are admissions of hurt in response to comments on student course evaluations, another topic Williams addresses: "They are awful and I am devastated. . . . I am deified, reified, and vilified in all sorts of cross-directions. I am condescending, earthy, approachable, and arrogant. Things are out of control in my classroom, and I am too much the taskmaster. I am a PNCNG (Person of No Color and No Gender) as well as too absorbed with ethnicity and social victimhood. . . . My writing on the blackboard is too small" (p. 95). *The Alchemy of Race and Rights: Diary of a Law Professor* (Cambridge: Harvard University Press, 1991).

   A similar sense of being easily targeted and vilified is spoken of by doris davenport, also an African American woman who puts a great deal of her self into her teaching: "Because I am so out as to who and what I am, I have been the target of numerous psychotic projections and reactions, from students and administrators alike. What has any of this to do with my being a Blacklesbian? Everything and nothing" (p. 222), in " 'Still Here': Ten Years Later . . . ," in Linda Garber, ed., *Tilting the Tower: Lesbians, Teaching, Queer Subjects* (New York: Routledge, 1994).

   Gail B. Griffin also writes of receiving a disturbing phone call in the night and of how an "immediate sense of shock and then sadness gives way to the old sense of nakedness, the vulnerability of women violated in the night by phones and other weapons" (p. 107). Once having been suspected of being a "man-hater," Griffin learns how hard it is to erase that reputation. As in my account, she speaks of her own lack of indifference to students: "Teachers want and need their students. . . . The Olympian professor who couldn't care less what they think is not one I can or want to be" (p. 112), in "Man Hating: Voices in the Dark," in *Calling: Essays on Teaching in the Mother Tongue* (Pasadena, Calif.: Trilogy Books, 1992), pp. 107–23.

A recent discussion of attacks on feminist scholarship and women's studies, of which my own experience was a small part, appears in Patrice McDermott, "On Cultural Authority: Women's Studies, Feminist Politics, and the Popular Press," *Signs* 20:3 (1995): 668–84. Toni A. H. McNaron describes feeling she is teaching in a "dangerous moment" because of a climate of "scare tactics from the academic right," in "Lesbian Resistance to the Anti-PC Debate," in Garber, *Tilting the Tower,* pp. 252–57. This climate is discussed more generally in the *Women's Review of Books* 9:5 (February 1992), a special issue on feminist responses to the anti-political correctness attacks; see also Marilyn Frye and Alice Kessler-Harris, "Forum: On Being Labeled Politically (In)Correct," *Signs* 17:4 (1992): 779–805. For parallels between the situations of women's and ethnic studies, see Johnella E. Butler and John C. Walter, eds., *Transforming the Curriculum: Ethnic Studies and Women's Studies* (Albany: State University of New York Press, 1991).

For additional works that discuss the need for separate women's spaces in universities and elsewhere, please see the notes to chapter 9.

7. LESBIAN IN ACADEME

1. In addition to *The Mirror Dance: Identity in a Women's Community* (Philadelphia: Temple University Press, 1983) and *Social Science and the Self: Personal Essays on an Art Form* (New Brunswick, N.J.: Rutgers University Press, 1991), my other previous works dealing with lesbianism are "Lesbian Identity and Community: Recent Social Science Literature," *Signs* 8:1 (1982): 91–108; and "Beyond 'Subjectivity': The Use of the Self in Social Science," *Qualitative Sociology* 8:4 (1985): 309–24, reprinted in *Social Science and the Self,* pp. 165–83. Lesbian community responses to *The Mirror Dance* are discussed in "Snapshots of Research," in *Social Science and the Self,* pp. 150–64.

2. Krieger, *The Mirror Dance,* p. 25.

3. Lesbian bases for theories of knowledge are discussed in Sandra Harding, "Thinking from the Perspective of Lesbian Lives," in *Whose Science? Whose Knowledge? Thinking from Women's Lives* (Ithaca, N.Y.: Cornell University Press, 1991), pp. 249–67; Diana Fuss, "Lesbian and Gay The-

ory: The Question of Identity Politics," in *Essentially Speaking: Feminism, Nature, and Difference* (New York: Routledge, 1989), pp. 97–112; and Teresa de Lauretis, *The Practice of Love: Lesbian Sexuality and Perverse Desire* (Bloomington: Indiana University Press, 1994), which offers a theory of lesbian subjectivity as part of an exploration of the inner psychic roots of lesbian desire and sexuality. In my view, all works that seek to identify ways that lesbian existence, subjectivity, or social life are unique point to bases for lesbian theories of knowledge; see the lesbian scholarship referred to in the notes for prior chapters and the introductory note on standpoint theories.

4. A discussion of "queer theory as male theory" can be found in Terry Castle, "A Polemical Introduction; or, The Ghost of Greta Garbo," in *The Apparitional Lesbian: Female Homosexuality and Modern Culture* (New York: Columbia University Press, 1993), pp. 12–15; says Castle, "When it comes to lesbians, many people have trouble seeing what's in front of them" (p. 2). Teresa de Lauretis, similarly, notes "a failure of representation, an enduring silence on the specificity of lesbianism in the contemporary 'gay and lesbian' discourse," *Differences* 3:2 (1991): vii. Donna Penn speaks of a queer "erasure" of lesbian experiences in "Queer: Theorizing Politics and History," *Radical History Review* 62 (1995): 24–42. Jacquelyn N. Zita discusses potential dangers for women in "the attempt to create an interdisciplinary area of queer studies," including the silencing of women's views and the "camping up of gender and the gutting out of feminism" (p. 262). She suggests that perhaps "a new rebellion of bride resisters is in order" (p. 271), in "Gay and Lesbian Studies: Yet Another Unhappy Marriage," in Garber, *Tilting the Tower*, pp. 258–76.

   A similar concern with the invisibility of women appears in Marilyn Frye, "Lesbian Feminism and the Gay Rights Movement: Another View of Male Supremacy, Another Separatism," in *The Politics of Reality: Essays in Feminist Theory* (Freedom, Calif.: The Crossing Press, 1983), pp. 128–51. Frye says of lesbians and gay men, "we deviate from very different norms" (p. 130) and points out that gay male effeminacy, and the male impersonation of women, displays no love of women, but rather is a "casual and cynical mockery of women." For women, "femininity is the trapping of oppression," while for men, it is more often "a naughtiness indulged in . . . by those who believe in their immunity to contamination" (p. 137).

5. For discussions of experiences of other lesbian faculty, some of them similar to my own, a recent important collection is Linda Garber, ed., *Tilting the Tower: Lesbians, Teaching, Queer Subjects* (New York: Rout-

ledge, 1994); see especially Mary Klages, "The Ins and Outs of a Lesbian Academic," pp. 235–42, for a discussion of job interview experiences. An important earlier collection is Margaret Cruikshank, ed., *Lesbian Studies: Present and Future* (Old Westbury, N.Y.: The Feminist Press, 1982); see especially Jane Gurko, "Sexual Energy in the Classroom," pp. 25–31, for a discussion of "particular sexual dynamics set off by a lesbian teacher" and of a pattern of unusually high student expectations that a lesbian teacher will be an especially good mother, often followed by a letdown (pp. 29–30). An important overview based on a recent study of sociologists is Verta Taylor and Nicole C. Raeburn, "Identity Politics as High-Risk Activism: Career Consequences for Lesbian, Gay, and Bisexual Sociologists," *Social Problems* 42:2 (1995): 252–73, including a discussion of how engaging in lesbian and gay scholarship has affected individual careers.

Additional personal accounts by lesbians include: Elenie Opffer, "Coming Out to Students: Notes from the College Classroom," in R. Jeffrey Ringer, *Queer Words, Queer Images: Communication and the Construction of Homosexuality* (New York: New York University Press, 1994), pp. 296–321; Judith McDaniel, "Is There Room for Me in the Closet? Or, My Life as the Only Lesbian Professor," in Margo Culley and Catherine Portuges, eds., *Gendered Subjects: The Dynamics of Feminist Teaching* (Boston: Routledge, 1985), pp. 130–35; Rebecca Mark, "Teaching from the Open Closet," in Elaine Hedges and Shelley Fisher Fishkin, eds., *Listening to Silences: New Essays in Feminist Criticism* (New York: Oxford University Press, 1995), pp. 245–59; Jacqueline Taylor, "Performing the (Lesbian) Self: Teacher as Text," in Ringer, *Queer Words,* pp. 289–95; and Ruthann Robson, "Pedagogy, Jurisprudence, and Finger-Fucking: Lesbian Sex in a Law School Classroom," in Karla Jay, ed., *Lesbian Erotics* (New York: New York University Press, 1995), pp. 28–39.

Henry Abelove discusses dilemmas posed by postmodernism for the teaching of lesbian and gay subjects, in "The Queering of Lesbian/Gay History," *Radical History Review* 62 (1995): 44–57; the idea of queering is also explored in Julia Wallace, "Queer-ing Sociology in the Classroom," *Critical Sociology* 20:3 (1994): 176–92. For accounts of teaching at many levels, see Kevin Jennings, ed., *One Teacher in Ten: Gay and Lesbian Educators Tell Their Stories* (Boston: Alyson, 1994). For experiences of students as well as of a lesbian teacher, see Harriet Malinowitz, *Textual Orientations: Lesbian and Gay Students and the Making of Discourse Communities* (Portsmouth, N.H.: Boynton/Cook Publishers, 1995).

8. A FEMINIST CLASS

1. Nancy J. Chodorow, "Family Structure and Feminine Personality," *Feminism and Psychoanalytic Theory* (New Haven: Yale University Press, 1989), pp. 45–65; see also her "Gender as a Personal and Cultural Construction," *Signs* 20:3 (1995): 516–44.

2. Carol Gilligan, *In a Different Voice: Psychological Theory and Women's Development* (Cambridge: Harvard University Press, 1982), pp. 1–63. Further discussion of relational themes appears in Carol Gilligan, Nona P. Lyons, and Trudy J. Hanmer, eds., *Making Connections: The Relational Worlds of Adolescent Girls at Emma Willard School* (Cambridge: Harvard University Press, 1990). For responses to Gilligan, see Linda K. Kerber et al., "On *In a Different Voice*: An Interdisciplinary Forum," *Signs* 11:2 (1986): 304–33.

3. Marjorie Harness Goodwin, "Directive-Response Speech Sequences in Girls' and Boys' Task Activities," in Sally McConnell-Ginet, Ruth Borker, and Nelly Furman, eds., *Women and Language in Literature and Society* (New York: Praeger, 1980), pp. 157–73. Goodwin's study of Philadelphia street children is presented more fully in her *He-Said-She-Said: Talk as Social Organization among Black Children* (Bloomington: Indiana University Press, 1991).

4. See, for example, Barrie Thorne, *Gender Play: Girls and Boys in School* (New Brunswick, N.J.: Rutgers University Press, 1993).

5. The class also reads a discussion of similar interpersonal boundary experiences in a different setting in Kesaya E. Noda, "Growing Up Asian in America," in Asian Women United of California, ed., *Making Waves: An Anthology of Writings by and about Asian American Women* (Boston: Beacon, 1989), pp. 243–51.

6. This sample of women's organizations is taken from student papers, spring 1991 and 1992.

7. The words used to describe women's organizational characteristics in this paragraph are partially quoted and partially paraphrased from student papers, spring 1991 and 1992.

8. Elizabeth Aries, "Interaction Patterns and Themes of Male, Female, and Mixed Groups," *Small Group Behavior* 7:1 (1976): 7–18.

9. Candace West and Don H. Zimmerman, "Small Insults: A Study of Interruptions in Cross-Sex Conversations between Unacquainted Persons," in Barrie Thorne, Cheris Kramarae, and Nancy Henley, eds., *Lan-*

guage, Gender and Society (Rowley, Mass.: Newbury House, 1983), pp. 103–18.

10. David N. Maltz and Ruth A. Borker, "A Cultural Approach to Male-Female Miscommunication," in John J. Gumperz, ed., *Language and Social Identity: Studies in International Sociolinguistics* (New York and Cambridge, England: Cambridge University Press, 1982), pp. 196–216.

11. Ann Harriman, "Communication," in *Women/Men/Management* (New York: Praeger, 1985), pp. 138–61. I also use Deborah Tannen, *You Just Don't Understand: Women and Men in Conversation* (New York: Ballantine, 1990), pp. 216–44; see, too, her *Talking from 9 to 5: How Women's and Men's Conversational Styles Affect Who Gets Heard, Who Gets Credit, and What Gets Done at Work* (New York: Morrow, 1994).

12. These observations are from Harriman, "Communication," in *Women/Men*, pp. 144–60; and from Nancy Henley, *Body Politics: Power, Sex, and Nonverbal Communication* (New York: Simon and Schuster, 1977), pp. 43–54.

13. Patricia J. Williams, "On Being the Object of Property," *Signs* 14:4 (1988): 12, reprinted in her *The Alchemy of Race and Rights: The Diary of a Law Professor* (Cambridge: Harvard University Press, 1991), pp. 216–36. We also read Kit Yuen Quan, "The Girl Who Wouldn't Sing," in Gloria Anzaldúa, ed., *Making Face, Making Soul, Haciendo Caras: Creative and Critical Perspectives by Women of Color* (San Francisco: Aunt Lute Foundation, 1990), pp. 212–20.

14. Kathy E. Ferguson, *The Feminist Case Against Bureaucracy* (Philadephia: Temple University Press, 1984), p. 94.

15. Ferguson, *The Feminist Case,* pp. 6–10, 92–99, and 182–212. On the Anita Hill case, we read Martha Mahoney, Susan Estrich, Louise Fitzgerald, and Anita Hill, *Southern California Law Review* 65:3 (1992), "Gender, Race, and the Politics of Supreme Court Appointments: The Import of the Anita Hill/Clarence Thomas Hearings," a special issue: 1393–1409 and 1445–1449. The critique of statistics on the situation of women comes from Susan Faludi, *Backlash: The Undeclared War Against American Women* (New York: Crown, 1991), pp. 363–70.

16. Betty Lehan Harragan, *Games Mother Never Taught You: Corporate Gamesmanship for Women* (New York: Warner, 1977), pp. 19–45 and 325–51. Other advice books I have used include: Rosemary Agonito, *No More "Nice Girl": Power, Sexuality, and Success in the Workplace* (Holbrook, Mass.: Bob Adams, 1993); Edith Gilson with Susan Kane, *Unnecessary Choices: The Hidden Life of the Executive Woman* (New York: Morrow,

1987); Sarah Hardesty and Nehama Jacobs, *Success and Betrayal: The Crisis of Women in Corporate America* (New York: Franklin Watts, 1986); Sue Joan Mendelson Freeman, *Managing Lives: Corporate Women and Social Change* (Amherst: University of Massachusetts Press, 1990); and Anita Roddick, *Body and Soul: Profits with Principles—the Amazing Success Story of Anita Roddick* (New York: Crown, 1991). Ferguson discusses the "success manuals for women" in *The Feminist Case,* pp. 184–87.

17. Rosabeth Moss Kanter, *Men and Women of the Corporation* (New York: Basic Books, 1977); I use especially "Secretaries," pp. 69–103, and "Minorities and Majorities," pp. 206–42. Kanter's *Men and Women* was issued in a second edition in 1993, with new commentary added by Kanter reassessing her original views. The original work, however, remains strong, both as a portrait and critique of gendered relationships in large-scale organizational life.

      A recent study of corporate organization with similar themes to Kanter is Angel Kwolek-Folland, *Engendering Business: Men and Women in the Corporate Office, 1870–1930* (Baltimore, Md.: Johns Hopkins University Press, 1994). See also Joan Acker, "Hierarchies, Jobs, and Bodies: A Theory of Gendered Organizations," *Gender and Society* 4:2 (1990): 139–58; Albert J. Mills and Peta Tancred, eds., *Gendering Organizational Analysis* (Newbury Park, Calif.: Sage, 1992); and for further stories of women's organizational dilemmas, Susan E. Chase, *Ambiguous Empowerment: The Work Narratives of Women School Superintendents* (Amherst: University of Massachusetts Press, 1995), and Gwendolyn Etter-Lewis, *My Soul is My Own: Oral Narratives of African American Women in the Professions* (New York: Routledge, 1993).

18. Nancy Mairs, *Plaintext: Deciphering a Woman's Life* (New York: Harper and Row, 1986), p. 57.

19. Pamela M. Fishman, "Interaction: The Work Women Do," in Barrie Thorne, Cheris Kramarae, and Nancy Henley, eds., *Language, Gender and Society* (Rowley, Mass.: Newbury House, 1983), pp. 89–101. Our other readings dealing with female gender as an "accomplishment" are Candace West and Don H. Zimmerman, "Small Insults," see note 9 (and their "Doing Gender," *Gender and Society* 1:2 [1987]: 125–51); Arlie Russell Hochschild, *The Managed Heart,* see note 21; and Judith Shapiro, "Transsexualism," see note 27.

20. Ursula Le Guin, "Bryn Mawr Commencement Address," in *Dancing at the Edge of the World: Thoughts on Words, Women, Places* (New York: Grove Press, 1989), pp. 147–60.

21. Arlie Russell Hochschild, "Gender, Status, and Feeling," in *The Managed Heart: Commercialization of Human Feeling* (Berkeley and Los Angeles: University of California Press, 1983), pp. 162–98.

22. We read Nancy F. Cott, *The Bonds of Womanhood: "Woman's Sphere" in New England, 1780–1835* (New Haven: Yale University Press, 1977), pp. 58–62; Cott draws on E. P. Thompson, "Time, Work-Discipline, and Industrial Capitalism," *Past and Present* 38 (1967): 56–79.

23. Kanter, *Men and Women of the Corporation*, p. 118; Le Guin, "Bryn Mawr Commencement Address," in *Dancing*, p. 154.

24. Marjorie L. DeVault, "Doing Housework: Feeding and Family Life," in Naomi Gerstel and Harriet Engel Gross, eds., *Families and Work* (Philadelphia: Temple University Press, 1987), pp. 178–91. A recent work on women's economies, including discussions of lesbian economies, is Loraine Edwalds and Midge Stocker, eds., *The Woman-Centered Economy: Ideals, Reality, and the Space In Between* (Chicago: Third Side Press, 1995). See also Barbara Brandt, *Whole Life Economics: Revaluing Daily Life* (Philadelphia: New Society Publishers, 1995); and Sheila Lewenhak, *The Revaluation of Women's Work* (London: Earthscan Publications, 1992).

25. Marilyn Loden, *Feminine Leadership, or How to Succeed in Business without Being One of the Boys* (New York: Times Books, 1985); I use especially "Teamwork," pp. 114–32. Similar themes appear in Sally Helgesen, *The Female Advantage: Women's Ways of Leadership* (New York: Currency/Doubleday, 1995). See also Kathleen Hall Jamieson, *Beyond the Double-Bind: Women and Leadership* (New York: Oxford University Press, 1995) for a literature synthesis.

26. The art of studying women's experiences that are difficult to describe is the focus of Marjorie L. DeVault, "Talking and Listening from Women's Standpoint: Feminist Strategies for Interviewing and Analysis," *Social Problems* 37:1 (1990): 96–116. See also her "Ethnicity and Expertise: Racial-Ethnic Knowledge in Sociological Research," *Gender and Society* 9:5 (1995): 612–31.

27. The invisibility of women's work is discussed in Marjorie L. DeVault, *Feeding the Family: The Social Organization of Caring as Gendered Work* (Chicago: University of Chicago Press, 1991), p. 56; and in Hochschild, *The Managed Heart*, p. 167. "Massage work" is discussed in Judy Edelstein, "In the Massage Parlor," in Frederique Delacoste and Priscilla Alexander, eds., *Sex Work: Writings by Women in the Sex Industry* (San Francisco: Cleis Press, 1987), pp. 62–69; erotic dancing is the subject of Judy

Helfand, "Silence Again," also in Delacoste and Alexander, *Sex Work*, pp. 266–70. Transsexualism is examined in Judith Shapiro, "Transsexualism: Reflections on the Persistence of Gender and the Mutability of Sex," in Julia Epstein and Kristina Straub, eds., *Body Guards: The Cultural Politics of Gender Ambiguity* (New York: Routledge, 1991), pp. 248–79.

28. Patricia Zavella, " 'Abnormal Intimacy': The Varying Networks of Chicana Cannery Workers," *Feminist Studies* 11:3 (1985): 541–57.

29. For other works discussing feminist teaching, please see chapter 10, note 9.

9. SEPARATISM

1. Helen Rogan, *Mixed Company: Women in the Modern Army* (Boston: Beacon, 1981); most losses are discussed on pp. 129–223. A further valuable discussion is Jean Zimmerman, *Tailspin: Women at War in the Wake of Tailhook* (New York: Doubleday, 1995).

2. Estelle Freedman, "Separatism as Strategy: Female Institution Building and American Feminism, 1870–1930," *Feminist Studies* 5:3 (1979): 512–29. See also her "Separatism Revisited: Women's Institutions, Social Reform, and the Career of Miriam Van Waters," in Linda K. Kerber, Alice Kessler-Harris, and Kathryn Kish Sklar, eds., *U.S. History as Women's History: New Feminist Essays* (Chapel Hill: University of North Carolina Press, 1995), pp. 170–88.

3. Marilyn Frye, "Some Reflections on Separatism and Power," in *The Politics of Reality: Essays in Feminist Theory* (Freedom, Calif.: Crossing Press, 1983), pp. 95–109. For further discussions of separatism, see Jackie Anderson, Maria Luisa "Papusa" Molina, and Maria Lugones, "Forum: Separatism Re-viewed," *Signs* 19:2 (1994): 435–57; Sarah Lucia-Hoagland and Julia Penelope, eds., *For Lesbians Only: A Separatist Anthology* (London: Onlywomen Press, 1988); Dana R. Shugar, *Separatism and Women's Community* (Lincoln: University of Nebraska Press, 1995); Verta Taylor and Leila J. Rupp, "Women's Culture and Lesbian Feminist Activism: A Reconsideration of Cultural Feminism," *Signs* 19:1 (1993): 32–61; and Nancy E. Whittier, *Feminist Generations: The Persistence of the Radical Women's Movement* (Philadelphia: Temple University Press, 1995).

4. Regina Markell Morantz-Sanchez, *Sympathy and Science: Women Physicians in American Medicine* (New York: Oxford University Press, 1985), pp. 88, 254, 356–59, and chapter 7, "Science, Morality, and Women Doctors," pp. 184–202.

5. Paula Giddings, *In Search of Sisterhood: Delta Sigma Theta and the Chal-*

lenge of the Black Sorority Movement (New York: William Morrow, 1988), pp. 5–22.

6. Bernice Johnson Reagon, "Coalition Politics: Turning the Century," in Barbara Smith, ed., *Home Girls: A Black Feminist Anthology* (New York: Kitchen Table–Women of Color Press, 1983), pp. 356–68.

7. Alma M. Garcia, "The Development of Chicana Feminist Discourse, 1970–1980," in Ellen Carol DuBois and Vicki L. Ruiz, eds., *Unequal Sisters: A Multicultural Reader in U.S. Women's History* (New York: Routledge, 1990), pp. 418–31. See also Reagon on the difference between "home" and "coalition," in "Coalition Politics," in *Home Girls*, p. 360.

8. Esther Ngan-Ling Chow, "The Feminist Movement: Where Are All the Asian American Women?" in Asian Women United of California, ed., *Making Waves: An Anthology of Writings by and about Asian American Women* (Boston: Beacon, 1989), pp. 362–77. See also my study, *The Mirror Dance: Identity in a Women's Community* (Philadelphia: Temple University Press, 1983), pp. 81–95, for a discussion of affinity groups within a lesbian community; and Esther Newton, for similar observations, in *Cherry Grove, Fire Island: Sixty Years in America's First Gay and Lesbian Town* (Boston: Beacon, 1993). For difficulties crossing barriers, see Virginia R. Harris and Trinity A. Ordoña, "Developing Unity Among Women of Color: Crossing the Barriers of Internalized Racism and Cross-Race Hostility," in Gloria Anzaldúa, ed., *Making Face, Making Soul, Haciendo Caras: Creative and Critical Writings by Women of Color* (San Francisco: Aunt Lute Foundation, 1990), pp. 304–16.

9. Babette Copper, Maxine Ethelchild, and Lucy Whyte, "Feminist Process: Developing a Non-competitive Process within Work Groups" (Berkeley, Calif.: self-published paper, August 1974), pp. 1–19. Although the collective had four members, three wrote the article.

10. Copper, Ethelchild, and Whyte, "Feminist Process"; and Deborah Tannen, "Women as Cooperative Overlappers," in *You Just Don't Understand: Women and Men in Conversation* (New York: Ballantine, 1990), pp. 203–5.

11. Joyce Rothschild-Whitt, "The Collectivist Organization: An Alternative to Rational-Bureaucratic Models," *American Sociological Review* 44 (August 1979): 509–27.

12. Anne Jardim, "From Hierarchy to Centrarchy," *Women's Review of Books* X:5 (February 1993): 27–28.

13. Carol Ascher, "Women Working with Women in the University," *Heresies* 2:3 (1979), "Women Working Together," a special issue: 58–63.

14. See, for example, Susan Porter Benson, *Counter Cultures: Saleswomen,*

Managers, and Customers in American Department Stores, 1890–1940 (Urbana: University of Illinois Press, 1986); and Greta Foff Paules, *Dishing It Out: Power and Resistance among Waitresses in a New Jersey Restaurant* (Philadelphia: Temple University Press, 1991).

15. For similar patterns in women's organizations despite feminist/traditional differences, see Mary Kay Asch, *Mary Kay: The Success Story of America's Most Dynamic Businesswoman* (New York: Harper and Row, 1987); Kathleen M. Blee, *Women of the Klan: Racism and Gender in the 1920s* (Berkeley and Los Angeles: University of California Press, 1991); Myra Marx Ferree and Patricia Yancey Martin, eds., *Feminist Organizations: Harvest of the New Women's Movement* (Philadelphia: Temple University Press, 1995); Kathleen P. Iannello, *Decisions Without Hierarchy: Feminist Interventions in Organization Theory and Practice* (New York: Routledge, 1992); Claudia Koontz, *Mothers in the Fatherland: Women, the Family, and Nazi Politics* (New York: St. Martin's, 1987); Bernice Johnson Reagon and Sweet Honey in the Rock, *We Who Believe in Freedom: Sweet Honey in the Rock . . . Still on the Journey* (New York: Anchor/Doubleday, 1993); Phyllis Schlafly, *The Power of the Positive Woman* (New Rochelle, N.Y.: Arlington House, 1977); Ann Firor Scott, *Natural Allies: Women's Associations in American History* (Urbana: University of Illinois Press, 1991); and Penny A. Weiss and Marilyn Friedman, eds., *Feminism and Community* (Philadelphia: Temple University Press, 1994). See also Jessie Bernard, *The Female World* (New York: The Free Press, 1981) for a comprehensive sociological effort to discern distinct patterns in separate female spheres.

16. The relationship between caring work, subordinance, and female gender is discussed in Kathy E. Ferguson, *The Feminist Case Against Bureaucracy* (Philadelphia: Temple University Press, 1984); Emily K. Abel and Margaret K. Nelson, *Circles of Care: Work and Identity in Women's Lives* (New York: State University of New York Press, 1990); and Marjorie L. DeVault, *Feeding the Family: The Social Organization of Caring as Gendered Work* (Chicago: University of Chicago Press, 1991).

17. These comments are from student papers, spring 1991 and 1992; all names have been changed.

18. Feelings about lesbianism in a women's college are discussed in Anne MacKay, ed., *Wolf Girls at Vassar: Lesbian and Gay Experiences, 1930–1990* (New York: St. Martin's, 1993); see also the novel by May Sarton, *The Small Room* (New York: Norton, 1961).

19. These and subsequent comments are from student papers on separatism and student course summary papers, spring 1991, 1992, and 1993.

1. Susan Krieger, *The Mirror Dance: Identity in a Women's Community* (Philadelphia: Temple University Press, 1983).

2. These comments are from student papers on *The Mirror Dance,* spring 1991.

3. Susan Krieger, "Beyond 'Subjectivity': The Use of the Self in Social Science," *Qualitative Sociology* 8:4 (1985): 309–24, also in *Social Science and the Self: Personal Essays on an Art Form* (New Brunswick, N.J.: Rutgers University Press, 1991), pp. 165–83.

4. For other analyses of the structure of *The Mirror Dance,* see Marjorie L. DeVault, "Women Write Sociology: Rhetorical Strategies," in Albert Hunter, ed., *The Rhetoric of Social Research* (New Brunswick: Rutgers University Press, 1990), pp. 97–110; and Mitchell Stevens, "Susan Krieger's *The Mirror Dance:* Lessons of a Deficient Sociology," *Studies in Symbolic Interaction* 13 (1992): 83–100. I have written about my teaching dilemmas in "Experiences in Teaching: Exposure, Invisibility, and Writing Personally," in *Social Science and the Self,* pp. 135–49. I now give this article to my classes to help the students understand my approach.

5. Evelyn Fox Keller, "A World of Difference," in *Reflections on Gender and Science* (New Haven: Yale University Press, 1985), pp. 158–76; see also her *A Feeling for the Organism: The Life and Work of Barbara McClintock* (San Francisco: W. H. Freeman, 1983).

6. This section begins with Joan Didion, "On Keeping a Notebook," in *Slouching Towards Bethlehem* (New York: Delta, 1968), pp. 131–41; and Nancy Mairs, "On Living Behind Bars," in *Plaintext: Deciphering a Woman's Life* (New York: Harper and Row, 1986), pp. 125–54. We also read Mairs' "Letter to Matthew" and "On Being Raised by a Daughter," in *Plaintext,* pp. 55–76. Patricia Hill Collins discusses "pivoting the center" in *Black Feminist Thought: Knowledge, Consciousness, and the Politics of Empowerment* (New York: Routledge, 1990), p. 236; we read pp. 221–38. The discussion of potter Maria Martinez is by Alice Marriott, "The Signatures," in *Maria: The Potter of San Ildefonso* (Norman: University of Oklahoma Press, 1948), pp. 227–35. Other readings on women's self-expression that I use are: Joan Didion, "Georgia O'Keeffe," in *The White Album* (New York: Simon and Schuster, 1979), pp. 126–30; bell hooks, "Talking Back," in Gloria Anzaldúa, ed., *Making Face, Making Soul, Haciendo Caras: Creative and Critical Perspectives by Women of Color* (San

Francisco: Aunt Lute Foundation, 1990), pp. 207–11; and Barbara Christian, "The Race for Theory," *Feminist Studies* 14:1 (1988): 67–79.

7. These comments are from student course summary papers, spring 1991 and 1992.

8. From a letter from a student, spring 1993.

9. Other works discussing feminist teaching and its dilemmas include: Mary Field Belenky, Blythe McVicker Clinchy, Nancy Rule Goldberger, and Jill Mattuck Tarule, *Women's Ways of Knowing: The Development of Self, Voice, and Mind* (New York: Basic Books, 1986), see especially "Toward an Education for Women" and "Connected Teaching," pp. 190–229; Margaret Cruikshank, ed., *Lesbian Studies: Present and Future* (Old Westbury, N.Y.: The Feminist Press, 1982), see especially "In the Classroom," pp. 23–99; Margo Culley and Catherine Portuges, eds., *Gendered Subjects: The Dynamics of Feminist Teaching* (Boston: Routledge, 1985); Sara Munson Deats and Lagretta Tallent Lenker, eds., *Gender and Academe: Feminist Pedagogy and Politics* (Lanham, Md.: Rowman and Littlefield, 1994); Joanna de Groot, "Roses and Thorns: Modest Thoughts on Prickly Issues," in Gabriele Griffin, ed., *Changing Our Lives: Doing Women's Studies* (London and Boulder, Colo.: Pluto, 1994), pp. 183–92, and Griffin, "Women's Studies Students," pp. 49–131; Marilyn Frye, "A Lesbian's Perspective on Women's Studies," in *Willful Virgin: Essays in Feminism, 1976–1992* (Freedom, Calif.: The Crossing Press, 1992), pp. 51–58; Diana Fuss, "Essentialism in the Classroom," in *Essentially Speaking: Feminism, Nature and Difference* (New York: Routledge, 1989), pp. 113–19.

In addition, see Jane Gallop, "A Reading in the Guise of an Introduction" and "The Teacher's Breasts," in *Pedagogy: The Question of Impersonation* (Bloomington: Indiana University Press, 1995), pp. 1–18 and 79–89; Linda Garber, ed., *Tilting the Tower: Lesbians, Teaching, Queer Subjects* (New York: Routledge, 1994); Gail B. Griffin, *Calling: Essays on Teaching in the Mother Tongue* (Pasadena, Calif.: Trilogy Books, 1992); bell hooks, *Teaching to Transgress: Education as the Practice of Freedom* (New York: Routledge, 1994) and "Toward a Revolutionary Feminist Pedagogy," in *Talking Back: Thinking Feminist, Thinking Black* (Boston: South End Press, 1989), pp. 49–54; Frances A. Maher and Mary Kay Thompson Tetrealt, "Toward Positional Pedagogies," in *The Feminist Classroom* (New York: Basic Books, 1994), pp. 201–27; Jean Fox O'Barr, *Feminism in Action: Building Institutions and Community through Women's Studies* (Chapel Hill: University of North Carolina Press, 1994), see especially "Rethinking Teaching and Learning: The 'We-They' Dichotomy," pp. 263–76; Barbara Omolade, "Invisible to the Naked Eye: Black Women and the Academy," in *The Rising Song of African American Women* (New York: Routledge, 1994), pp. 103–51; and Patricia J. Williams, *The Alchemy of Race and Rights: Diary of a Law Professor* (Cambridge: Harvard University Press, 1991), see especially "Crimes Without Passion," pp. 80–97.

Compositor:	J. Jarrett Engineering, Inc.
Text:	12/14.5 Adobe Garamond
Display:	Perpetua and Adobe Garamond
Printer and binder:	Thomson-Shore, Inc.